# McCormick/Schilling's
# New SPICE COOKBOOK

# McCormick/Schilling's

# *New* SPICE COOKBOOK

*Edited
by
Jack Felton*

*A Benjamin* **B** *Company Book*

Produced and published by The Benjamin Company, Inc.
21 Dupont Avenue
White Plains, NY 10605
Library of Congress Cataloging-in-Publishing Data
McCormick/Schilling new spice cookbook
416 p.   17.8 x 25.4 cm.
Includes index.
ISBN 0-87502-251-0
1. Cookery.    2. Cookery, International.   3. Spices   I. McCormick
& Company (Sparks, Md.)  II. Title: New spice cookbook.
TX714.M3   1994
641.5--dc20
94-33284
CIP

Printed and bound in the United States of America
First Printing: September 1994

～

*This cookbook is dedicated to
our former Chairman and CEO,
BAILEY A. THOMAS,
who taught us to seek joy in living.*

～

# Preface

Seasoning is not just a matter of taste. It is an art. Appealing foods created from a palette of spices and flavors have pleased discriminating palates for centuries. This ancient art form mixes aroma, eye appeal, chemistry, instinct, experience, history, skill, and care.

This McCormick cookbook presents a whole world of flavorful recipes that are picture-perfect and fun. Some, designed for today's lifestyles, are easy family recipes. Others provide promises of fine dining. In the third section you'll find ideas and recipes that make entertaining enjoyable for both the guests and the host or hostess.

The art of cooking begins with imagination and testing new ideas. We hope our palette of spice suggestions and recipes tempts you to rediscover the exotic flavor of an ancient spice, a new use for a familiar favorite, or entices you to try a new spice you do not know. Using these ideas, you can create your own works of art!

We believe "spice is the variety of life!"

JACK FELTON
*Vice President*
*Corporate Communications*
*McCormick & Company, Incorporated*

# Acknowledgments

All books have to be written, proofed, and printed with care, but the recipes in cookbooks must also be kitchen-tested for flavor and taste, and to make sure they are doable. These recipes have had clever and creative crafting by flavor experts and technicians in the Kitchens of McCormick. For all of this tedious and time-consuming work, we thank the following:

| | | | |
|---|---|---|---|
| Ellen Gibb | Lorraine Kealiher | Betsy Voss | Laurie Wilson |
| Marianne Gillette | Mary Randisi | Carolyn Wille | Merle Wilson |

A special thank you also is extended to Barbara Bloch, of The Benjamin Company, for her valuable editorial perceptions and suggestions.

McCormick gratefully acknowledges permission granted by Turner Entertaining Company for references to *Casablanca*. We also extend special thanks to the American Spice Trade Association for the line illustrations of spice plants.

For design, layout, and photographic concepts, we thank Diane Hamel and Danette High of McCormick and Benjamin's designer, Phil Grushkin.

In addition, we thank all those McCormick employees who served as taste testers for recipes. Without the dedication of all of these people, this book would not have been possible.

# CONTENTS

~

## INTRODUCTION

## EASY FAMILY RECIPES

# FINE DINING

# ENTERTAINING

# INDEX

# HISTORY OF SPICES

**THE HISTORY OF SPICES** parallels the history of the exploration of our world.

The use of herbs probably began accidentally when a caveman wrapped meat in the leaves of a nearby bush. To his surprise, he discovered this enhanced the taste of the meat, as did certain nuts, seeds, berries — and even bark.

In ancient times, spices and herbs were also used as a way to mask the often unpleasant taste and odor of food. Because there were so few ways to keep food fresh, the value of spices to Europeans in the late Middle Ages grew to a point that can hardly be imagined today. A handful of cardamom was worth as much as a poor man's yearly wages, and many slaves were bought and sold for a few handfuls of peppercorns.

Arab traders were the first to introduce spices into Europe. Realizing that they controlled a commodity in great demand, the traders kept their sources of supply secret and made up fantastic tales of the dangers involved in obtaining spices.

However, when it became known that the true sources of these precious spices and herbs were in Asia and India, world exploration began in earnest. Not only did Columbus, Magellan, and others claim the lands they "discovered" for their sovereigns, but their ships brought back to Europe samples of plants, fruit, seeds, spices, and "flavorings" they found.

Once the sources of supply were identified, the major powers set up monopolies trading in these commodities. Often the country with the strongest navy was able to gain control of the areas where spices originated. The Spanish, Portuguese, Dutch, and British empires all enjoyed leading roles for a time. In fact, the last of these great spice monopolies, the Dutch, remained in existence until the outbreak of World War II.

With the discovery of the Caribbean Islands and Central America, new spices were added to the world's cuisine, notably red pepper, vanilla, and allspice. Some of these became extremely popular in Europe, and then, centuries later, were reintroduced in the United States by immigrants.

The popularity of spices during the entire period of European expansion, from the 15th to the 18th centuries, cannot be exaggerated. Spice cookery reached extremes of complexity, especially in puddings and meat dishes, and the combinations of spices used might seem strange to modern palates. Hot spices from the Orient, such as pepper, ginger, and cloves, were frequently mixed with native flavors such as fennel and coriander. Sweet seasonings, such as anise, nutmeg, and mint, were often added for good measure. These were the staple seasonings of the Renaissance diet. These same seasonings have survived in many different combinations and are widely used in spice cookery today.

As the Arab monopoly of the spice trade declined, the great colonizing nations of Europe fought for supremacy. At first, the Portuguese and Spanish, whose sea captains and navigators were supreme early voyagers, enjoyed virtual dominion over the spice trade. Their sphere of influence extended into India and Burma and even the Philippines. In 1493, Pope Alexander VI divided the New World between Spain and Portugal. In the 1500s, Spain was the dominant spice merchant; then England and Holland successfully challenged her.

In the late 17th century, America benefited indirectly from the spice trade. Boston-born Elihu Yale grew up in England, where he worked as a clerk for the British East India Company, which held a monopoly on all trade with India. The company's ships brought the first cargo of nutmeg and cloves from the Moluccas in Indonesia. Yale eventually became governor of Madras, India, and his spice fortune helped endow Yale University.

In the late 18th and early 19th centuries, Americans became directly involved in the spice trade as the sleek clipper ships of New England began to dominate world trade. So many pepper voyages were undertaken from New England to Sumatra that the price of pepper dropped to less than three cents a pound in 1843, a disastrous slump that affected many aspects of American business. Ultimately, the New England spice trade fell off sharply when piracy in the Java and China Seas made long voyages for pepper too dangerous. Meanwhile, the American spice business, like the rest of the country, was moving west. In 1835, American settlers in Texas developed chili powder by combining various ground red peppers from Mexico, thus adding new dimensions to American taste. Later, once the gold rush had subsided, herbs were grown commercially in California. Mustard seed was grown in North Dakota, Montana, and Canada's prairie provinces.

Our cuisine has great variety because America was settled by people from many nations who, in their native lands, enjoyed distinctively spiced dishes. The move to America often made it difficult for immigrants to obtain their favorite flavoring materials. At the same time, the different, more plentiful supply of food eliminated some of the need for heavy spicing. And many times, the newer generation — to its own loss — deliberately tried to depart from the traditional dishes of the old country. Only in recent times has the increase in international travel created a vogue for food seasoned with spices from all over the world.

The spice trade has changed over the years. In some cases, the prices and production of spices are controlled by native governments or groups of growers. Travel, however, is still an integral part of the business of McCormick spice procurement. In an average year, our buyers travel hundreds of thousands of miles in search of information about the quality of various herbs and spices and to track political and climatic conditions that might disrupt usual sources of supply.

Weather historically has had an impact on crop size, quality, and price. The life cycle of spices and herbs, from initial planting to harvesting, can be as little as three months for most herbs to as long as six to eight years for some tree spices. Typically, allspice, nutmeg, and cloves can be harvested between six and eight years after planting. Vanilla and pepper vines take three years to mature. If a storm destroys a portion of existing plantations, years of shortages, coupled with price increases, can follow.

In the 20th century, another problem has gained major importance. Political upheavals, such as the Communist takeover of Vietnam, can restrict sources of supply. This was of major importance because Vietnamese cassia (cinnamon) is considered among the world's finest. Indonesia is another significant source.

Iran was the premier supplier of cumin seed before the Islamic revolution. Again, political conditions made this source temporarily unavailable. India and Turkey have picked up most of the cumin seed business once held by Iran. These pressures, both national and political, make alternate sources of supply as critical today as they were to the early explorers.

Today, with spice use so prevalent and the cost relatively low, it is hard to imagine that these fragrant bits of leaves, seeds, and bark were once so coveted and costly. For centuries wars were waged, new lands discovered, and the earth circled, all in the quest of spices. Below is a brief chronological listing that provides a "flavor" of the influence spices have had on history.

2600 B.C.  *Ancient records show that onion and garlic were fed to laborers who built the Great Pyramids.*

1920 B.C.  *Biblical history tells of Joseph's jealous brothers selling him to a spice caravan.*

1453 B.C.  *The Greeks used wreaths made of bay leaves to honor champions of their Olympic Games.*

950 B.C.  *Arabs gained control of the spice trade. Their geographic position made them the natural middlemen between the spice lands of the East and the markets in the West. Although the Arabs actually bought their spices from the Indians, Chinese, and Javanese, they invented fantastic tales regarding the true sources of the spices. This folklore enabled them to maintain lucrative positions as middlemen.*

460-377 B.C. *Hippocrates wrote of over 400 medicinal uses for spices. Alexandria, Egypt, became the greatest spice-trading port of the eastern Mediterranean. The spice trade that passed through the city was so important that one of the gates was named the Pepper Gate.*

50 B.C.  *Romans introduced mustard seed to England.*

65 A.D.  *Funeral rites for Nero's wife used more than a year's supply of cinnamon.*

| | |
|---|---|
| 300 | *Constantinople was founded as a spice-trading center. The demand for spices spread rapidly throughout Europe. To understand the popularity of spices, one must remember that during this time many foods, especially meat, were barely palatable. All meat was butchered in the fall and heavily salted. A dash of pepper, ginger, or other spices could improve the taste of almost any meal.* |
| 410 | *Rome was brought under siege and Alaric the Visigoth demanded 3,000 pounds of pepper as ransom for the city.* |
| 595 | *Mohammed wed a wealthy spice-trading widow. His followers combined missionary work with spice trading in the East to build the first spice monopoly.* |
| 641 | *Constantinople fell to the Arabs. The Arabs controlled the geographic area from Spain to China and dominated the spice trade until about A.D. 1100.* |
| 1179 | *The Guild of Pepperers was founded in London. This later became the present Grocery Trade Association.* |
| 1200 | *During this time, many small towns kept their accounts in pepper. Spices were so valuable that dockworkers were required to work with their pockets sewn shut.* |
| 1298 | *After many years, Marco Polo returned from China and told the world the true origins of many spices.* |
| 1418 | *Prince Henry of Portugal formed a navigational college in the hope of discovering a direct route to spice-producing countries.* |
| 1471 | *Portuguese sailors crossed the equator for the first time.* |
| 1486 | *Dias discovered the Cape of Good Hope, opening new trade routes around the African continent.* |
| 1492 | *Columbus, seeking a direct route to the Spice Islands, discovered America. He returned to Europe with allspice and capsicum peppers from the West Indies.* |
| 1498 | *The most significant event in spice history occurred when Vasco de Gama reached Calcutta on the west coast of India. This allowed Europe to set up trade directly with the spice-producing countries of the East.* |
| 1519-1522 | *Seeking a more direct route to the Spice Islands, Magellan discovered a water passage around South America and his ship became the first to circumnavigate the world.* |
| 1529 | *Charles V of Spain sold all rights to the Spice Islands to Portugal. One of the smallest of the European countries, Portugal quickly became one of the richest.* |
| 1580 | *Sir Francis Drake traveled around the world searching for the most direct route to the Spice Islands.* |

| | |
|---|---|
| 1600 | *The British East India Company was formed to trade in spices. Two years later, the Dutch East India Company was formed.* |
| 1640 | *The Dutch seized Malaysia and gained control of the spice trade.* |
| 1658 | *The Dutch controlled Ceylon (now Sri Lanka) and later captured the pepper ports on the Malabar Coast of India. The English also strengthened their position in India.* |
| 1780 | *The Dutch and English went to war over control of the spice trade.* |
| 1786 | *Off the west coast of the Malay Peninsula, the English established Penang, which later became the major Eastern pepper port.* |
| 1797 | *The United States entered the spice trade when Captain John Carnes returned from Sumatra with the first large cargo of pepper.* |
| 1799 | *The English took control of the spice trade and the Dutch East India Company was dissolved.* |
| 1821 | *The first spice-grinding company in the United States was started in Boston.* |
| 1835 | *Chili powder was invented in Texas.* |
| 1873 | *Pirates interrupted the world spice trade.* |
| 1889 | *McCormick & Company, Incorporated, was founded to sell fruit flavors.* |
| 1896 | *McCormick entered spice marketing with the purchase of a small Philadelphia firm.* |
| 1907 | *The American Spice Trade Association (ASTA) was founded.* |
| 1910 | *California began chili pepper production.* |
| 1931 | *Dehydrated onion and garlic went on the market.* |
| 1965-1975 | *The Vietnam War interrupted cinnamon trading with Saigon, the premier source.* |
| 1968 | *McCormick began to visit source countries to ensure spice quality.* |
| 1971 | *Spice trading with China reopened.* |
| 1980s | *California became a prime source of herbs such as basil, mint, etc.* |
| 1987 | *McCormick began global sourcing of spices through joint partnerships with growers.* |
| 1989 | *McCormick & Company, Incorporated, celebrated its 100th anniversary with sales of over $1 billion.* |
| 1990s | *Using modern agricultural techniques, Egypt regained some of its glory as a major source of herbs.* |

# ALL ABOUT SPICES

The term "spice" or "spices" is often used in a general sense to mean any aromatic flavoring material of vegetable origin. It is also often used in a more specific sense, together with the terms "herbs," "seeds," "blend," and "condiment," as defined below.

SPICES: *Aromatic natural products that are the dried seeds, buds, fruit or flower parts, bark, or roots of plants, usually of tropical origin.*

HERBS: *Aromatic leaves and sometimes the flowers of plants, usually grown in a climate similar to the Mediterranean.*

SEEDS: *Aromatic, dried, small, whole fruit of plants, usually of temperate climates.*

BLEND: *A mixture of spices, herbs, seeds, or other flavoring materials either ground or whole.*

CONDIMENT: *Any spice, herb, or seed, but more frequently a pungent, prepared mixture of seasonings, sometimes in liquid form. Condiments are often served as an accompaniment to food.*

## *Allspice* (*Pimenta diocia*)

SPICE DESCRIPTION: Allspice is the dried, unripened fruit of a small evergreen tree. The fruit is a pea-size berry that is sun-dried to a reddish brown color. Though its flavor is suggestive of a blend of clove, cinnamon, and nutmeg, allspice is a single spice. The aroma is pleasant and clove-like. Outside the United States, allspice is known as pimento (from the Spanish word pimienta for "pepper") because Columbus thought the berries of the allspice plant resembled unripened peppercorns.

Allspice is grown in Jamaica, but alternate sources include Guatemala, Honduras, Mexico, and the Leeward Islands. Historically, Jamaican allspice has been considered superior because it has a higher oil content and better appearance and flavor than any other. Jamaican allspice has a clove-like aroma, while the Honduran and Guatemalan varieties have a characteristic bay rum flavor.

HISTORY: Allspice was discovered by Columbus in 1494, but was not recognized or used as a spice until the early 17th century.

**FORMS AND COMMON USAGE:** Available both whole and ground, allspice blends well with other spices and is present in many spice mixtures. It can be used in both savory and sweet dishes and is commonly added to meat, gravies, ketchup, pickling mixes, pies, cakes, cookies, relishes, and preserves. Allspice adds rich, warm flavor to many dishes that are cooked for a long period of time.

Allspice is also used in Jamaican soup and meat stews to provide a traditional flavor. German sauerbraten depends on allspice for balance and subtlety, and recipes for many American fruit pies, cookies, and cakes call for allspice.

# *Anise Seed* (*Pimpinella anisum*)

**SPICE DESCRIPTION:** Anise seed has a sweet, licorice-like flavor and is a slow-growing annual herb of the parsley family. The seed, planted in early spring, produces a plant that grows to a height of about three feet. Clusters of white flowers appear three months after planting and seeds are harvested a month later. The seeds are threshed and dried outdoors. At harvest, the seeds are a light greenish gray color, crescent shaped, and about  one-fifth of an inch long. Though the anise seed has an unmistakable licorice flavor, it is not related to the European plant whose roots are the source of true licorice.

Turkey, Spain, and Egypt are sources of anise seed. Of these, the bolder, more flavorful Spanish seed is considered a premium seed.

**HISTORY:** In Rome, during the first century, anise was used as a flavoring in a popular spice cake that, baked in bay leaves, was believed to prevent indigestion. In 1305, the English collected a toll on anise seed to fund repairs to the London Bridge. A popular English condiment, it was also used to perfume the clothing worn by King Edward IV. Anise is one of the oldest cultivated spices and was known to the early Egyptians, Greeks, and Romans. Pliny the Elder claimed that if anise seed were placed under a pillow, it would prevent bad dreams. The Romans began to use anise as a food flavoring in the Middle Ages. In 1619, the Virginia Assembly enacted a law requiring each family to plant at least six anise seeds each year. The Shakers used anise as a medicinal herb.

**FORMS AND COMMON USAGE:** Anise is sold as the whole seed. It may retain its flavor qualities and strength for up to three years if stored properly.

Anise seed is commonly used to give a licorice-like flavor to spice cakes, cookies, breads, sweets, and beverages, including the cordial anisette. The extract may be used to add a licorice-like flavor to cakes, icings, candies, and cookies.

Portuguese and Italian recipes often call for anise seed. German and Italian bakers use anise in cookies, coffee cakes, and sweet rolls. Sometimes Scandinavian rye bread is flavored with anise instead of caraway.

# *Basil* *(Ocimum basilicum)*

**HERB DESCRIPTION:** Basil, also called sweet basil, is a member of the mint family. Over 150 varieties of basil are grown. Basil is native to India but is grown commercially all over the Mediterranean region and in California. Known as the "royal herb" to ancient Greeks, it is very versatile. With an aroma that is like mint and tea, it blends well with tomatoes and is essential in most tomato-sauced Italian dishes.

**HISTORY:** The botanical name for basil is derived from the Greek "to be fragrant," even though many Greeks disliked basil. They believed that scorpions bred under basil pots and one Greek writer insisted that basil existed "only to drive men insane." In India, however, Hindus believed that if a leaf of basil were buried with them, it would serve as their passport to heaven.

**FORMS AND COMMON USAGE:** Basil is available in leaf form. It is used as a seasoning for pizza, spaghetti sauce, sausage, soup, tomato juice, dressings, and salads. Many Italian cooks prefer to use basil instead of oregano. Basil is also a common flavoring in Thai cuisine.

# *Bay Leaves* *(Laurus nobilis)*

**HERB DESCRIPTION:** Bay leaves, also known as bay laurel, are harvested from the evergreen laurel tree that is native to the Mediterranean region. They have a woody, astringent flavor with a pleasant, slightly minty aroma. Bay leaves are imported primarily from Turkey.

**HISTORY:** Bay leaves have long been associated with honor and celebration and therefore, were used in wreaths to crown victors. Champions of the Olympic Games wore garlands of bay leaves. The word "baccalaureate," signifying the successful completion of one's bachelor studies, means "laurel berries." Bay leaves have always had a reputation for protection against lightning, witchcraft, and evil.

**FORMS AND COMMON USAGE:** Bay leaves are robust, strongly aromatic, and indispensable to most cuisines, especially French, Mediterranean, and Indian. They are used to flavor all kinds of meat and vegetable dishes, soup, sauces, and occasionally custards. Bay leaves should always be removed before food is served.

# Caraway Seed *(Carum carvi)*

**SPICE DESCRIPTION:** Caraway has a sharp, pleasant, slightly bitter flavor with a sweet undertone. Caraway seed gives rye bread its characteristic flavor, which resembles a blend of dill and anise. Most caraway is grown in Eastern Europe, Holland, and Egypt. Because of its uniform shape, consistent color, and oil content, Dutch caraway is considered the premium seed. Egyptian caraway is milder than Dutch caraway.

**HISTORY:** Caraway seed is believed to have been cultivated and used in Europe longer than any other condiment. The seeds themselves have been found in debris of the earliest lake dwellings in Switzerland. As early as the first century, Dioscorides, a renowned Greek physician, recommended its use as a tonic for "pale girls." By the Middle Ages, caraway was cultivated widely throughout Europe and later was even mentioned by Shakespeare in his plays.

**FORMS AND COMMON USAGE:** Caraway is available as the whole seed. Many German recipes call for caraway seed in bread, dishes made with sauerkraut, and sauerbraten. Austrian cooks use caraway seed in stews, and Italians boil chestnuts with caraway seed prior to roasting.

# Cardamom Seed *(Elettaria cardamomum)*

**SPICE DESCRIPTION:** Cardamom has a grapefruit-like, floral flavor with some green and woody notes and a menthol undertone. The flavor somewhat resembles ginger. Cardamom is the dried, unripened fruit of the perennial *Elettaria cardamomum*. The tiny, brown, aromatic seeds, which are slightly pungent to the taste, are enclosed in pale cream-colored pods.

Two varieties are grown in India but cardamom is also cultivated in Guatemala and Sri Lanka. Indian cardamom is considered premium quality: the Malabar variety, more rounded in shape, has a pleasant mellow flavor; the Mysore variety, which is ribbed and three-cornered, has a slightly harsher flavor. Guatemalan cardamom compares favorably with that of Indian origin.

**HISTORY:** Cardamom was grown in the garden of the king of Babylon in 721 B.C. The ancient Greeks and Romans used cardamom in perfumes and it is used in the cosmetic industry today.

**FORMS AND COMMON USAGE:** Cardamom is available whole and ground. Whole cardamom seed has long been used as a breath freshener. Turkish coffee is flavored with cardamom and many Scandinavian bakers use cardamom in pastries and breads. Indian curries contain cardamom as one of many spices.

# Celery Seed and Celery Salt *(Apium graveolens)*

**SPICE DESCRIPTION:** Celery seed is harvested from a wild variety of the celery plant that is native to the Mediterranean region. The seeds are oval in shape and light brown in color. They are so tiny that it takes 750,000 of them to make a pound. The principal sources of celery seed are India and China. Celery salt is a blend of ground celery seed and fine salt. Use celery seed sparingly and enjoy its aromatic and slightly bitter flavor.

**HISTORY:** The history of celery actually dates back to "smallage," a wild, bitter, marsh plant. The ancient Greeks and Romans used celery for its medicinal properties, and it was popularly believed to be an aphrodisiac. In the Middle Ages, Italian farmers began to cultivate "smallage," but it was not until the 19th century that celery seed began appearing in recipes.

**FORMS AND COMMON USAGE:** Celery seed is available whole, ground, or mixed with salt. It is used primarily as a flavoring in salads (especially potato), sauces, pickling, soup, tomato juice, and meat. It is also an integral part of the flavoring of traditionally prepared crabs and other seafood.

# Chili Powder

**SPICE DESCRIPTION:** Chili powder is a blend of ground spices with an earthy, slightly sweet, and sometimes hot flavor. Some of these spices include oregano, cumin, garlic, and ground chili pepper. This spice blend usually dominates food rather than enhancing it.

**HISTORY:** The Aztecs used a similar spice blend, but chili powder as we know it was developed in Texas in 1835.

**FORMS AND COMMON USAGE:** Chili powder is available in both hot and mild blends. Mexican and other Latin American dishes depend on chili powder for their characteristic flavor.

# Chives *(Allium schoenoprasum)*

**SPICE DESCRIPTION:** Chives have a mild scallion flavor. The hollow leaves of this bulbous plant are quickly freeze-dried to preserve fresh color and flavor.

**HISTORY:** Chives, like their more pungent cousins onion and garlic, have a long history of seasoning foods. Traditionally grown in the cooler climates of the Northern Hemisphere, chives are frequently grown in small gardens at home.

**FORMS AND COMMON USAGE:** Chives enhance fish, veal, pork, and chicken. Chives are often used in soups such as tomato, potato, and cucumber, or with baked potatoes, dips, and salads. They are excellent when used in scrambled eggs or as a garnish.

# Cilantro *(Coriandrum sativum)*

**SPICE DESCRIPTION:** Cilantro has a bold flavor often described as a mixture of sage, parsley, and citrus. In Mexican dishes and salsas, cilantro is the "indescribable" flavor note that sets them apart. Cilantro is the young leaves of the *Coriandrum sativum* herb. The seed of the mature plant is coriander, a different flavor.

**HISTORY:** Cilantro is believed to be one of the earliest plantings in North America, dating back to 1670; however, it is mentioned in earlier writings as one of the plants that grew in the Hanging Gardens of Babylon.

**FORMS AND COMMON USAGE:** Cilantro adds pungent flavor to many Latin American and Asian dishes such as soup, steamed fish, and noodle dishes. It is also used in Indian chutneys, Moroccan stews, and Thai salads. It is often called "Chinese parsley."

# Cinnamon

*(Cinnamomum, C. zeylanicum burmannii, C. loureiril, C. cassia)*

SPICE DESCRIPTION: Cinnamon has a characteristic woody, musty, earthy, and sweet flavor. It is warming to taste. Most cinnamon brought into the United States is actually cassia but goes by the name cinnamon.

Cassia is the bark from the genus *Cinnamomum*, which grows in Southeast Asia. It is a member of a botanical family comprised of evergreen trees of the tropics and subtropics.

"True" cinnamon (*C. zeylanicum*) comes from Sri Lanka. Like all spices, cinnamon was originally harvested in the wild. Today, however, most is grown plantation-style. Although the best quality cinnamon comes from older trees, plantation owners and farmers cannot afford to wait 20 to 30 years to harvest their crop and therefore most trees are harvested after 10 years. At harvest, the bark is stripped off and put in the sun, where it curls into the familiar form called "quills." Four species of the tree provide raw material for the world's cinnamon trade.

The major origins of cinnamon are Indonesia, Sri Lanka, China, and Vietnam.

HISTORY: Cinnamon and cassia are two of the oldest known spices. The ancient Egyptians used them for both cosmetics and embalming. As early as 1500 B.C., the Egyptians sent buying expeditions to present-day Somalia because it was near ancient spice-trading sea routes. Cassia and cinnamon grow in China and Southeast Asia. The true sources of cinnamon and cassia were once a mystery. The Arab traders who supplied the Greeks and Romans invented fables about the geographic origins and gathering of cinnamon and cassia so their role as middlemen in the trade would not be disturbed. Cinnamon was one of the first spices to be sought in 15th and 16th century European explorations. Indirectly, it led to the discovery of America.

FORMS AND COMMON USAGE: Cinnamon is an important baking spice. It is available whole, as cinnamon sticks, and ground. In ground form, it is used in cakes, buns, cookies, and pies. In stick form, cinnamon is used to flavor beverages, such as coffee, cider, tea, and hot chocolate.

# Cloves *(Syzygium aromaticum)*

SPICE DESCRIPTION: The flavor of cloves is strong, fruity, and sweet—almost hot. They have a penetrating, astringent flavor that leaves a numbing sensation in the mouth. Cloves are the dried, unopened, nail-shaped flavor buds of an evergreen tree. The word "clove" comes from the French *clou*, meaning "nail."

Cloves are believed to be native to the Molucca Islands of Indonesia. Today, the majority of cloves imported to the United States come from the Indian Ocean basin, where clove trees cover thousands of acres of the islands. The largest grower of cloves today is Indonesia, where they are used to flavor local cigarettes.

The clove tree is propagated by seed. After the seeds have been transplanted to fields, the first crop can be harvested when the trees are six to eight years old. At harvest, the unopened buds are removed from the trees by hand and spread in the sun to dry for several days.

**HISTORY:** The first references to cloves are found in Oriental literature of the Han period in China under the name "tongue spice." Courtiers were required to hold cloves in their mouths when addressing the emperor during the Han dynasty, 206 B.C. to A.D. 220. From the eighth century on, cloves became one of the major spices in European commerce. In the 18th century, seeds of the clove tree were stolen from the Dutch by French traders to break the Dutch monopoly in the spice trade.

**FORMS AND COMMON USAGE:** Cloves are available both whole and ground. Whole cloves are popular for flavoring ham, pork, pickled fruit, onions, gravy, and syrup. Ground cloves are an internationally popular spice. More than half the world's production of cloves is used in the manufacture of clove-flavored cigarettes in Indonesia.

Ground cloves are used in spice cake, pumpkin pie, fruitcake, gingerbread, chili sauce, ketchup, and in combination with many other spices.

# *Coriander Seed* (*Coriandrum sativum*)

**SPICE DESCRIPTION:** Coriander is the dried ripe fruit of the herb *Coriandrum sativum*. The tannish brown seed has a sweet, slightly lemony flavor.

Most coriander is produced in Canada, Morocco, Romania, and Egypt, but China and India also offer limited supplies. Romanian and Chinese coriander are typically darker in appearance than the other types.

Coriander leaves are called cilantro.

**HISTORY:** Moses compared the color of manna to coriander seed. The ancient Greeks and Romans used it in love potions. Coriander was introduced in Massachusetts before 1670 and was one of the first herbs grown in America by the colonists.

**FORMS AND COMMON USAGE:** Coriander is available as whole seed and ground and is a principal ingredient in curry powder. Middle Eastern, Indian, Russian, North African, and Mexican recipes include coriander for its distinctive flavor. Coriander seed is a pleasant addition to potato salad, hot dogs, apple pie, poached fish, or bean, pea, and lentil soup.

# *Cumin* *(Cuminum cyminum)*

**SPICE DESCRIPTION:** Cumin is the dried seed of an herb from the parsley family. The yellowish brown seed, which resembles caraway, has a penetrating musty, earthy flavor with some green, grassy nuances. The major sources of cumin are India, Turkey, Pakistan, and China. The correct time for planting cumin seed is dependent on the arrival of the monsoon season.

**HISTORY:** Babylonian and Assyrian doctors used cumin in drugs and it was used as a food preservative by early Greeks and Romans. The cumin seed is referenced in both the biblical Old Testament (Isaiah 28:27) and New Testament (Matthew 23:23). In the Middle Ages, cumin was believed to keep both chickens and lovers from wandering. More recently, cumin has become popular because of its use in many Mexican dishes.

**FORMS AND COMMON USAGE:** Cumin is available as whole seed and ground. It is a principal ingredient in both chili powder and curry powder. Middle Eastern, Mexican-Indian, and North African recipes often include cumin.

# *Curry Powder*

**SPICE DESCRIPTION:** Curry powder is a blend of 15 or more ground spices. Flavors vary according to the use or the creator of the blend. All curry blends have a rich, warm, earthy, and pungent flavor with a great many overtones. The characteristic golden color comes from turmeric. Curry powder may contain ginger, fenugreek, cloves, cinnamon, cumin, and pepper, as well as other spices that determine the character of a particular type of curry powder.

**HISTORY:** The name "curry" probably was derived from the Indian word *kari,* meaning "spice." Curry powder originated in India, where people mix their own spices for different curries. Curry is also a popular dish in England.

**FORMS AND COMMON USAGE:** Curry powder is available in mild or hot blends. Curry powder is usually intended to be the dominant flavor but it also may be used in small amounts simply to enhance the flavor of foods such as corn bread, stuffed eggs, soup, and sour cream dips.

# *Dill* *(Anethum graveolens)*

**SPICE DESCRIPTION:** Dill is an annual of the parsley family and is related to anise, caraway, coriander, cumin, and fennel. It is native to Europe but is now grown commercially in California. Dill is available both as dill weed (the green leaf portion) and as dill seed. Dill seed is purchased from India or China. The seeds are light brown in color, strongly aromatic, and warming to the taste. Dill weed has a subtle, anise-like, sweet flavor.

**HISTORY:** Dill is reputed to have a calming effect on the digestive tract. It was given to crying babies, thus deriving its name from the Old Norse, *dilla,* meaning "to lull." Dill was believed to have magical properties and was used as a weapon against witchcraft. Dill was also reputed to cure hiccups, stomachaches, insomnia, and bad breath. In medieval times, injured knights are said to have burned dill seeds on their open wounds to speed healing.

**FORMS AND COMMON USAGE:** Dill is available as the whole seed and as chopped leaves, called dill weed. Dill weed is used in salads, sauces, egg dishes, and especially in seafood dishes. Dill seed is used primarily to flavor pickles and in bread, potato, and vegetable dishes. Dill is characteristically used in Russian, Middle Eastern, and Indian cooking.

# *Fennel Seed* (Foeniculum vulgare)

**SPICE DESCRIPTION:** Fennel seed is the dried fruit of a perennial in the parsley family. Tall and hardy, this plant has finely divided, feathery green foliage and golden yellow flowers. Because fennel is grown in dry areas, seed can be sown only after the spring monsoon. Seeds are ready for harvest when they harden and turn a greenish gray. The plants are then cut by hand and dried. The fennel seed has a warm, sweet, agreeable flavor and an odor similar to licorice and anise seed.

Today, the three largest sources of fennel seed are India, Egypt, and China. Of these, Egyptian fennel is considered the premium because of its consistent flavor, size, color, and cleanliness. In countries where fennel is grown, it is sometimes used like a bank account by farmers who bring it to market when they need cash. For this reason, buyers constantly monitor the market to buy only the freshest available.

**HISTORY:** Since ancient times, fennel seed has been enjoyed as a condiment and valued for its supposed medicinal qualities. In ancient Greece, it was considered a symbol of success. In fact, the Greek word for fennel is "marathon," because the Greek victory over the Persians in 470 B.C. at Marathon was fought on a field of fennel. In more recent history, the Puritans referred to it as the "meeting seed" because it was a favorite practice to chew the seed during meetings. Throughout the centuries, fennel has been used in medicines to relieve everything from a toothache to colic.

**FORMS AND COMMON USAGE:** Fennel is available as whole seed and is popular in pickling mixtures. Italian foods include fennel seed in sausage, spaghetti sauces, fish dishes, and bakery products. Fennel is also used in German bread and cookies, Polish borscht, English soup, Spanish bakery products, and in Chinese cuisines.

# *Garlic* (Allium sativum)

**SPICE DESCRIPTION:** Garlic, a member of the lily family, has been eaten for centuries as a reputed cure for toothaches, tuberculosis, and evil demons. The edible bulb grows under the ground. Most garlic is grown commercially in California, Texas, Egypt, and Mexico. It has a strong, pungent green flavor and is one of the most popular seasonings used today.

**HISTORY:** Garlic has been cultivated in Egypt, China, and India since before the beginning of recorded history. Egyptian priests placed garlic on the altars of the gods, and several garlic bulbs were found in the tomb of Tutankhamen. Garlic was used as a food by the Egyptian slaves who built the pyramids and by ancient Greeks and Romans. Hippocrates warned that garlic was bad for the eyes but good for the body. The ancients thought the smell of garlic would drive away serpents and scorpions. Books have been written on the benefits of garlic in maintaining good health and curing or preventing a variety of diseases. Medical research is still investigating the health benefits of garlic.

**FORMS AND COMMON USAGE:** Garlic can be conveniently purchased as fresh bulbs, dehydrated powder, minced flakes, and blends with salt. It adds flavor to almost any dish. Garlic is especially popular in Italian cuisine and throughout the Mediterranean region and Asia. Use it sparingly to begin with and add small acounts until it suits your taste.

**EQUIVALENTS:** One-eighth teaspoon garlic powder or dehydrated minced garlic is equivalent to one average-size clove of fresh garlic. One-half teaspoon garlic salt is equivalent to one average-size clove of fresh garlic. Be sure to reduce the amount of salt in a recipe when using garlic salt.

# *Ginger* (Zingiber officinale)

**SPICE DESCRIPTION:** The flavor of ginger is pungent, lemon/citrus, warm, and sweet. Growing ginger requires a consistently warm and moist climate with ample sunshine and heavy rainfall. The plant is propagated by dividing and planting the root-like structures called rhizomes. After about a full year of growth, the rhizomes are dug up, washed, boiled, and laid in the sun to dry for about eight days. The principal countries exporting dried ginger are India, Jamaica, and China.

**HISTORY:** Long cultivated by the ancient Chinese and Hindus, ginger was one of the first Oriental spices known in Europe. The Latin name, *Zingiber*, means "shaped like a horn" and refers to the roots, which resemble a deer's antlers. Throughout the early centuries, ginger was thought to have medicinal powers. In fact, King Henry VIII of

England recommended ginger as a remedy in the great plague of the 16th century. It is often used by pregnant women for "morning sickness."

Toward the end of the 19th century, ginger was commonly sprinkled on top of beer or ale and then stirred into the drink with a hot poker — thus, ginger ale.

**FORMS AND COMMON USAGE:** Ginger is available ground, whole (gingerroot), and crystallized. Chinese cooks use ginger to add zest to many dishes. Americans use ginger as the principal flavoring in gingersnaps and gingerbread and to round out the flavor of pumpkin pie. Ginger is also a common flavoring in the cooking of Germany, North Africa, and India. Crystallized ginger, which is fresh gingerroot cooked in syrup and dried, is used as a confection or condiment.

# Lemon Peel and Orange Peel

**SPICE DESCRIPTION:** Both lemon and orange peel are the dried natural rind of the fresh fruit. The flavor of the dehydrated peel is very similar to that of the grated fresh peel.

**HISTORY:** Native to India, lemons have been grown around the Mediterranean Sea since the first century. Sweet oranges were not known until about the 15th century. Although the fruit is grown in almost every subtropic region, most commercial peel comes from California.

**FORMS AND COMMON USAGE:** Substitute slightly less or an equal amount of lemon peel or orange peel for freshly grated peel in a recipe.

# Marjoram *(Origanum majorana)*

**HERB DESCRIPTION:** Marjoram is a member of the mint family and has a taste similar to oregano. The marjoram plant is a low, bushy perennial that grows 12 to 18 inches high. The majority of the crop is sourced in the Nile Valley of Egypt. Marjoram has a distinctly aromatic green and pleasant woody flavor, with a slightly bitter undertone.

**HISTORY:** Marjoram was well known in the Greco-Roman era. The ancient Greeks believed that if marjoram grew on a grave, the deceased would enjoy eternal peace and happiness. It was used as a medicine by Hippocrates. In the Middle Ages, it was said to be a stimulant, nerve tonic, and cure for asthma, coughs, indigestion, rheumatism, toothaches, and heart conditions.

**FORMS AND COMMON USAGE:** Available in both leaf and ground forms, marjoram should be used sparingly at first. It complements the flavor of chicken and turkey stuffing, vegetable and bean soup, as well as tomato sauces. Marjoram also enhances the flavor of many meat dishes.

# Mint *(Mentha spicata)*

**HERB DESCRIPTION:** Mint, also called spearmint, is native to Europe and Asia but is now sourced out of California and Egypt. It has an aromatic, sweet flavor with a cool aftertaste. Mint grows wild all over the world. It is cultivated mainly in Europe and the United States for its essential oil.

**HISTORY:** Mint was named by the Greeks after the mythical character Menthe. Menthe fought with Pluto's wife who turned her into the mint plant. Mint was used by ancient Assyrians in rituals to their fire god. The ancient Hebrews scattered mint leaves on the synagogue floor so each footstep would produce a fresh whiff of fragrance. Spearmint was used by ancient Greeks and Romans as an aromatic herb and in perfumes and bath scents. Mint has long been the symbol of hospitality.

**FORMS AND COMMON USAGE:** Mint is available in leaf form and is wonderful for flavoring main dishes such as lamb, as well as summer fruit desserts and beverages. It combines well with lamb, ham, carrots, potatoes, and tomatoes. Mint is popular in Tunisian, Middle Eastern, Indian, Thai, and Greek cuisines.

# Mustard Seed

*(Brassica hirta* - yellow or white; *Brassica juncea* - brown or black)

**SPICE DESCRIPTION:** Mustard has a clean, fresh aroma and a pungent, biting flavor. Mustard seed can be grown in most temperate climates and is widely grown throughout the world. Two main types of mustard seed are grown as a spice: yellow and brown. The seed used as the whole spice or in ground form is the yellow seed. The brown or Oriental seed is used mostly in the preparation of hot mustards. Mustard seed is planted in early spring and is an annual that grows about 24 inches high, producing bright yellow flowers with four petals. Mustard pods are rough and hairy, containing the small yellowish seeds that are about one-twelfth of an inch in diameter.

Although mustard seed is grown commercially in the western United States, most seed is imported from Canada. The Canadian seed is preferred because of its uniform golden color and minimum stem and chaff content.

HISTORY: "A tale without love is like beef without mustard; an insipid dish." This quote taken from the work of French humorist Anatole France seems to reflect accurately the popularity of mustard. The seed derives its name from the Latin *mustum,* meaning "mustseed," because the seed was processed in Roman-occupied Britain by saturating it with grape juice or "must." From early times, mustard has been used as both a medicine and condiment. Even today, "mustard plaster" is sometimes used in the treatment of rheumatism, arthritis, and some respiratory illnesses. The Spanish padres in California scattered mustard seed to mark the trails from mission to mission. These trails of mustard plants can still be found near some early missions.

FORMS AND COMMON USAGE: Mustard seed is most commonly used in its processed form, either as ground mustard or a prepared (wet) mustard. Ground mustard enhances meat, fish, poultry, sauces, salad dressings, cheese, and egg dishes. Unlike most other aromatic spices, ground mustard has no aroma when dry. It must be moistened for about ten minutes to develop its sharp, hot, tangy flavor. The whole seed is used in pickling, boiled with beets, cabbage, or sauerkraut, and as a garnish for salads.

# *Nutmeg and Mace* (Myristica fragrans)

SPICE DESCRIPTION: Nutmeg is called the "two for one spice." Both the nut-like seed and its covering (mace) are used. Piney and citrus-like flavors combine with sweet and bitter tastes to provide nutmeg's distinctive flavor. The flavor of mace is similar to nutmeg but it is more delicate. Both spices are derived from the peach-like fruit of the nutmeg tree. Nutmeg is the pit, or  seed, of the nutmeg fruit. Surrounding the hard shell of the pit is mace, a brilliant red, lacy, net-like membrane.

The nutmeg tree thrives in sheltered valleys close to the sea on hot, moist tropical islands. The primary sources of nutmeg and mace are Indonesia and Grenada.

HISTORY: Connecticut is known as "The Nutmeg State" because of its importance in the nutmeg trade. History books sometimes include tales of slick Yankee peddlers selling whittled wooden "nutmegs" to unsuspecting housewives.

FORMS AND COMMON USAGE: Nutmeg is available both whole and ground. Mace is sold primarily in the ground form. Nutmeg and mace are most commonly used in flavoring sweet foods such as puddings, cakes, and cookies. They are also used in meat products such as sausage. Nutmeg is also delicious sprinkled on eggnog.

# *Onion* *(Allium cepa)*

**SPICE DESCRIPTION:** Onions, along with their relative garlic, are members of the lily family. They can be grown from seed or bulblets (sets) in almost any temperate climate. Onions are believed to be native to southwestern Asia and are among the oldest known cultivated plants. Today onion is sourced out of California and Egypt. Onion has a characteristic pungency and bittersweet taste that complements many foods and cuisines.

**HISTORY:** Onions were cultivated by the ancient Babylonians. Onions, like garlic, were placed on the altars of the gods by the ancient Egyptians and were also fed to the slaves who built the pyramids. In the late 15th century, Columbus was believed to have brought the onion to the Dominican Republic, from where it quickly spread to Mexico, Central and South America, and to North America. For many years, it was believed that onions would help to heal gunpowder burns. In 1864, Ulysses S. Grant advised the government that he would not move any of his armies without onions, whereupon three carloads were immediately shipped to him.

**FORMS AND COMMON USAGE:** Onions are an important flavoring in almost every country in the world. When combined with other ingredients, onion flavor is rarely overwhelming or assertive. Onion is available as onion powder and instant minced onion.

**EQUIVALENTS:** One tablespoon onion powder equals one medium-size fresh onion. One tablespoon instant minced onion equals one-quarter cup minced raw onion.

# *Oregano* *(species of Lippia, Origanum)*

**HERB DESCRIPTION:** Oregano is the dried leaf of a perennial that is native to both the Mediterranean region and Mexico. Oregano that comes from Mexico has a different flavor from oregano that comes from the Mediterranean area. The Mexican plant *(Lippia)* is the more potent and is used primarily in chili powder and Mexican cooking. The Mediterranean form *(Origanum)* is sourced primarily in Turkey and Greece and has a slightly bitter, minty taste. It is used primarily in pasta sauces and pizza. Similar in flavor to marjoram, it is not as sweet and is slightly more pungent and bitter.

**HISTORY:** The Greek word "oregano" means "joy of the mountain." Since the early days of ancient Rome, oregano has been used as a flavoring for vegetables, wine, meat, and fish. The herb was not used widely in the United States until the end of World War II. Returning GIs liked its flavor so much that use jumped 400%.

**FORMS AND COMMON USAGE:** Oregano, which is available in both leaf and ground forms, is an essential ingredient in Italian, Greek, and Mexican cuisines. Use oregano in your favorite ethnic dishes as well as in fresh garden salads, egg dishes, and quick breads.

# *Paprika* *(Capsicum annuum)*

**SPICE DESCRIPTION:** Paprika is the dried, ground pod of a sweet red pepper. It is mildly flavored and prized for its brilliant red color.

Paprika is produced primarily in Spain, central Europe, and the United States. Historically, the central European varieties were more pungent, but they now exhibit a sweetness similar to Spanish paprika. Hungarian paprika is characterized by a hotter taste, achieved in recent times by adding hot, red capsicum pepper to ground paprika.

**HISTORY:** Early Spanish explorers took red pepper seeds back to Europe, where the plant gradually lost its pungent taste and became "sweet" paprika.

A Hungarian scientist won the Nobel Prize for research on the vitamin content of paprika. Pound for pound, it has a higher content of vitamin C than citrus fruit.

**FORMS AND COMMON USAGE:** Paprika, always sold in ground form, is one of the most popular seasonings.

Paprika is a colorful garnish for light-colored food such as fish, potatoes, eggs, and cheese dishes. It is the principal seasoning in Hungarian goulash and often is used in French dressing. To retain its red color, paprika should be kept in the refrigerator.

# *Parsley* *(Petroselinum crispum)*

**HERB DESCRIPTION:** Parsley is native to the rocky shores of the Mediterranean region. The curly leaf variety, chiefly grown in California, is the main source of dehydrated parsley flakes. Parsley has a slightly mild green taste that complements most dishes.

**HISTORY:** Parsley was used to flavor and garnish food as early as the third century B.C. The name "parsley" comes from the Greek word *petros,* meaning "stone," because the plant was often found growing among rocks. In ancient times, wreaths were made with parsley and were worn to prevent intoxication. Parsley was brought to the New World by the colonists.

**FORMS AND COMMON USAGE:** Parsley is available fresh or as dried flakes. This herb helps bring out the flavor of other herbs and seasonings and is a popular component of herb blends and seasonings. It adds both flavor and visual appeal to salads, soup, pasta, butters, shellfish, meat, and poultry.

# *Pepper* *(Piper nigrum)*

**SPICE DESCRIPTION:** Black pepper has a sharp, penetrating aroma and a characteristic woody, piney flavor. It is hot and biting to the taste. White pepper has a similar but more earthy flavor.

White pepper and black pepper are both produced from the berry of the vine *Piper nigrum.* For white pepper, the berry is picked when fully ripe. The outer layer of skin is removed, leaving the dried, grayish white kernel. For black pepper, the berries are picked while still green, allowed to ferment, and are then dried until they shrivel and turn a brownish black color.

Pepper grows on a vine that must be supported by a host tree or stake in order to survive. The supported vines grow up to 100 feet long, but to facilitate harvest, vines are trained to grow only five or six feet high. Pepper vines require three years to mature and produce peppercorns, but the vines will continue to produce for many years.

Pepper is one of the most important spices in the world, and there are four major growing areas: India, Brazil, Indonesia, and Malaysia.

**HISTORY:** Because pepper can be stored for many years without losing its flavor and aroma, it has long been known as the master spice. Pepper was so precious in ancient times that it was used as money to pay taxes, tributes, dowries, and rent. It was weighed like gold and used as a common medium of exchange. In A.D. 410, when Rome was captured, 3,000 pounds of pepper were demanded as ransom.

**FORMS AND COMMON USAGE:** Pepper is available as whole peppercorns, ground black pepper, coarse ground black pepper, cracked black pepper, white peppercorns, ground white pepper, and freeze-dried green peppercorns.

Black and white pepper are widely used in recipes of almost every nation on earth. White pepper is especially popular in Europe, where it is used in fish dishes and light-colored sauces. Black pepper is used in the German cookie pfeffernüsse.

# *Red Pepper* *(Capsicum [C. annuum] frutescens)*

SPICE DESCRIPTION: Red pepper is the dried ripened fruit pod of *Capsicum frutescens*, one of the most pungent capsicums native to tropical America, the West Indies, and much of South America. Red pepper has a hot, pungent flavor. Use with caution!

Although there is no botanical relationship between the capsicum pods of the Western world and the true pepper berries (peppercorns) of the Eastern world, the misnomer "pepper" has stuck with the red pods down through the centuries. A wide variety of sweet and pungent peppers came from the small capsicum pepper found by Columbus. They evolved in other climates as the great Portuguese navigators took the plant around the world.

HISTORY: It was only a quirk of history that gave the capsicum its name, pepper. Spanish explorers of the islands of the New World found little red-colored vegetable pods, which the Indians used in cooking to impart a sharp bite to food. In what may have been innocent confusion, or perhaps a little face-saving, the Spaniards named their discovery *pimienta,* their word for "pepper."

FORMS AND COMMON USAGE: Red pepper is available ground and crushed. Ground red pepper, often called "cayenne," is used in many spice blends, where it adds color and flavor to Mexican and Italian dishes. Chinese, Thai, Indian, Indonesian, and North African recipes also call for red pepper. Crushed red pepper is often sprinkled on salads and Italian foods at the table.

# *Pickling Spice*

SPICE DESCRIPTION: Pickling spice is a specially blended mixture of whole and broken cinnamon, allspice, mustard seed, coriander, bay leaves, ginger, chilies, cloves, black pepper, mace, and cardamom.

FORMS AND COMMON USAGE: It is perfect for flavoring pot roast, spiced fruit, shrimp, sauerkraut, and, of course, for pickling. Place a tablespoon or two of pickling spice in a cheesecloth bag so it is easy to remove at the end of the cooking process.

# *Poppy Seed* *(Papaver somniferum)*

**SPICE DESCRIPTION:** Poppy seeds are very small in size, nut-like in flavor, and can be cultivated in most temperate regions of the world. Throughout the years, varieties of poppies that have high seed yield and low narcotic potential have been developed. Poppy seeds are so tiny that each pod may contain hundreds of seeds. The color of the seed can range from white to blue to black.

Poppy seed is produced in various countries including the Netherlands, Australia, Romania, and Turkey. The Dutch variety, noted for its uniform slate blue color, is recognized as the best quality seed.

**HISTORY:** Poppy seed has been cultivated for over 3,000 years. The tiny poppy seed actually comes from the plant that produces opium. The botanical name for the poppy flower means "sleep bearing." Poppies were even used in the *Wizard of Oz* to put Dorothy to sleep. The seed does not have this effect. Compared to the history of opium, the seed's history is quite peaceful, with mention of its use as a condiment as early as the first century A.D. The red poppy flower has been the symbol of fallen warriors throughout history and was adopted as the emblem to commemorate Veterans Day in the United States.

**FORMS AND COMMON USAGE:** Poppy seed is sold only in the whole form and can be used as a topping or as an ingredient in bread, rolls, cakes, and cookies. Poppy seed butter is used with rice, noodles, fish, and vegetables. Poppy seed filling is used in pastries and strudel.

# *Poultry Seasoning*

**HERB DESCRIPTION:** Poultry seasoning is a mixture of ground thyme, sage, marjoram, rosemary, black pepper, and nutmeg.

**FORMS AND COMMON USAGE:** Poultry seasoning was created mainly to season stuffing but it also adds unusual flavor to many other dishes. Use it to add special flavor to all poultry, pork, or veal dishes.

# Rosemary *(Rosmarinus officinalis)*

**HERB DESCRIPTION:** Rosemary is leaves from a perennial shrub of the mint family that is native to the Mediterranean area. The slender, slightly curved leaves are grayish green in color and resemble pine needles. Rosemary has a distinctive fresh, sweet, piney aroma and flavor. Today, rosemary is grown in France, Spain, Portugal, and the former Yugoslavia.

**HISTORY:** Rosemary has been used extensively since 500 B.C. In ancient Greece, it was recognized for its alleged ability to strengthen the brain and memory. Greek students braided rosemary into their hair to help them with their exams. Rosemary's name joins two Latin words meaning "dew of the sea" because it thrives where fog and salt spray meet. It is also known as the herb of remembrance. In *Hamlet,* Ophelia said, "There's rosemary, that's for remembrance." Even today, it is placed on the graves of English heroes. Rosemary was used by the American colonists to scent soap.

**FORMS AND COMMON USAGE:** Rosemary is available in leaf form. Its distinctive flavor blends well with lamb, pork, potatoes, carrots, stews, marinades, fish, poultry, and bread. Rosemary is especially appealing on grilled or skewered meat and in roasted potato dishes.

# Saffron *(Crocus sativus)*

**SPICE DESCRIPTION:** Saffron is the most expensive spice in the world. It is the dried stigma of the saffron crocus flower. The stigmas must be harvested by hand and it takes 225,000 of them to make one pound of saffron. Saffron is used both for color and for its pleasantly bitter flavor. Use sparingly; a little goes a long way.

**HISTORY:** Saffron is native to the Mediterranean area and most imported saffron comes from Spain. The ancient Assyrians used saffron for medicinal purposes. The Greeks and Romans used it to perfume their luxurious baths. The bright orange-yellow color also made saffron useful as a dye.

**FORMS AND COMMON USAGE:** A few threads of saffron are enough to flavor and color several servings of rice or paella. Scandinavian recipes call for saffron in cakes, rolls, and pastries. French, Spanish, and South American dishes often include saffron.

# *Sage* *(Salvia officinalis)*

**HERB DESCRIPTION:** Sage is a hardy evergreen shrub of the mint family. It is native to the Mediterranean and has been traditionally sourced from the former Yugoslavia. It is also available in Italy, Russia, Albania, Turkey, and Greece. The herb is distinctively aromatic and fragrant with slightly medicinal, piney, and bitter flavors.

**HISTORY:** Sage was used during the Middle Ages to treat many maladies including fevers, liver disease, and epilepsy. The herb was used in England to make a tea that was considered a pleasant and healthful beverage. One common belief was that sage strengthened the memory, hence a sage, or a wise man, always had a long memory. In the 9th century, Charlemagne had sage included among the herbs grown on the imperial farms in Germany. During the 17th century, the Chinese exchanged three or four pounds of their tea with Dutch traders for one pound of European sage leaves.

**FORMS AND COMMON USAGE:** Sage is available in leaf, rubbed or crushed, and ground forms. It is used to flavor pork, especially pork sausage, other kinds of meat, and poultry stuffing. Sage is an important flavoring in the classic dish saltimbocca.

# *Savory* *(Satureja montana)*

**HERB DESCRIPTION:** Savory has a flavor that is a cross between thyme and mint. It grows well in most temperate climates and is native to southern Europe and the Mediterranean region. Most commercial savory comes from the Adriatic coast of Croatia. Savory is available in both summer and winter varieties. Cultivated summer savory is slightly milder than the winter variety, which some prefer. Savory has a slightly peppery, minty, and medicinal flavor that blends well with other herbs.

**HISTORY:** Savory, with its peppery flavor, was known to the Romans before the first lots of true pepper were imported from India. In the first century B.C., Virgil grew savory as ambrosia for his bees, believing that it made their honey taste better. In the Middle Ages, savory was used as a flavoring for cakes, pies, and puddings.

**FORMS AND COMMON USAGE:** Savory is available in ground form and gives a piquant flavor to many dishes. Use savory in a favorite bean soup, meat loaf, hamburgers, eggs, or poultry.

# Sesame Seed *(Sesamum indicum)*

**SPICE DESCRIPTION:** Also known as benne seed, sesame is a small, oval shaped seed that has a rich, nut-like flavor when roasted.

Most of the sesame seed sold in the United States is grown in Mexico, Central America, and China. Sesame is among the most nutritious of the seeds. It is 25 percent protein and contains two amino acids lacking in many other sources of vegetable protein. Sesame seed, an annual herb, is harvested by hand and may range in color from yellowish white to red, brown, and black. Most of the seed that comes to the United States is pearly white with a glossy finish.

**HISTORY:** Sesame seed may be the oldest condiment known to man and probably was the first crop grown for its edible oil. The Babylonians made sesame cakes, wine, and brandy and used the oil for cooking and toiletries. Sesame was used by the Egyptians as a medicine as early as 1500 B.C. "Open Sesame" was the magical password that opened the entrance to the cave in *Ali Baba and the Forty Thieves*. This reference is perhaps attributable to the fact that ripe sesame seed pods open with a sharp pop at the slightest touch. Late in the 17th and 18th centuries, slaves brought the seed to America. In some parts of the South, it is still known as "benne," which was its name in the African (Bantu) dialect.

**FORMS AND COMMON USAGE:** Sesame seed is sold whole, and is widely used. Bread stick, cracker, and bread bakers, as well as snack food manufacturers and health food companies all use sesame seed. Its high protein content makes this seed popular with the health food industry. Hulled sesame is the principal ingredient in the Middle Eastern confection halvah. Toasted sesame is used on a variety of bakery products. Sesame oil is considered a specialty salad and cooking oil. Tahini is a paste made from ground sesame seeds.

# *Tarragon* (*Artemisia dracunculus*)

**HERB DESCRIPTION:** Tarragon is one of the most aromatic of herbs and a favorite of connoisseurs because of its intriguing flavor. Tarragon is harvested from a shrub-like perennial and has floral licorice-like flavor, reminiscent of anise. Although available in other varieties, French is preferred because of its smoother, glossier leaves and more aromatic, pungent flavor. California is the usual source for U.S. consumers. Tarragon gives a distinctive flavor to classic béarnaise sauce and tarragon vinegar.

**HISTORY:** The English word "tarragon" originates from the French word *estragon* or "little dragon," which is derived from the Arabic *tarkhun*. Some believe the herb was given this name because of its supposed ability to cure the bites of venomous reptiles, while others believe the plant was so named because of its coiled, serpent-like roots. Although alluded to briefly in the 13th century as a seasoning for vegetables, a sleep-inducing drug, and a breath sweetener, tarragon did not become well known until the 16th century. Around 1550, it was introduced into England.

**FORMS AND COMMON USAGE:** Tarragon is a versatile herb that complements fish, green salads, and chicken dishes. It is also used to prepare infused vinegars. In Cajun cuisine, tarragon is used to marinate carrot salads and as a complement to seafood, casseroles, and marinades.

# *Thyme* (*Thymus vulgaris, T. hyemalis*)

**HERB DESCRIPTION:** Thyme, a member of the mint family, is native to the Mediterranean region. It grows best in a mild climate in a well-drained, sunny location. Although the herb grows well in much of southern Europe, most thyme is sourced from Spain. It has a warm, pleasant, medicinal, green, and aromatic flavor.

**HISTORY:** The name "thyme," derived from Greek, has been given many meanings including courage, sacrifice, and "to fumigate." Thyme was a symbol of courage and bravery over 2,000 years ago in Greece. The linkage of thyme with courage continued well into the Middle Ages, when ladies embroidered a sprig of thyme on the scarves of knights. Assyrian doctors and chemists recognized the medicinal properties of thyme and used it as a fumigant. The ancient Greeks and Romans used it to flavor cheese and liquor.

**FORMS AND COMMON USAGE:** Thyme is available in both leaf and ground forms. Use it as a flavoring in chowders, meat, Creole seafood dishes, poultry dressing, and tomatoes. Thyme is also a wonderful seasoning in many vegetarian dishes, especially bean soup.

# *Turmeric* *(Curcuma longa)*

**SPICE DESCRIPTION:** Turmeric is the dried root of a plant similar in size and related to ginger. Its flavor is woody and earthy.

India is the primary exporter of turmeric, although Peru, Haiti, and Jamaica are additional sources. It thrives in hot, moist, tropical climates with well-drained soil.

**HISTORY:** The use of turmeric as a coloring agent for food and fabric dates as far back as 600 B.C. Marco Polo, in 1280, mentioned turmeric in notes of his travels in China: "There is also a vegetable that has all the properties of true saffron, as well as the smell and the color, and yet it is not really saffron." In medieval Europe, turmeric was known as "Indian saffron." Since then, turmeric has been used as an inexpensive substitute for saffron.

**FORMS AND COMMON USAGE:** Turmeric is sold in ground form. While turmeric has little retail demand as an individual spice flavor, it is one of the major ingredients in curry powder, a mixture of many spices including ginger, fenugreek, cloves, cinnamon, cumin, and black and red pepper. Turmeric is also used in pickles and relishes and to flavor and color prepared mustard.

# *Vanilla* *(Vanilla planifolia)*

**SPICE DESCRIPTION:** Vanilla extract is made from the bean-like fruit of an orchid plant, *Vanilla planifolia*. This accounts for 99 percent of the vanilla imported into the United States. Another species, *Vanilla tahitensis* (Tahitian vanilla) is also used in small amounts. The vanilla plant is native to Mexico. Vanilla is now also grown on the Indian Ocean islands of Madagascar and Comoro as well as in Indonesia, Uganda, Tonga, and Mexico.

Through a laborious process, vanilla flowers are hand-pollinated and the resultant beans are allowed to mature for nine months. The vanilla on the vine looks like long thin green beans. The curing process, which develops the complex flavors, begins once the beans have been picked. Each country of origin has its own method for curing the beans. The beans must undergo a boiling or blanching process to stop maturation and then undergo sweating and drying processes. These processes include covering the beans, keeping them warm for several days to "sweat," and then using the sun or dryers. The beans are dried for several hours each day for several months until the curing process is complete. After curing, the beans are imported into the United States for extraction.

**HISTORY:** History says that vanilla was enjoyed by the Aztecs in a drink called *xoco-latl*, which was made from cocoa and vanilla beans. It was this drink that Cortés sampled and brought back to Spain with reports it contained magical powers. Europeans mixed vanilla beans with their tobacco for smoking and chewing and considered it a miracle drug. It wasn't until the 1880s that vanilla became universally accepted as a powerful food flavoring with no particular medicinal properties.

FORMS AND COMMON USAGE: Vanilla extract, a popular flavoring in cakes, cookies, and puddings, is a versatile flavoring that can also be used with many other different kinds of food. It rounds out flavors in a variety of dishes and is especially pleasant with seafood. Add a dash of pure vanilla extract to melted butter served with lobster. Use vanilla extract with heavy cream, yogurt, or dairy sour cream to top strawberries or fresh fruit salads.

Vanilla beans are also available. Use the whole beans to flavor sugar, custards, and coffee.

Make your own vanilla sugar by combining 1 cup of sugar with a 3-inch piece of vanilla bean. Blend in a food processor until the vanilla bean has been reduced to tiny specks. Store the vanilla sugar in a tightly closed container. Sprinkle it on cereal, fruit, or waffles. Use it when baking cakes and cookies. It is especially good when used as the sugar in homemade ice cream.

# OTHER EXTRACTS / FLAVORINGS

• *Pure Almond Extract* has a smooth, cherry-like, nutty flavor that enhances a variety of foods and is especially good with fruit dishes. It can be used to flavor coffee beans, cakes, cookies, and icings.

• *Pure Anise Extract* is derived from anise seed. It has a subtle licorice overtone and is used often in Italian cookies. Since this extract is robust in flavor, start with a small amount, taste, then add more, if desired. One teaspoon of extract has the flavor strength of 1½ teaspoons anise seed.

• *Banana Extract* enriches natural banana flavor and teams up well with strawberry and almond flavors. Try adding ½ to 1 teaspoon of extract to your next batch of banana bread or to the custard in a banana cream pie.

• *Black Walnut Extract* works well with other extracts such as vanilla and anise. It does not have as pronounced a flavor as walnut itself, but it adds a nice background flavor. Add it to mayonnaise for a delicious Waldorf salad.

• *Brandy Extract* adds a festive note to many foods. To substitute brandy extract for brandy in a recipe, use one part of extract for each five parts of brandy called for in the recipe. Add a splash to eggnog, too.

• *Butter Flavor Extract* adds the flavor of butter, without the fat and calories, to many recipes. However, butter flavor cannot replace the fat required in baked goods such as cakes, cookies, and bread. Add ¼ teaspoon extract to water when cooking vegetables for butter flavor without adding calories.

- *Cherry Extract* adds the juicy flavor of ripe cherries and a pretty pink color to food. Add it to whipped cream to decorate a dessert.

- *Chocolate Extract* is a special favorite of chocolate lovers on a diet. They use this extract to make a low-calorie milk shake. It contains only eight calories per teaspoon! This extract also can be used with cocoa to create a more intense chocolate flavor.

- *Coconut Extract* will add a hint of the tropics to a basic cake. Its clear color makes it a perfect addition to a white icing. It also provides a great flavor in smooth frosty drinks.

- *Pure Lemon Extract* comes from the oil in the lemon rind. Its flavor is characteristic of the rind. It is excellent as flavoring for baked goods and other desserts — but not for use as a substitute for lemon juice in a recipe.

- *Maple Flavor Extract* will add excellent flavor to pancake syrup. Try it in a sweet potato casserole for a harvest flavor. It is delicious in baked beans, too. Homemade ice cream can also be flavored with this extract.

- *Pure Mint Extract* is a blend of spearmint and peppermint. It has a robust flavor and should be used in smaller amounts than the other extracts. Add it to apple jelly to accompany a lamb dish.

- *Pure Orange Extract* is made from the oil in the orange rind. The flavor characteristic is that of the rind. It is useful for flavoring desserts — but is not a good substitute for orange juice in recipes.

- *Pure Peppermint Extract* is made from the oil of peppermint and is robust in flavor. Add it to divinity or sugar cookie dough for holiday treats.

- *Pineapple Extract* permits you to enjoy the fresh flavor of pineapples any time. Team it with coconut extract to make a piña colada milk shake or add it to whipped topping for a special flavor.

- *Rum Extract* may be substituted for small amounts of rum in a recipe. Use 2 tablespoons of extract for 1 tablespoon of dark rum, or 1 tablespoon of extract for 5 tablespoons of light rum. It is good in cakes, cookies, and sauces, but not recommended if more than ¼ cup of rum is called for in a recipe.

- *Strawberry Extract* has the mildest flavor of all the extracts. It adds fruity flavor to toppings, cakes, and milk shakes. It also helps intensify the flavor of dishes that call for fresh strawberries.

- *Vanilla, Butter & Nut Flavor* is the ultimate in pound cake flavoring. The rich combination of vanilla, butter flavor, and nut flavor adds interest to custards and cookies as well. Add a teaspoon to your next pumpkin pie.

## BEEF FLAVOR BASE

Beef flavor base is the seasoned extract of beef and may be used as a base for beef broth and stock. Omit salt in recipes when you use this flavor base. Use it in French onion soup, meat gravy, beef stew, pot roast, barbecue sauce, and pilaf. It also adds flavor to hamburgers and meat loaf.

## CHICKEN FLAVOR BASE

Chicken flavor base is the seasoned extract of chicken. As a broth it adds flavor to casseroles and stews. Omit salt in recipes when using this versatile flavor base. Use it in soup, gravy, and stuffing. Add it to the water when cooking rice, vegetables, or pasta.

## BON APPÉTIT®

Bon Appétit is a blend of salt and ground seasonings that can be used to enhance the flavor of many foods. It is an extremely versatile seasoning and has a celery seed character. Be sure to decrease the amount of salt in your recipe when using Bon Appétit. This blend is delicious on meat dishes, soups, vegetables, and salad dressings. Use Bon Appétit to sprinkle on freshly steamed or stir-fried vegetables in the kitchen or at the table.

## CALIFORNIA STYLE GARLIC BLENDS

**Garlic Pepper** is a perfect blend of coarse ground garlic, black pepper, just the right amount of salt, and a touch of sweet bell pepper. It is the ultimate garlic seasoning, specially created for garlic lovers. Sprinkle it on steak, chicken, pork, or fish. Mix it into ground beef or turkey when making burgers and meatballs, or add it to salads, vegetables, pasta, or rice. It can also be added to marinades, dips, and cheese spreads — and it does not contain MSG.

**Garlic Powder** is a distinctive combination of natural, coarse ground garlic blended with a touch of parsley. One-quarter of a teaspoon is the equivalent of one average-size clove of fresh garlic.

**Garlic Salt** is a blend of coarse ground natural garlic, salt, and a touch of parsley. It provides the fresh flavor of garlic with just a shake. Garlic salt is delicious sprinkled on potatoes, pasta, and salad. It can be stirred into cooked vegetables and soup, and it can be added to steaks or chicken before grilling.

## CHINESE FIVE SPICE

Chinese Five Spice is a classic blend of spices used in Oriental dishes. It also adds an intriguing flavor to other foods. It has a sweet flavor with a hint of licorice and is added to roast pork, roast duck, and barbecued spareribs.

## HOT SHOT!® PEPPER BLEND

Hot Shot! is a zesty combination of coarsely ground black pepper and ground red pepper. Use it in cooking or sprinkle it on food at the table. Sprinkle on tossed salads, baked potatoes, and vegetables. Toss with pasta, add it to potato salad, or sprinkle it over stir-fried chicken.

## ITALIAN SEASONING

This robust mixture of herbs is designed to give food a characteristic Italian flavor. The salt-free blend of marjoram, thyme, rosemary, savory, sage, oregano, and basil imparts a classic Italian herb flavor. It is a versatile blend that can be used with a wide variety of foods: zucchini, eggplant, tomatoes, pizza, herb bread, dips, salad dressing, meat loaf, pot roast, veal, chicken, and fish. Italian seasoning adds extra flavor when sprinkled on poultry, seafood, meat, vegetables, and fish before grilling, broiling, sautéing, roasting, or braising.

## LEMON & PEPPER SEASONING

Lemon and pepper seasoning adds a distinct spicy lemon flavor to food. Use it on meat, poultry, fish, broccoli, asparagus, and artichokes. Sprinkle it on steaks or fish before broiling and add it to salad dressings. Use it at the table to sprinkle on salads, vegetables, or meat.

## MONTREAL STEAK SEASONING

This seasoning is a robust blend of coarsely ground black pepper, salt, and spices. It is a tasty and versatile seasoning blend that can be used to shake or rub on food or in a marinade. It is excellent on steaks, burgers, and roasts.

## OLD BAY® SEASONING

This unique blend of spicy seasonings was initially developed for use on seafood, but it is also delicious on many other kinds of food. It does not contain MSG. The Old Bay Seasoning was developed over 50 years ago and sold along the Baltimore waterfront. The name was taken from a steamship line then in operation on the Chesapeake Bay. Most cooks on the East Coast associate Old Bay with the blue crab, but in fact, it is used on shrimp, other seafood, poultry, French fries, and vegetables as well.

## SALAD SUPREME® SEASONING

Salad Supreme is a blend of seasonings that adds a unique and delightful flavor to salad greens, pasta salads, and vegetable salads. It also adds zest to meat, eggs, potatoes, and French bread.

### SEASON-ALL® SEASONED SALT

This versatile blend of ingredients includes salt and ten spices gathered from around the world. Use it instead of salt, in cooking and at the table. Season-All is an easy way to add just the right seasoning to a wide variety of foods.

The use of Season-All provides more savory salads, better burgers, and spicy pasta, poultry, fish, and vegetables. Sprinkle it on eggs and cottage cheese. Add it to casseroles, soup, stew, pot roast, and gravy. Shake it on meat as it grills and use it to add flavor and improve the appearance of meat cooked in a microwave oven.

Season-All is available in several varieties including spicy, garlic, and peppered. It is also available in a version that has 75 percent less sodium than regular Season-All.

### SEASONED PEPPER

Seasoned pepper is a pungent blend of black pepper with sweet pepper undertones. It can be used on meat, in salads, or for variety instead of black pepper.

### THAI SEASONING

Thai Seasoning is a delightful blend of chili pepper, ginger, coriander, cumin, cinnamon, and star anise, with just the right amount of heat to tease the tongue. It adds a delicious exotic flavor to vegetables and meat. Use it in stir-fry dishes, marinades, and rice.

# SEASONING BLENDS TO MAKE YOURSELF

### MEAT AND VEGETABLE BLEND

*1 tablespoon Marjoram Leaves*  
*1 tablespoon Basil Leaves*  
*1 teaspoon Celery Seed*  
*1 teaspoon Thyme Leaves*  
*1 teaspoon Onion Powder*

Combine all ingredients and store in airtight container. Shake well before using.

SUGGESTED USES: Sprinkle over hamburgers before cooking; add 1 teaspoon of blend for each pound of ground meat when making meat loaf; add ½ teaspoon of blend to 2 cups of vegetables during cooking; sprinkle over chicken before grilling.

### HERB BLEND FOR SOUP, STEWS, MEAT, AND POULTRY

*1 tablespoon Thyme Leaves*  
*1 tablespoon Marjoram Leaves*  
*2 teaspoons Rosemary Leaves*  
*1 teaspoon Rubbed Sage*

Grind all ingredients in blender, food processor, or with mortar and pestle. Store in airtight container. Use in place of salt when cooking or sprinkle over cooked food.

# GENERAL COOKING INSTRUCTIONS

∼

## *Using Spices in Cooking*

Tastes differ greatly; therefore, it's very difficult to give exact and precise directions for seasoning. What may be the ultimate taste to one person may be objectionable to another. The seasoning of food must be adjusted to suit the tastes of those being served. One important rule to remember is that seasonings should be used in small quantities, particularly a new or unfamiliar flavor. More seasoning can always be added if desired, but it's almost impossible to correct or remove seasoning if too much has been used.

The art of seasoning is to *enhance the natural flavors* of food, never to overpower it. Exceptions might be curry, some sauces, chili, or Thai food, where "heat" is a personal preference.

Spices and herbs make it possible to serve food with an almost unlimited variety of flavors. They can enhance the aroma, taste, and appearance of food. Spice and herb cookery does not have to mean preparing complicated, time-consuming, or expensive recipes. Nor does it have to mean long preparation or the creation of fancy, hot, exotic dishes, although you might find special dishes fun to prepare occasionally.

Well-seasoned food is food made to taste especially good — food given extra excitement and a "whole world of flavor" through the proper use of spices and herbs. This cookbook is designed to help you "season with taste."

Special attention to seasoning is required in microwave cooking. It takes time for spices and herbs to fully release their flavors when they are combined with food. The flavors are released during cooking, chilling, or adequate standing time. But microwave cooking, which has become synonymous with fast cooking, usually does not provide enough time for flavors to be fully released. Therefore many recipes are *not* appropriate for conversion to microwave cooking. When recipes are converted to microwave cooking, it usually is necessary to adjust the amount of seasoning used to compensate for the reduction in cooking time. Since ground spices release flavor more readily than whole spices, ground spices are usually preferred as a seasoning for food cooked in a microwave oven.

## Storage of Spices

- Spices and herbs will keep for a long time if they are stored in airtight containers, away from heat, moisture, and light.

- Do not store spices and herbs over the stove, dishwasher, or sink or near a window.

- Although spices and herbs do not spoil, they do lose their strength over time. The storage life of properly stored spices and herbs is approximately five years for whole spices, one to two years for ground spices, and six months for leafy herbs.

## Preparation Tips

- Read the entire recipe and assemble all ingredients and equipment before you begin to cook.

- Do not sprinkle spices and herbs directly from a container into a steaming pot. Steam hastens the loss of flavor and also causes the caking of spices and herbs.

- In spice cookery, recipes may be doubled or halved successfully if all ingredient amounts are multiplied or divided exactly by two. If a larger than double quantity is needed, make the recipe three or more times as needed, then combine the food.

- Tie whole spices in a cheesecloth or fabric bag for easy removal.

- When selecting fresh fruit and vegetables, be sure they are free of blemishes and have fresh, bright color. Trim stems and roots and cut according to recipe directions.

## Measuring Tips

- Always measure carefully and accurately. Measure liquids in a measuring cup designed especially to measure liquid. Liquid measuring cups have headspace above the cup mark to prevent liquid from spilling out. Measure dry ingredients in nested measuring cups that don't have any headspace so ingredients can be leveled with a small spatula or table knife for accuracy.

- To measure ⅛ teaspoon of a dry ingredient, measure a level ¼ teaspoon and then remove half of the measured ingredient.

- To measure honey or molasses, lightly grease or oil the cup or spoon before measuring the ingredient. If you don't, the measurement will not be accurate because some of the honey or molasses will adhere to the utensil.

- If a recipe calls for 1 cup chopped nuts or other ingredient, the nuts must be chopped before measuring. In a recipe calling for 1 cup nuts, chopped, the nuts are measured first and then chopped. If a recipe calls for 1 cup sifted flour, the flour is sifted first and then measured. If a recipe calls for 1 cup flour, sifted, measure the flour first and then sift it.

- When measuring brown sugar, always pack it firmly in the cup.

# Baking Tips

- When adding flour to cake batter, be careful not to overmix.

- When adding flour alternately with liquid, always start and end with flour.

- Always use the pan size specified in baking. A change in pan size requires an adjustment in baking and cooling times and can change the appearance, texture, and flavor of the finished product.

- After fluting the edge of pastry, press or crimp under rim of pie plate in several places to prevent shrinkage of crust.

- Preheat the oven before baking. Allow 15 to 20 minutes for the oven to reach the correct temperature.

- When using a glass cake pan, decrease the oven temperature by 25°F.

- Use an oven thermometer in the center of the oven to check oven temperature.

- Bake (or roast) with oven rack in center position unless recipe specifies a higher or lower position.

- To test a cake for doneness, insert a cake tester, skewer, or toothpick in the center of the cake. If it comes out clean, the cake is done. Another way to test for doneness is to touch the center of the cake gently with a finger. If no imprint remains when you remove the finger, the cake is done.

- To determine if a yeast dough has doubled in size, punch two fingers into dough. If impression remains, dough has doubled.

# Tips for Cooking Fish and Seafood

- Most varieties of fish are fully cooked when they flake easily with a fork.

- As a general rule, it's not necessary to turn fish when broiling or baking.

- Baste fish and shellfish during cooking with marinade, juices, or drippings to keep them moist when baking or broiling.

- For moist, tender shrimp, cook in well-seasoned, boiling water 5 minutes or just until pink.

- Spiced, steamed shrimp, popular in many sections of the country, require 10 to 15 minutes cooking time. Place shrimp on rack in steamer, add a small amount of water, and sprinkle generously with spices and herbs. Cover and steam. Steamed shrimp will be firmer and less moist than boiled shrimp.

- Cover frozen rock lobster tails (it is not necessary to thaw them) with salted water and heat to boil. Cook 3 minutes longer than the ounce weight of largest lobster tail, as in 10 minutes for 7-ounce lobster tail.

- Crab meat should be picked over carefully to remove cartilage and any bits of shell.

## Sauce and Gravy Tips

- Arrowroot is ideal for thickening pie fillings and sauces because it turns very clear when thickened and does not mask other flavors.

- When sauces are made in a double boiler, never allow the water in the bottom pan to touch the bottom of the top pan.

- If hollandaise sauce, béarnaise sauce, or any rich butter-egg sauce separates during preparation, add 1 to 2 teaspoons boiling water to sauce, stirring briskly.

- Overcooking can cause custards, rice pudding, and custard-type bread puddings to turn watery.

## Beverage Tips

- Freeze carbonated drinks, fruit juices, or a small amount of a punch mixture in a ring mold or loaf pan to make an ice ring or ice block that can be floated in the punch without diluting the flavor.

- Tea tends to get cloudy when refrigerated. Even though the cloudiness does not affect tea flavor, it does affect the way tea looks. Cloudiness can be removed by adding a small amount of boiling water to the tea.

## Miscellaneous Tips

- When deep-frying food, pan must be deep enough to allow 3 inches between the surface of fat and top of the pan in order to prevent overflow of fat and reduce chance of fire. Never cover a container when heating oil or when deep-frying.

- When cooking in a microwave oven, use a nonmetal container so microwaves can pass through the container and the food can be cooked evenly from all directions.

- Use low heat when cooking eggs or cheese.

- To hard-cook eggs, cover with cold water, heat to boil, remove from heat, cover, and let stand 10 to 20 minutes. Hard-cooked eggs will keep for 1 week in the refrigerator.

- A baking pan, referred to in this book, is ovenproof, usually shallow, and uncovered unless specified otherwise. A casserole is deep and usually has a cover.

- Vegetables retain their original color and most of their nutrient value when cooked quickly in a small amount of water in a saucepan with a tight-fitting cover. Vegetables also retain color and nutritional value when cooked in a microwave oven.

- Stir cooked rice with a fork to fluff it.

- Scallions and green onions are the same vegetable. The name depends on the area in which you live.

# Food Handling and Safety Tips

- Raw meat and poultry should be refrigerated no longer than two days after purchasing before they are cooked or frozen.

- When preparing raw meat, poultry, or eggs, discard packaging materials immediately. Use hot soapy water to thoroughly clean work surfaces and utensils that have been in contact with these foods. Work surfaces can be sanitized with a solution of 2 teaspoons of bleach in 1 quart of water.

- Don't thaw frozen food on a counter. Thaw it in the microwave oven or in the refrigerator.

- Perishable food should not be left out for longer than 1 hour when the temperature is 85°F or hotter.

- Store leftover food in small containers so the food can cool quickly. When cool, cover and refrigerate.

- Perishable food should be cooked at an oven temperature of at least 325°F, never lower.

- Store shelf-stable food in a cool, dry place. Don't store canned food in any location where the temperature goes below 32°F or above 85°F.

- Fresh eggs can be refrigerated 3 to 5 weeks.

- Cook egg yolks and egg whites until firm.

- Food mixtures containing raw eggs should be cooked to 160°F and stored in the refrigerator after cooking. According to the American Egg Board, "A meringue made with 3 egg whites, placed over a hot pie filling, and baked at 350°F, should reach 160°F in about 15 minutes. A meringue that has more than 3 egg whites will require 25 to 30 minutes at 325°F. Refrigerate meringue pies until ready to serve."

- If you are concerned about using the raw egg whites in several of the desserts in this cookbook, the American Egg Board recommends the following: "For further safety, combine the egg whites with the sugar in the recipe (using a minimum of 2 tablespoons of sugar per egg white) and beat over hot water or over low heat in a heavy saucepan until the whites stand in soft peaks. Without sugar, the whites will coagulate too rapidly and produce an unsatisfactory meringue."

- For safety, the American Egg Board also recommends cooking raw egg yolks used in dishes such as cold soufflés, chiffons, and mousses. It is important to note that *at least* 2 tablespoons of liquid per yolk should be added during cooking, otherwise, the result will be scrambled eggs.

# Tips for Cooking Meat and Poultry

- The most accurate way to judge the doneness of meat or poultry is with a meat thermometer. See Meat and Poultry Roasting Charts.

- To check meat for doneness, insert the thermometer into the thickest part of the meat. Be sure the bulb doesn't rest on fat or bone.

- To check poultry for doneness, insert thermometer so the bulb is in the center of the inside thigh muscle or the thickest part of the breast meat. If a meat thermometer is not used, test for doneness by moving the drumstick from side to side. When it moves easily, the bird is cooked.

- The USDA now recommends that fresh pork, other meat, eggs, fish, and poultry be cooked to a minimum internal temperature of 160°F. For those who prefer the flavor of more well-done meat, it can be cooked to 170°F or 180°F. Many of the recipes in this book recommend the higher temperatures in order to allow flavors to develop.

- Never thaw raw meat and refreeze without cooking.

# Meat Roasting Chart

| MEAT | OVEN TEMPERATURE | MINIMUM INTERNAL TEMPERATURE INDICATED ON MEAT THERMOMETER | WEIGHT OF MEAT | COOKING TIME PER POUND |
|---|---|---|---|---|
| Beef | 325°F | 160°F | 6 to 8 pounds | 18 to 20 min. *rare* 22 to 25 min. *medium* 27 to 30 min. *well-done* |
| Pork, fresh | 350°F | 160°F | 3 to 7 pounds | 35 to 40 min. |
| Ham, Precooked | 325°F | 130°F | 10 to 12 pounds | 12 to 15 min. |
| Ham, Smoked (uncooked) | 325F° | 160°F | 10 to 14 pounds | 18 to 20 min. |
| Lamb | 325°F | 160°F | 3 to 5 pounds | 30 to 35 min. |
| Veal | 325°F | 160°F | 5 to 8 pounds | 25 to 30 min. |

## Poultry Roasting Chart

| POULTRY | OVEN TEMPERATURE | MINIMUM INTERNAL TEMPERATURE INDICATED ON MEAT THERMOMETER | WEIGHT OF UNSTUFFED POULTRY | TOTAL COOKING TIME |
|---|---|---|---|---|
| Turkey | 325°F | 180°F in thigh, 170°F in breast, and 165°F in stuffing* | 12 to 16 pounds | 4 to 4½ hours |
| Chicken | 375°F | 180°F | 4 to 6 pounds | 2½ to 3½ hours |
| Duckling | 325°F to 350°F | 180°F | 4 to 5 pounds | 2 to 3 hours |
| Capon | 325°F to 350°F | 180°F | 6 to 8 pounds | 2½ to 3½ hours |
| Goose | 325°F | 180°F | 10 to 12 pounds | 4 to 5 hours |

*Stuffed birds require a slight increase (30 minutes) in cooking time.*

# Cooking Terms

**Al dente**  To cook pasta until it offers a slight resistance to the bite.

**Bake**  To cook in an oven or oven-type appliance. It is generally referred to as roasting when meat is cooked uncovered.

**Baste**  To moisten meat or other food during cooking by spooning or brushing food with liquid to add flavor and to prevent surface of food from drying out. The liquid is usually melted fat, meat drippings, fruit juice, sauce, marinade, or water.

**Beat**  To stir thoroughly and vigorously with a wire whisk, spoon, hand-beater, fork, or electric mixer to incorporate air into food.

**Blanch**  To partially cook vegetables or fruit in boiling water for 1 to 2 minutes.

**Blend**  To mix 2 or more ingredients thoroughly.

**Boil**  To cook in liquid that is at boiling temperature. Bubbles will rise continually and break on the surface. "To the boiling point" refers to a temperature of 200°F reached just before bubbles break the surface.

**Braise**  To brown meat or poultry in a small amount of liquid or fat, then cook over low heat in a covered utensil.

**Bread**  To coat a food with bread crumbs, cracker crumbs, or other food prior to cooking. The surface may be coated with beaten egg or other liquid first.

**Brew**  To steep or let stand in hot water to extract flavor, as in tea.

**Broil**  To cook under direct heat or over an open flame.

**Brown**  To cook food in a small amount of fat with moderate or high heat until it is browned.

**Candy**  To cook fruit or vegetables in sugar or syrup.

**Caramelize**  To heat sugar, or food containing sugar, over medium heat, stirring constantly, until a brown color develops.

**Chill**  To cool in refrigerator, but not freeze.

**Chop**  To cut food into small pieces with a knife, chopper, or other sharp tool, blender, or food processor.

**Coat**  To spread food with, or dip it into, a substance such as flour or sauce until it is covered. To cover with a thin layer of flour, sugar, nuts, crumbs, seeds, or spices.

**Coats a spoon**  To cook a mixture used for a sauce or soft custard until it is thick and forms a film on a metal spoon.

**Combine**  To stir 2 or more ingredients together to form a mixture of uniform consistency.

**Cream**  To mix 1 or more foods (usually fat and sugar) with a spoon or an electric mixer until soft, smooth, and creamy.

**Crisp-tender**  To cook just until tender but not soft or limp.

**Cube**  To cut food into pieces with 6 equal sides.

**Curdle**  To form clots in a smooth liquid (such as milk) with heat or acidic food such as lemon juice or vinegar.

**Cut**  To divide food with a knife or scissors.

**Cut in**  To distribute solid fat throughout dry ingredients using 2 knives or a pastry blender until flour-coated fat particles are the desired size.

**Dash**  About half of ⅛ teaspoon of a spice or seasoning.

**Deep-fry**  To cook food in enough hot fat (350°F) so food is submerged or will float.

**Dice**  To cut food into very small cubes.

**Dilute**  To thin a liquid or to reduce flavor by adding liquid.

**Dissolve**  To make a solution such as sugar in water; to melt or liquefy.

**Dredge**  To cover or coat with flour or other fine substances such as bread crumbs or cornmeal.

**Drippings**  The fat and juices obtained when cooking meat, poultry, seafood, or fish.

**Drizzle**  To pour a liquid over the surface of food in a fine, thread-like stream.

**Dust**  To sprinkle on food lightly; to coat with flour or sugar.

**Flake**  To break food into small pieces, usually with a fork.

**Flute/Fluting**  To crimp the edge of a crust to prevent shrinkage and create an attractive edge. After fluting, press under rim in several places to prevent shrinkage.

**Fold**  To combine 1 ingredient, usually a light or delicate ingredient, with another heavier ingredient by gently turning the mixture with a spoon or spatula to minimize loss of air. Two motions are used: cutting vertically through the mixture and sliding it across the bottom of the bowl and up the other side.

| | |
|---|---|
| **Fry** | To cook in fat. A small amount of fat is used for panfrying or sautéing; deep-fat fried foods are submerged in fat. |
| **Garnish** | To add decorative touches (usually edible) to food that is ready to be served. |
| **Glaze** | To coat with a glossy mixture that enhances both flavor and appearance of food such as meat, vegetables, and desserts. |
| **Grate** | To produce particles of a specific size by rubbing food such as carrots or cheese on a grater. |
| **Grease** | To rub the surface of a pan or dish with fat to prevent food from sticking. |
| **Grease and flour** | To rub the surface of a pan or dish with fat and then dust it with a small amount of flour to prevent food from sticking. |
| **Grill** | To cook food on a rack over direct heat. |
| **Grind** | To reduce food to small particles by cutting or crushing the food mechanically in a grinder, blender, or food processor. |
| **Julienne** | To cut meat, fruit, or vegetables into long, thin strips. |
| **Knead** | To work dough with the heel of a hand or with the kneading attachment of a mixer in order to develop the structure of bread. |
| **Lukewarm** | A temperature of about 95°F. Lukewarm liquids and food feel neither hot nor cold when tested on the inside of the wrist. |
| **Marinade** | A seasoned sauce, usually a combination of an oil and acid (fruit juice or vinegar), in which meat and other kinds of food are soaked. |
| **Marinate** | To let food stand in a marinade to season and tenderize it. Marinade is discarded unless the recipe calls for it to be used in cooking. |
| **Meringue** | A foam of beaten egg whites and sugar that is baked. A soft meringue may be baked as topping of a single-crust pie; a baked hard meringue is used as a shell for berries or other dessert fillings. |
| **Microcook** | To cook food in a microwave oven using high-frequency radio waves that cook food quickly. |
| **Mince** | To chop or cut food into very small pieces (⅛ inch or less). |
| **Mix** | To combine 2 or more ingredients into a uniform mixture by stirring or using an electric mixer. |
| **Panbroil** | To cook, uncovered, over high heat on a hot surface (usually in a frying pan), pouring off accumulated fat. |

| | |
|---|---|
| **Panfry** | To cook, uncovered, over high heat in a small amount of fat. |
| **Parboil** | To boil food in water or other liquid until food is partially cooked. Cooking is usually completed by another method. Also called blanching. |
| **Peel** | To remove the outer covering or skin of fruit and vegetables such as potatoes, carrots, oranges, or bananas. |
| **Punch down** | To deflate a risen yeast dough by pushing it down with the fist. This step is necessary to allow formation of smaller, more uniform air pockets. |
| **Purée (v.)** | To blend food in a blender or food processor until smooth. |
| **Purée (n.)** | A smooth paste made by pressing food through a fine sieve or food mill; also a thick sauce made from puréed vegetables or fruit. |
| **Reconstitute** | To restore concentrated food such as nonfat dry milk or frozen orange juice to original form by adding water. |
| **Reduce** | To decrease volume of liquid by rapid boiling. |
| **Rehydrate** | To restore water lost during drying by soaking or by cooking the dehydrated food in liquid. |
| **Rice** | To force cooked vegetables through a ricer or fine colander to break the food into small particles. |
| **Roast** | To cook meat, poultry, or vegetables, uncovered, in an oven. |
| **Sauté** | To brown or cook food in a small amount of hot fat. |
| **Scald** | To heat liquid to just under the boiling point. Also refers to placing fruit and vegetables in boiling water for 1 minute to aid in removing the skin. |
| **Scallop** | To bake food that usually has been cut into pieces, in a sauce or other liquid. |
| **Score** | To mark cuts, notches, or lines on the surface of meat or food to increase tenderness, prevent the fat from curling, or make food look attractive. |
| **Sear** | To brown the surface of food quickly in a skillet or on a grill over high heat in order to seal in juices. |
| **Shred** | To cut or tear into small, usually long, narrow pieces. |
| **Simmer** | To cook food over low heat in liquid that is just below the boiling point (about 180°F to 210°F). Bubbles will form slowly and break apart just below the surface. Bubbles should not be visible on surface. |

| | |
|---|---|
| **Skewer** | A long pin of wood or metal upon which food is placed to hold it during cooking or serving. Also to position food on a "skewer." |
| **Steam** | To cook food in steam over boiling water in a closed container. |
| **Steep** | To let a food stand in a heated liquid that is below the boiling point in order to extract flavor or color, as in tea. |
| **Stew** | To simmer food in liquid. |
| **Stir** | To mix ingredients with a circular motion. |
| **Stir-fry** | To fry thinly sliced food quickly in a little hot oil, stirring with a tossing motion. |
| **Strain/Drain** | To remove liquid from food by placing it in a strainer or colander. |
| **Thicken** | To make a thin paste by mixing flour, cornstarch, or arrowroot with an equal amount of cold water and then stirring the paste into a hot liquid and cooking it, stirring, until the liquid has thickened. |
| **Toss** | To mix ingredients gently with 2 forks or a fork and spoon. To coat salad ingredients with dressing. |
| **Whip** | To beat rapidly with a whisk, fork, or mixer in order to incorporate air into food and produce expansion of food. |

# Emergency Substitutions

It is always best to use the ingredients specified in a recipe. However, if a substitution is necessary, you can use the following suggestions:

| *If you don't have*: | *Use:* |
|---|---|
| 1 cup cake flour | 1 cup minus 2 tablespoons all-purpose flour |
| 1 tablespoon cornstarch (for thickening) | 2 tablespoons all-purpose flour |
| 1 tablespoon Arrowroot | 2 tablespoons all-purpose flour or 1 tablespoon cornstarch |

| *If you don't have:* | *Use:* |
| --- | --- |
| 1 teaspoon baking powder | ½ teaspoon Cream of Tartar plus ¼ teaspoon baking soda |
| 1 package (¼ ounce) active dry yeast | 1 cake compressed yeast |
| 1 cup granulated sugar | 1 cup firmly packed brown sugar or 2 cups sifted confectioners sugar |
| 1 cup honey | 1¼ cups sugar plus ¼ cup milk or water |
| 1 cup corn syrup | 1 cup sugar plus ¼ cup milk or water |
| 1 square (1 ounce) unsweetened chocolate | 3 tablespoons unsweetened cocoa powder plus 1 tablespoon vegetable shortening or cooking oil |
| 1 cup heavy cream, whipped | 2 cups whipped dessert topping |
| 1 cup light cream | 1 tablespoon melted butter plus enough milk to make 1 cup |
| 1 cup dairy sour cream | 1 cup plain yogurt plus 3 tablespoons melted butter |
| 1 cup reduced-fat buttermilk | 1 tablespoon lemon juice or vinegar plus enough 2% milk to make 1 cup (let stand 5 minutes before using), or 1 cup 2% milk plus 1¾ teaspoons Cream of Tartar, or 1 cup plain yogurt |
| 1 cup whole buttermilk | Same as above, but use whole milk |
| 1 cup whole milk | ½ cup evaporated milk plus ½ cup water, or 1 cup water plus ⅓ cup nonfat dry milk powder |
| 1 cup canned tomatoes | 1⅓ cups cut-up fresh tomatoes simmered 10 minutes |

| *If you don't have:* | *Use:* |
| --- | --- |
| 2 cups tomato sauce | ¾ cup tomato paste plus 1 cup water |
| 1 cup tomato juice | ½ cup tomato sauce plus ½ cup water |
| 1 small onion, chopped (⅓ cup) | 1 teaspoon Onion Powder or 1 tablespoon Instant Minced Onion |
| 1 medium-size onion, chopped (⅔ cup) | 1 tablespoon Onion Powder or ¼ cup Instant Chopped Onion |
| 1 medium-size clove garlic | ⅛ teaspoon Garlic Powder |
| 1 teaspoon chopped fresh ginger | ¼ teaspoon Ground Ginger |
| 1 tablespoon prepared mustard | 1 teaspoon Ground Mustard (in cooked mixtures) |
| 1 tablespoon fresh herbs | 1 teaspoon any dry leafy herbs |
| 1 teaspoon grated fresh orange or lemon peel | Slightly less, or equal amounts of dehydrated Lemon or Orange Peel |
| 1 teaspoon Pure Vanilla Extract | 1 teaspoon Vanilla Powder |
| 1 teaspoon Pure Anise Extract | 1½ teaspoons Anise Seed |
| 5 teaspoons brandy | 1 teaspoon Brandy Extract |
| 1 tablespoon dark rum | 2 tablespoons Rum Extract |
| 5 tablespoons light rum | 1 tablespoon Rum Extract |
| 1 tablespoon sherry | 1 tablespoon Pure Sherry Extract |

# Common Food Equivalents

| Ingredient | Unit or weight | Equivalent |
| --- | --- | --- |
| Apples | 1 medium-size | 1 cup sliced |
| Bananas | 1 medium-size | ⅓ cup mashed |
| Bell peppers | 1 large | 1 cup chopped |
| Butter, margarine or other fat | ¼ stick<br>½ stick (⅛ lb.)<br>1 stick (¼ lb.)<br>2 sticks (½ lb.)<br>4 sticks (1 lb.) | 2 tablespoons<br>¼ cup<br>½ cup<br>1 cup<br>2 cups |
| Cabbage | 1 lb. (1 small head) | 5 cups shredded |
| Carrots | 1 lb. (6 to 8 medium-size) | 2½ cups shredded or 2¼ cups chopped |
| Celery | 1 stalk | ½ cup chopped |
| Cheese | 1 lb. | 4 to 4½ cups grated |
| Chicken breasts | 1½ lbs. (2 whole medium-sized breasts) | 2 cups cooked, chopped chicken |
| Chocolate | 1 oz. | 1 square |
| Coconut | 1 lb. | 5 cups shredded |
| Cranberries | 12 oz. | 3 cups |
| Cream, heavy | ½ pint (1 cup) | 2 cups whipped cream |
| Cream cheese | 3-oz. package | 6 tablespoons |
| Currants | 1 lb. | 3 cups |
| Dates, pitted | 1 lb. | 2½ cups |

| Ingredient | Unit or weight | Equivalent |
| --- | --- | --- |
| Eggs, whole | 3 medium-size | Approx. ½ cup |
| Egg whites | 4 medium-size | Approx. ½ cup |
| Egg yolks | 3 medium-size | Approx. ¼ cup |
| Flour, all-purpose | 1 lb. | 4 cups (sifted) |
| Flour, cake | 1 lb. | 4½ cups (sifted) |
| Flour, rye | 1 lb. | 4½ cups to 5 cups (unsifted) |
| Flour, whole-wheat | 1 lb. | 3½ cups (unsifted) |
| Fruit and peels, candied | 1 lb. | 3 cups (cut-up) |
| Gelatin, unflavored | 1 envelope | 1 tablespoon |
| Green beans | 1 lb. (4 cups) | 2½ cups cooked |
| Lemon | 1 medium-size | 2 to 3 tablespoons juice, 1½ to 2 teaspoons grated rind |
| Lettuce | 1 medium-size head | 6 cups torn into bite-size pieces |
| Lime | 1 medium-size | 2 tablespoons juice, 1½ teaspoons grated rind |
| Macaroni | 1 cup (3¼ oz. uncooked) | 2 to 2½ cups cooked |
| Noodles | 1 cup (1⅓ oz. uncooked) | 1 to 1½ cups cooked |

| Ingredient | Unit or weight | Equivalent |
|---|---|---|
| Nuts, whole (shelled) | | |
| almonds | 1 lb. | 3½ cups |
| peanuts | 1 lb. | 3 cups |
| pecans | 1 lb. | 4 cups |
| walnuts | 1 lb. | 4 cups |
| Orange | 1 medium-size | ¼ to ⅓ cup juice, 3 to 4 teaspoons grated peel |
| Peaches, pears | 1 medium-size | ½ cup sliced |
| Potatoes | 1 lb. (3 medium-size) | 2 cups cubed or 1¾ cups mashed |
| Raisins | 1 lb. | 3¼ cups |
| Rice | 1 lb.<br>1 cup (uncooked)<br>1½ cups packaged precooked | 2 cups<br>3 cups cooked<br>3 cups cooked |
| Spaghetti | 8 oz. | 4 cups cooked |
| Spinach | 1 lb. | 12 cups torn into bite-size pieces |
| Strawberries | 4 cups whole | 4 cups sliced |
| Sugar: | | |
| brown | 1 lb. | 2¼ cups firmly packed |
| confectioners | 1 lb. | 3 to 5 cups |
| granulated | 1 lb. | 2 cups |
| superfine | 1 lb. | 2 cups |
| Tomatoes | 1 medium-size | ½ cup chopped |

## *Equivalent Measurements*

Dash (used frequently in spice and herb cookery) = less than ⅛ teaspoon

3 tsp. = 1 tbsp.

1 cup = ½ pint

2 cups = 1 pint

2 pints (4 cups) = 1 quart

4 quarts (liquid) = 1 gallon

8 quarts (solid) = 1 peck

4 pecks = 1 bushel

16 ounces = 1 pound

## *Tablespoon Measurements*

4 tbsp. = ¼ cup

5 tbsp. + 1 tsp. = ⅓ cup

8 tbsp. = ½ cup

10 tbsp. + 2 tsp. = ⅔ cup

12 tbsp. = ¾ cup

14 tbsp. = ⅞ cup

16 tbsp. = 1 cup

## *Abbreviations*

tsp. = teaspoon

tbsp. = tablespoon

pt. = pint

qt. = quart

pk. = peck

bu. = bushel

oz. = ounce or ounces

lb. = pound or pounds

sq. = square

min. = minute or minutes

hr. = hour or hours

mod. = moderate or moderately

doz. = dozen

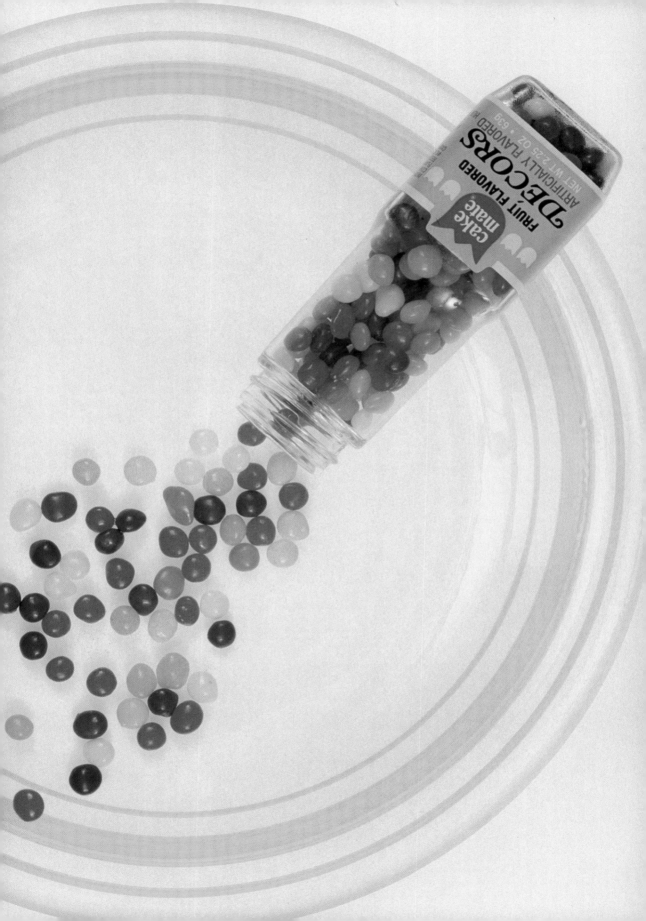

# EASY FAMILY RECIPES

～

**AMERICAN LIFESTYLES** and work patterns have changed. So have mealtimes and menus. Gone are the days when hours were spent in food preparation. Today, families want food that is tasty, satisfying, healthy, and convenient. But homemakers also want recipes that are easy and fast – and fun!

This section suggests ideas for Easy Family Recipes. Most are simple, contain healthy ingredients, and can be completed in about twenty minutes. But Ah! the good taste is still there. Other sections of this spice cookbook offer elegant recipes for Fine Dining and Entertaining.

We believe many of these recipes will become new favorites for your family.

## APPETIZERS / SOUPS

## Caraway-Cheese Spread

*1 container (12 ounces) Cheddar cheese spread, room temperature*

*2 teaspoons Instant Minced Onion*

*1½ teaspoons Caraway Seed*

*1 teaspoon Worcestershire sauce*

*½ teaspoon Season-All Seasoned Salt*

*Celery stalks, cherry tomatoes, jicama sticks, endive leaves, and/or assorted crackers to serve*

1. Place cheese in bowl, add seasonings, and stir until well combined.

2. Cover and refrigerate at least 2 hours.

3. Spread on assortment of vegetables and/or crackers and arrange on serving dish.

*Makes about 1½ cups*

# Hot Crab Dip

1 cup mayonnaise

1½ cups shredded Cheddar cheese, divided

1½ teaspoons Old Bay Seasoning

1 teaspoon Worcestershire sauce

¼ teaspoon Ground Mustard

1 pound crab meat, picked over *

Assorted crackers, cocktail bread, and/or pita chips to serve

1. Preheat oven to 350°F.

2. Place mayonnaise, ¾ cup cheese, Old Bay Seasoning, Worcestershire, and mustard in medium-size bowl and stir to combine. Add crab meat to mayonnaise mixture and fold in gently.

3. Spoon into 1-quart casserole, smooth top, and sprinkle with remaining ¾ cup cheese and a dash additional Old Bay Seasoning.

4. Bake in preheated 350°F oven 15 minutes or until mixture begins to bubble around edges.

5. Serve immediately with assorted crackers, cocktail bread, and/or pita chips.

*Makes about 5 cups*

* (See page 47)

# Fresh Tomato Salsa

4 medium-size tomatoes, chopped

1 medium-size onion, chopped

1 can (4 ounces) chopped green chilies, undrained

¼ cup chopped fresh cilantro or 4 teaspoons Cilantro Leaves

1 tablespoon Lemon & Pepper Seasoning

1½ teaspoons Instant Minced Garlic

Tortilla chips to serve

1. Place all ingredients except tortilla chips in medium-size bowl and stir until well combined.

2. Spoon into serving dish, cover, and refrigerate at least 1 hour.

3. Serve with tortilla chips.

*Makes about 4 cups*

# Creamy Dill Dip

1 cup dairy sour cream

1 cup mayonnaise

1 tablespoon Dill Weed

1 tablespoon Instant Minced Onion

1 tablespoon Bon Appétit

Red or green bell pepper strips;
carrot, celery, or jicama sticks;
broccoli or cauliflower florets;
mushrooms; cherry tomatoes;
and/or radishes to serve

1. Place all ingredients except raw vegetables in medium-size bowl and stir until well combined.

2. Spoon into serving dish, cover, and refrigerate at least 1 hour.

3. Serve with raw vegetables.

*Makes about 2 cups*

# Warm Cranberry Brie

1 wheel (8 ounces) Brie

⅓ cup crushed cranberry sauce

2 tablespoons brown sugar

¼ teaspoon Rum Extract or Pure
    Orange Extract

⅛ teaspoon Ground Nutmeg

2 tablespoons chopped pecans

Assorted crackers and/or cocktail
    bread to serve

1. Remove top rind of Brie to within ¼ inch of edge all the way around.

2. Lightly coat cookie sheet with no-stick cooking spray and place Brie on cookie sheet. Set aside.

3. Preheat oven to 500°F.

4. Place cranberry sauce, sugar, extract, and nutmeg in small bowl and stir until well combined. Spread over top of Brie to edge of rind and sprinkle with pecans.

5. Bake in preheated 500°F oven 4 to 5 minutes.

6. Remove to serving dish with spatula, surround with assorted crackers and/or cocktail bread, and serve immediately.

*Makes 8 servings*

# Creamy Cinnamon Fruit Dip

1 package (8 ounces) cream cheese, softened

2 tablespoons brown sugar

2 tablespoons milk

1 teaspoon Ground Cinnamon

1 teaspoon Pure Vanilla Extract

¼ teaspoon Pure Orange Extract

¼ teaspoon Ground Nutmeg

Fresh fruit slices to serve

1. Place all ingredients except fruit in medium-size bowl and beat until smooth and well combined.

2. Spoon into serving dish, cover, and refrigerate until ready to serve.

3. Serve with slices of fresh fruit.

*Makes about 1 cup*

TIP:

Sprinkle fruit slices with fresh lemon juice to keep them from turning brown.

# Salmon-Cheese Spread

1 package (8 ounces) cream cheese, softened

1 tablespoon prepared horseradish

1 tablespoon lemon juice

1¼ teaspoons Bon Appétit

½ teaspoon Onion Powder

¼ teaspoon Ground Red Pepper

1 can (14¾ ounces) red salmon, drained and bones removed

Assorted crackers to serve

1. Place cream cheese, horseradish, lemon juice, Bon Appétit, onion powder, and red pepper in medium-size bowl and stir well to combine.

2. Add salmon to cream cheese mixture and work salmon into mixture gently with fork.

3. Spoon into serving dish, cover, and refrigerate at least 1 hour.

4. Serve with assorted crackers.

*Makes about 3 cups*

# Spicy Black Bean Dip

1 can (15 ounces) black beans,
  undrained
1 teaspoon Ground Cumin
1 teaspoon Chili Powder
¼ teaspoon Oregano Leaves

¼ teaspoon Garlic Salt
⅛ to ¼ teaspoon Ground Red Pepper
1 cup chopped tomato
Pita chips, bagel chips, and/or
  tortilla chips to serve

1. Drain beans, reserving 2 tablespoons liquid. Rinse and drain beans and place in blender or food processor.
2. Add reserved 2 tablespoons bean liquid, cumin, chili powder, oregano, garlic salt, and red pepper to blender. Cover and process just until beans are coarsely chopped.
3. Spoon into saucepan and cook over medium-low heat 5 minutes, stirring occasionally. Add tomato and cook 5 minutes, stirring occasionally.
4. Serve warm with chips.

*Makes about 1½ cups*

# Trail Mix

1 cup unsalted peanuts
1 cup raisins
1 cup semisweet chocolate morsels
½ cup dried banana slices
½ cup sunflower seeds

OR

4 cups of your favorite mixture
*  *  *
1 Vanilla Bean
1 Cinnamon Stick

1. Place trail mixture in medium-size bowl.
2. Add vanilla bean and cinnamon stick.
3. Cover tightly and set aside overnight or for several days.
4. Remove vanilla bean and cinnamon stick and save to use another time.

*Makes 4 cups*

# Spicy Chicken

2 pounds chicken wing drumettes,
   about 16 pieces

¾ cup ketchup

2 teaspoons Instant Minced Onion

2 teaspoons Worcestershire sauce

2 teaspoons prepared yellow mustard

1 teaspoon Hot Shot!
   Pepper Blend

½ teaspoon Chili Powder

½ teaspoon Garlic Powder

Lettuce to serve, if desired

1. Preheat oven to 375°F.

2. Line bottom and sides of 15 x 10-inch baking pan with aluminum foil.
   Arrange drumettes in single layer on foil. Bake in preheated 375°F oven
   15 minutes.

3. Place remaining ingredients in small bowl and stir well to combine. Brush
   half of sauce over drumettes and bake 15 minutes.

4. Turn drumettes over and brush with remaining sauce. Bake 15 minutes or
   until done.

5. Remove to serving dish with tongs and serve immediately on bed of lettuce.
   (Be sure to provide lots of napkins.)

*Makes 4 servings*

**MUSTARD**

# Chicken Quesadillas

½ pound boneless, skinless chicken breasts, cut into small strips

1 jalapeño pepper, seeded and chopped

1 cup chopped tomato

2 tablespoons chopped fresh onion

¾ teaspoon Ground Cumin

½ teaspoon Oregano Leaves

½ teaspoon Garlic Powder

2 flour tortillas (each 6 inches round)

¼ cup (4 tablespoons) shredded Cheddar cheese

1. Coat medium-size nonstick skillet with no-stick cooking spray. Add chicken and sauté over medium-high heat 3 minutes.

2. Add jalapeño pepper, tomato, onion, cumin, oregano, and garlic powder. Sauté 2 minutes, remove from heat, and set aside.

3. Preheat oven to 450°F.

4. Lightly coat cookie sheet with no-stick cooking spray. Place tortillas on cookie sheet, spread half reserved chicken mixture over each tortilla, and sprinkle each with 2 tablespoons cheese.

5. Bake in preheated 450°F oven 7 to 9 minutes.

6. Remove tortillas to cutting surface with spatula and cut each tortilla into 6 wedges.

*Makes 6 servings*

# Spiced Shrimp

COCKTAIL SAUCE

1 cup ketchup

1½ teaspoons Old Bay Seasoning

½ teaspoon prepared horseradish

* * *

1 pound medium-size shrimp in shells

½ cup water

½ cup cider vinegar

1 tablespoon Old Bay Seasoning

1 teaspoon salt

1. Place ketchup, 1½ teaspoons Old Bay Seasoning, and horseradish in small bowl and stir to combine. Place in serving dish, cover, and refrigerate to chill.

2. Rinse shrimp and set aside.

3. Place water, vinegar, 1 tablespoon Old Bay Seasoning, and salt in medium-size saucepan and stir. Cover and heat to boil.

4. Add shrimp to saucepan. Reduce heat to medium, stir gently, cover, and cook until shrimp are tender, about 5 minutes.

5. Drain, peel, and devein shrimp.

6. Shrimp may be served hot, room temperature, or chilled. Serve with Cocktail Sauce.

*Makes 4 servings*

# *Cream of Chicken Soup*

*1 tablespoon vegetable oil*

*1½ pounds boneless, skinless chicken breasts, cubed*

*¾ cup diced celery*

*½ cup all-purpose flour*

*1 can (13¾ ounces) chicken broth*

*1 cup water*

*½ pound mushrooms, thinly sliced*

*1 teaspoon Onion Powder*

*½ teaspoon Thyme Leaves*

*¼ teaspoon Ground White Pepper*

*¼ cup milk*

1. Heat oil in large saucepan. Add chicken and celery and sauté until tender.

2. Sprinkle flour over chicken and celery and stir to mix well.

3. Pour chicken broth and water into saucepan slowly, stirring constantly.

4. Add remaining ingredients except milk. Heat to boil, reduce heat, cover, and simmer 30 minutes.

5. Stir in milk and simmer just until milk is heated.

*Makes 6 servings, 1 cup each*

# Turkey-Corn Chowder

*1 can (13¾ ounces) chicken broth*
*½ cup chopped green bell pepper*
*¼ cup chopped red bell pepper*
*2 tablespoons Instant Minced Onion*
*½ teaspoon Bon Appétit*
*½ teaspoon Garlic Powder*
*⅛ teaspoon Ground Black Pepper*

*2 medium-size red potatoes, peeled and chopped*
*2 cans (17 ounces each) cream-style corn*
*1 cup cooked, cubed turkey or chicken*

1. Place chicken broth, green and red bell peppers, and seasonings in 3-quart saucepan and stir to combine. Cover and heat to boil.
2. Add potatoes to saucepan, cover, reduce heat, and simmer 45 minutes.
3. Stir in corn and turkey, cover, and simmer 10 minutes.

*Makes 6 servings, 1 cup each*

## SALADS

# Special Turkey Salad

DRESSING
*1 cup mayonnaise*
*1 tablespoon honey*
*½ teaspoon Curry Powder*
*¼ teaspoon Celery Salt*
*     ⋆   ⋆   ⋆*

*3 cups cooked, cubed turkey or chicken*
*1 cup seedless grapes*
*½ cup pecan halves*

1. Place dressing ingredients in medium-size bowl and stir until well combined.
2. Add turkey, grapes, and pecans and stir gently to coat with dressing.
3. Spoon into serving dish, cover, and refrigerate at least 1 hour.

*Makes 6 servings, 1 cup each*

# Curried Shrimp Salad

2 cups fast-cooking brown rice

1 tablespoon Instant Minced Onion

1 pound medium-size shrimp,
  cooked, peeled, and deveined

1 cup frozen peas, thawed

½ cup chopped red bell pepper

DRESSING

1 cup mayonnaise

1 tablespoon white wine vinegar

1½ teaspoons Curry Powder

½ teaspoon Celery Salt

½ teaspoon Ground Red Pepper

1. Cook rice according to package directions, adding minced onion to cooking water.

2. Place rice, shrimp, peas, and chopped red bell pepper in large salad bowl.

3. Place dressing ingredients in small bowl and stir to combine. Spoon over rice mixture and stir gently to coat.

4. Cover and refrigerate at least 1 hour.

*Makes 6 servings, 1 cup each*

# Baked Turkey-Pasta Salad

2 cups cooked, cubed turkey

1 cup cooked elbow macaroni

½ cup thinly sliced celery

¼ cup slivered green bell pepper

1 teaspoon Instant Minced Onion

½ cup mayonnaise

¾ teaspoon Season-All Seasoned Salt

¼ teaspoon Basil Leaves

⅛ teaspoon Ground Black Pepper

⅛ teaspoon Dill Weed

⅛ teaspoon Crushed Red Pepper

1. Preheat oven to 350°F.

2. Place turkey, macaroni, celery, green bell pepper, and minced onion in 2-quart casserole and stir gently to combine.

3. Mix mayonnaise and seasonings in small bowl. Stir into turkey mixture and toss gently to coat.

4. Bake in preheated 350°F oven 15 to 20 minutes or until heated through.

*Makes 4 servings, 1 cup each*

# Snappy Tuna Salad

1 can (6⅛ ounces) chunk-style tuna, drained

2 tablespoons mayonnaise

2 tablespoons chopped celery

1 teaspoon Instant Minced Onion

¾ teaspoon Lemon & Pepper Seasoning

Lettuce and tomato wedges to serve

Lemon slices to garnish

1. Place tuna, mayonnaise, celery, minced onion, and seasoning in small bowl and stir to combine. Cover and refrigerate at least 30 minutes.

2. Serve on bed of lettuce surrounded by tomato wedges and garnished with lemon slices.

*Makes 2 servings, ¾ cup each*

VARIATION:

Serve in pita pockets or on bread with lettuce and sliced tomatoes.

# Tortellini Salad

1 package (9 ounces) cheese tortellini

1 carrot, thinly sliced

1 scallion, sliced

¼ cup chopped red bell pepper

1 can (2¼ ounces) sliced ripe olives, drained

DRESSING

3 tablespoons red wine vinegar

3 tablespoons olive oil

2 teaspoons Dijon-style mustard

½ teaspoon Garlic Powder

¼ teaspoon Italian Seasoning

1. Cook tortellini according to package directions. Rinse under cold water to stop cooking and drain well.

2. Place pasta and vegetables in large salad bowl.

3. Place dressing ingredients in 1-cup glass measure and beat with fork until well combined.

4. Pour dressing over pasta and vegetables and toss gently to coat. Cover and refrigerate at least 2 hours.

*Makes 4 servings, 1 cup each*

# Tuna Salad Niçoise

½ pound small red potatoes, quartered

½ pound green beans, trimmed

DRESSING

⅓ cup olive oil

2 tablespoons red wine vinegar

½ teaspoon Garlic Salt

½ teaspoon Ground Mustard

½ teaspoon Pepper Medley Seasoning

     * * *

Lettuce

2 cans (6⅛ ounces each)
     chunk-style tuna, drained

1 pint cherry tomatoes, halved

1 small red onion, sliced and
     separated into rings

½ cup small pitted ripe olives

1. Place potatoes in steamer basket set over boiling water. Cover and steam 5 minutes. Add beans to steamer, cover, and steam 5 minutes or until vegetables are tender.

2. Place steamed vegetables in bowl and refrigerate to chill.

3. Place dressing ingredients in 1-cup glass measure. Beat with fork until well combined.

4. Arrange lettuce on serving dish. Flake tuna and arrange in center of dish.

5. Arrange potatoes, beans, tomatoes, onion rings, and olives around tuna. Sprinkle with dressing.

*Makes 6 servings, ¾ cup each*

**GARLIC**

*Tuna Salad Niçoise*

# Dilly Potato Salad

3 pounds red potatoes, quartered

½ pound green beans, trimmed

½ cup chopped fresh onion

½ cup chopped celery

1 can (2¼ ounces) sliced ripe
   olives, drained

DRESSING

¼ cup vegetable oil

2 tablespoons white wine vinegar

2½ teaspoons Season-All Seasoned Salt

2 teaspoons Dill Weed

2 teaspoons Ground Mustard

1. Cook potatoes in lightly salted boiling water 5 to 6 minutes. Add beans and cook 2 minutes or just until potatoes are fork tender. Drain and rinse under cold water to stop cooking. Set aside to cool slightly.
2. Place potatoes and beans in large salad bowl and add onion, celery, and olives. Toss gently to combine.
3. Place dressing ingredients in 1-cup glass measure and beat with fork until well combined.
4. Pour dressing over vegetables and toss gently to coat. Cover and refrigerate at least 4 hours.

*Makes 10 servings, 1 cup each*

# Poppy Seed Fruit Salad

DRESSING

¼ cup vegetable oil

2 tablespoons lemon juice

2 tablespoons honey

½ teaspoon Poppy Seed

¼ teaspoon Ground Ginger

¼ teaspoon Ground Mustard

\*   \*   \*

4 cups assorted chopped fresh fruit

1. Place dressing ingredients in 1-cup glass measure and beat with fork until well combined.
2. Place fruit in large salad bowl, pour dressing over, and toss gently to coat.
3. Cover and refrigerate at least 1 hour.

*Makes 4 servings, 1 cup each*

*Dilly Potato Salad*

# Holiday Coleslaw

1 head (2 to 2½ pounds) cabbage, chopped, shredded, or grated

2 medium-size carrots, shredded

1 medium-size green bell pepper, chopped

DRESSING

½ cup cider vinegar

⅓ cup sugar

¼ cup light corn syrup

¼ cup vegetable oil

1 teaspoon Parsley Flakes

½ teaspoon Celery Seed

½ teaspoon Garlic Salt

½ teaspoon Onion Salt

½ teaspoon Lemon & Pepper Seasoning

1. Place cabbage, carrots, and green bell pepper in large salad bowl and toss to mix.

2. Place dressing ingredients in 2-cup glass measure and beat with fork until well combined.

3. Pour dressing over cabbage mixture and stir well.

4. Cover and refrigerate overnight.

*Makes 8 servings, 1 cup each*

# Black Bean and Rice Salad

1 can (13¾ ounces) chicken broth

¼ cup water

1 cup long grain rice

1 can (15 ounces) black beans, drained and rinsed

1 red bell pepper, chopped

½ green bell pepper, chopped

½ medium-size red onion, chopped

DRESSING

3 tablespoons olive oil

3 tablespoons orange juice

1 tablespoon red wine vinegar

2 teaspoons Cilantro Leaves

1½ teaspoons Ground Cumin

1 teaspoon California Style Garlic Salt

½ teaspoon Chili Powder

1. Heat chicken broth and water to boil in 2-quart saucepan. Add rice, cover, reduce heat, and simmer 20 minutes or until all liquid has been absorbed. Fluff rice with fork.

2. Place rice, beans, red and green bell peppers, and onion in large salad bowl and stir gently to combine.

3. Place dressing ingredients in 1-cup glass measure and beat with fork until well combined.

4. Pour dressing over rice mixture and stir gently. Cover and refrigerate at least 4 hours.

*Makes 8 servings, 1 cup each*

# Avocado, Orange, and Spinach Salad

*1 pound spinach*

*½ pound mushrooms, sliced*

*½ medium-size red onion, thinly sliced*

DRESSING

*¼ cup olive oil*

*2 tablespoons cider vinegar*

*1 tablespoon sugar*

*1 tablespoon Lemon & Pepper Seasoning*

\* \* \*

*1 avocado, peeled, pit removed, and sliced, to serve*

*1 can (11 ounces) mandarin oranges, drained, to serve*

1. Remove tough stems from spinach and wash thoroughly to remove sand. Dry with paper towels or in salad spinner.

2. Tear spinach into pieces and place in large salad bowl with mushrooms and onion.

3. Place dressing ingredients in 1-cup glass measure and beat with fork until well combined.

4. When ready to serve, pour dressing over spinach mixture and toss to coat. Garnish with avocado slices and mandarin oranges.

*Makes 6 servings, 1 cup each*

# Fresh Green Bean Salad

*1 pound green beans, trimmed and blanched*

*1 small red onion, thickly sliced*

*1 cup cherry tomatoes, halved*

*½ cup drained and rinsed cooked chickpeas*

DRESSING

*2 tablespoons vegetable oil*

*2 tablespoons water*

*1 tablespoon red wine vinegar*

*1 teaspoon Basil Leaves*

*¼ teaspoon Ground Mustard*

1. Place beans, onion, tomatoes, and chickpeas in large salad bowl.
2. Place dressing ingredients in 1-cup glass measure and beat with fork until well combined.
3. Pour dressing over vegetables and toss gently. Cover and refrigerate at least 2 hours.

*Makes 8 servings, ½ cup each*

# MEAT

# Sizzlin' Steak Burgers

*1 teaspoon Montreal Steak Seasoning*

*1 pound lean ground beef*

*4 slices Gouda, Gruyère, Havarti, Jarlsberg, or crumbled blue cheese (optional)*

1. Preheat grill.
2. Mix steak seasoning into meat and form meat into 4 equal-size patties.
3. Grill patties 5 to 6 minutes on each side or to desired doneness. Add slice of cheese to each patty 1 minute before cooking is completed.

*Makes 4 servings, 3 ounces each*

# Hamburgers Plain and Fancy

BASIC BURGERS

*1 pound lean ground beef*

*1 tablespoon Instant Minced Onion*

*½ teaspoon salt or to taste*

*¼ teaspoon Pepper Medley Seasoning*

*⅛ teaspoon Garlic Salt*

1. Preheat grill, broiler, or skillet.
2. Mix all ingredients lightly but thoroughly. Do not overmix.
3. Shape mixture into 4 patties. Cook to desired doneness on grill or broiler or in preheated nonstick skillet.

*Makes 4 hamburgers, 3 ounces each*

VARIATIONS:

Red Hot Burgers: Add 1 tablespoon Crushed Red Pepper to ground beef to make very hot burger. For milder burger, add ½ teaspoon Crushed Red Pepper instead.

Oriental Burgers: Add ¼ teaspoon Ground Ginger, 1 teaspoon Lemon Peel, and 1 teaspoon soy sauce to ground beef.

Texas Barbecued Cheeseburgers: Add 2 tablespoons soy sauce, 2 teaspoons Chili Powder, and 2 teaspoons California Style Garlic Pepper to ground beef. Top each burger with 2 tablespoons shredded Cheddar cheese about 2 minutes before burger reaches desired doneness. Cook just until cheese has melted.

Herb Burgers: Add 1 teaspoon Parsley Flakes, ½ teaspoon Celery Salt, ¼ teaspoon Ground Marjoram, and ⅛ teaspoon Ground Thyme to ground beef.

ONION

# Weeknight Chili

*1 pound lean ground beef or ground turkey*

*1 can (15 ounces) red kidney beans, undrained*

*1 can (8 ounces) tomato sauce*

*1 tablespoon white vinegar*

*2 tablespoons Chili Powder*

*2 tablespoons Instant Minced Onion*

*1 teaspoon sugar (optional)*

*¼ teaspoon Garlic Salt*

*Sliced scallions and dairy sour cream to serve, if desired*

*Shredded Cheddar cheese to garnish*

1. Cook meat in 3-quart saucepan over medium-high heat 4 to 5 minutes or until no longer pink, stirring constantly. Drain off excess fat.
2. Stir in beans, tomato sauce, vinegar, chili powder, minced onion, sugar if using, and garlic salt. Heat just to boil, reduce heat immediately, cover, and simmer 20 minutes, stirring occasionally.
3. Serve topped with sliced scallions and dairy sour cream. Garnish with shredded Cheddar cheese.

*Makes 4 servings, 1 cup each*

# Beef Barbecue

*2 pounds lean ground beef*

*1½ cups ketchup*

*¼ cup pickle relish*

*2 tablespoons Worcestershire sauce*

*1½ teaspoons Season-All Seasoned Salt*

1. Cook meat in large skillet over medium-high heat 4 to 5 minutes or until no longer pink, stirring constantly. Drain off excess fat.
2. Stir in remaining ingredients, reduce heat, and simmer 10 minutes.

*Makes 8 servings, ½ cup each*

# Spicy Meat Pockets

*1 pound lean ground beef*

*½ pound Kielbasa or chorizo sausage, chopped*

*½ Spanish onion, chopped*

*1 small green bell pepper, chopped*

*1 jar (4 ounces) chopped pimientos, drained*

*1½ teaspoons Ground Cumin*

*1 teaspoon Thyme Leaves*

*¼ to ½ teaspoon Crushed Red Pepper*

*¼ teaspoon Garlic Salt*

*¼ teaspoon Ground Black Pepper*

*1 package (15 ounces) of 2 refrigerated pie crusts*

*1 egg, beaten*

1. Preheat oven to 400°F. Lightly grease cookie sheet and set aside.

2. Place ground beef, sausage, onion, and green bell pepper in large skillet and cook over medium-high heat, stirring, 7 minutes or until meat is no longer pink. Drain off excess fat.

3. Add pimientos, cumin, thyme, red pepper if using, garlic salt, and black pepper. Cook 10 minutes, stirring occasionally.

4. Unfold 1 pie crust on 1 end (not in center) of prepared cookie sheet. Spread half of meat mixture on half of pie crust to within 1 inch of edge of crust. Brush 1-inch border of crust with beaten egg.

5. Fold other half of pie crust over meat to encase it and press edges of crust together with fork. Brush top of crust with beaten egg and pierce top in several places to allow steam to escape.

6. Repeat with second pie crust and remaining meat mixture.

7. Bake in preheated 400°F oven 20 minutes or until crust is golden brown.

8. Cut each pocket into 4 wedges and serve hot.

*Makes 8 servings*

TIP:

If using chorizo sausage rather than Kielbasa, omit Crushed Red Pepper.

# Cajun Meat Loaf with Salsa

1 egg, lightly beaten

½ cup ketchup

1 teaspoon hot pepper sauce

1 teaspoon salt or to taste

¾ teaspoon Ground Black Pepper

¾ teaspoon Ground Red Pepper

½ teaspoon Chili Powder

½ teaspoon Ground Cumin

¼ teaspoon Garlic Powder

¼ teaspoon Onion Powder

1½ pounds lean ground beef

¾ cup dry bread crumbs

Mild or hot salsa to serve

1. Preheat oven to 350°F. Lightly grease jelly-roll pan and set aside.
2. Place egg, ketchup, and seasonings in large bowl and mix until well combined.
3. Add ground beef and bread crumbs to bowl and mix lightly but thoroughly.
4. Shape into 8 x 3 x 2-inch oval loaf and place on prepared pan. Bake in preheated 350°F oven 50 to 60 minutes.
5. Remove to serving platter, slice meat loaf, and serve with salsa.

*Makes 6 servings, 3 ounces each*

# Peppered Flank Steak

2 tablespoons Dijon-style mustard

1 teaspoon honey

1 teaspoon Coarse Ground Black Pepper

½ teaspoon Garlic Salt

1-pound flank steak

1. Preheat grill.
2. Combine mustard, honey, pepper, and garlic salt.
3. Spread mustard mixture on both sides of steak and let stand 5 minutes.
4. Grill steak to desired doneness. Thinly slice against grain before serving.

*Makes 4 servings, 3 ounces each*

# Quick Beef Marinade

MARINADE

¼ cup soy sauce

¼ cup olive oil

1 teaspoon Lemon & Pepper  Seasoning

1 teaspoon Garlic Powder

\* \* \*

Sirloin or top loin steak,
up to 2 pounds

1. Combine all marinade ingredients in order given in 1-cup glass measure. Beat with fork until well combined.
2. Place steak in shallow glass or stainless steel dish and pour marinade over. Cover and refrigerate at least 30 minutes, turning meat after 15 minutes.
3. Preheat grill or broiler.
4. Remove steak from marinade, discard marinade, and grill or broil steak to desired doneness.

*Makes ½ cup marinade*

# Beef and Vegetable Skewers

3 tablespoons vegetable oil

2 tablespoons soy sauce

1 tablespoon red wine vinegar

1 teaspoon California Style Garlic Powder

¾ teaspoon Hot Shot! Pepper Blend

1-pound boneless sirloin steak, cut into 1½-inch cubes

Assorted vegetables such as
12 large mushroom caps,
12 firm cherry tomatoes,
12 wedges red or green bell
peppers, and/or 12 small
white onions

1. Combine oil, soy sauce, vinegar, and seasonings in 1-cup glass measure. Beat with fork until well combined.
2. Pour into self-closing plastic bag or shallow glass or stainless steel dish. Add meat and toss to coat. Cover if using dish and refrigerate at least 2 hours, turning meat occasionally.

3. Preheat grill.

4. Remove meat from marinade and discard marinade. Spear meat and vegetables onto metal skewers and grill 10 to 15 minutes, turning frequently.

*Makes 6 servings, 1½ cups each*

TIP:

Since meat and vegetables do not take exactly the same amount of time to cook, you can control cooking time for different ingredients by separating the ingredients and putting them on separate skewers. For example, onions will take longer to cook than tomatoes.

# Beef and Snow Pea Stir-Fry

*1½ teaspoons cornstarch*

*½ teaspoon Garlic Powder*

*¼ teaspoon Ground Ginger*

*2 tablespoons soy sauce*

*⅓ cup water*

*2 teaspoons vegetable oil*

*1-pound boneless sirloin steak, cut into thin strips*

*1 red bell pepper, cut into strips*

*¼ pound snow peas, thawed if frozen*

*Hot cooked rice to serve, if desired*

1. Place cornstarch, garlic powder, and ginger in 1-cup glass measure and stir. Add soy sauce and stir to smooth paste. Stir in water and set aside.

2. Heat oil in wok or large skillet. Add meat and sauté 4 to 5 minutes. Remove meat to plate with slotted spoon and set aside.

3. Add red bell pepper and snow peas to wok and sauté 5 minutes or until crisp-tender.

4. Pour reserved cornstarch mixture over vegetables and stir in reserved meat. Heat to boil, reduce heat, and simmer, uncovered, just until sauce thickens. Serve over hot cooked rice.

*Makes 4 servings, 1 cup each*

# Santa Fe Beef Salad

MARINADE

3 tablespoons vegetable oil

2 tablespoons lime juice

2 tablespoons soy sauce

1 tablespoon water

1¼ teaspoons Lemon & Pepper
    Seasoning

1 teaspoon Garlic Powder

SALAD INGREDIENTS

1-pound boneless sirloin steak,
thinly sliced

6 cups assorted salad greens

1 red bell pepper, cut into long strips

1 yellow bell pepper, cut into long strips

1 scallion, sliced

*  *  *

Guacamole Dip, homemade (page 161)
    or ready-made, to serve

Tortilla chips to serve

1. Place marinade ingredients in self-closing plastic bag or shallow glass or stainless steel dish. Mix to combine. Add steak slices and turn to coat meat evenly. Let stand 15 minutes.

2. Arrange salad greens on large serving plate and set aside.

3. Heat large skillet over high heat. Add steak and marinade. Cook quickly, stirring constantly, 2 to 3 minutes. Spoon meat over salad greens.

4. Top salad with bell pepper strips and sprinkle with scallion. Serve with Guacamole Dip and tortilla chips.

*Makes 4 servings*

**PEPPER**

# Angel Hair Pasta with Sausage and Herbs

*1 pound sweet Italian sausage*

*¼ cup butter or margarine*

*½ pound mushrooms, quartered*

*1 medium-size red onion, chopped*

*1 teaspoon Parsley Flakes*

*1 teaspoon Basil Leaves*

*1 teaspoon Italian Seasoning*

*1 teaspoon Garlic Salt*

*½ teaspoon Fennel Seed*

*½ cup grated Romano cheese*

*16 ounces angel hair pasta, cooked and drained*

1. Break up sausage into large skillet. Sauté over medium-high heat 5 to 6 minutes or until thoroughly cooked, stirring constantly. Drain off excess fat and set aside.

2. Melt butter in large saucepan over medium heat. Add mushrooms, onion, and seasonings. Cook, stirring, 5 minutes.

3. Add reserved sausage to saucepan and cook 10 minutes.

4. Add sausage mixture and cheese to hot cooked pasta and toss gently. Spoon into serving dish and garnish with additional cheese, if desired.

*Makes 8 servings, 1½ cups each*

# Seasoned Pork Cutlets

*1 teaspoon Thyme Leaves*

*1 teaspoon Onion Powder*

*⅛ teaspoon Ground Black Pepper*

*4 pork or turkey cutlets*

*2 teaspoons olive oil*

1. Combine thyme, onion powder, and pepper. Sprinkle on both sides of pork cutlets.

2. Heat oil in nonstick skillet and panfry cutlets on both sides until thoroughly cooked.

*Makes 4 servings, 3 ounces each*

# Delicious Spareribs

*1 cup honey*

*1 cup soy sauce*

*2 tablespoons Curry Powder*

*2 teaspoons Instant Minced Garlic*

*4 pounds spareribs*

1. Preheat oven to 375°F.
2. Combine honey, soy sauce, curry, and minced garlic.
3. Place spareribs in baking pan and brush sauce on both sides. Bake in preheated 375°F oven 1 hour or until thoroughly cooked, basting frequently with sauce.

*Makes 4 servings, 4 ounces each*

# Sesame Pork

*1 tablespoon Sesame Seed*

*1 pound boneless lean pork, cut into ⅛-inch strips*

*1 tablespoon orange juice*

*1 teaspoon sesame oil*

*½ teaspoon Ground Ginger*

*½ teaspoon Garlic Powder*

*3 scallions, sliced*

*1 teaspoon cornstarch*

*1 tablespoon soy sauce*

*Hot cooked rice to serve, if desired*

1. Place sesame seed in nonstick skillet and cook over medium heat, stirring, until lightly browned. Remove seeds and set aside.
2. Place meat in dish. Place orange juice, oil, ginger, and garlic powder in 1-cup glass measure and beat with fork until well combined. Pour over meat and stir to coat. Let stand 10 minutes.
3. Spoon into skillet, add scallions, and stir-fry 10 minutes or until meat is thoroughly cooked.
4. Place cornstarch in small dish. Add soy sauce and stir until smooth. Add to skillet and cook just until sauce thickens.
5. Sprinkle with reserved sesame seed and serve over hot cooked rice.

*Makes 4 servings, 3 ounces each*

# Seasoned Pork Roast

*2 teaspoons Garlic Salt*
*½ teaspoon Ground Black Pepper*
*1 to 2-pound boneless pork roast*
*¼ cup honey*

*1 teaspoon prepared horseradish*
*1 teaspoon Ground Ginger*
*Orange slices and sprigs of Italian
    parsley to garnish*

1. Preheat oven to 350°F.
2. Combine garlic salt and pepper. Rub over roast.
3. Place roast on rack in roasting pan and roast in preheated 350°F oven 40 minutes per pound.
4. Combine honey, horseradish, and ginger. Baste roast with honey mixture during last 30 minutes of cooking.
5. Remove to carving board and let stand about 5 minutes before slicing. Garnish with orange slices and sprigs of parsley.

*Makes 4 to 6 servings*

**GINGER**

*Seasoned Pork Roast*

# POULTRY

## Chicken Olé

1 tablespoon vegetable oil

1 pound boneless, skinless chicken
  breasts, cut into strips

1 can (16 ounces) whole-kernel
  corn, drained

1 can (15 ounces) tomato sauce

1 can (4 ounces) chopped
  green chilies, undrained

1½ teaspoons Chili Powder

1 teaspoon Onion Powder

Tortilla chips and shredded
  Cheddar cheese to serve

1. Heat oil in large skillet over medium-high heat. Add chicken strips and cook 5 minutes, stirring frequently.

2. Stir in corn, tomato sauce, chilies, chili powder, and onion powder. Heat to boil, reduce heat to medium-low, and cook 10 minutes, stirring occasionally.

3. To serve, spoon mixture over tortilla chips and top with cheese.

*Makes 4 servings*

## Chicken and Vegetable Skewers

¼ cup vegetable oil

¼ cup dry white wine or white cooking wine

2 teaspoons Lemon & Pepper Seasoning

1 teaspoon sugar

½ teaspoon California Style Garlic Powder

½ teaspoon Rosemary Leaves

1 pound boneless, skinless chicken breasts,
  cut into 1½-inch cubes

Assorted vegetables such as
  12 mushroom caps,
  12 onion wedges or
  parboiled small white
  onions, 12 wedges red or
  green bell peppers,
  12 cocktail tomatoes,
  12 thick slices zucchini
  and/or 12 thick slices
  yellow squash

1. Place oil, wine, and seasonings in 1-cup glass measure and beat with fork until well combined. Pour into self-closing plastic bag or shallow glass or stainless steel dish.

2. Add chicken cubes to marinade and toss or stir to coat. Cover if using dish and refrigerate at least 2 hours.

3. Preheat grill.

4. Remove chicken from marinade and discard marinade.

5. Spear chicken and vegetables onto metal skewers and grill 10 to 15 minutes or until chicken is thoroughly cooked, turning frequently.

*Makes 6 servings, 1½ cups each*

# Southwest White Chili

SPICE BLEND

*1 teaspoon California Style Garlic Powder*

*1 teaspoon Ground Cumin*

*½ teaspoon Oregano Leaves*

*½ teaspoon Cilantro Leaves*

*⅛ to ¼ teaspoon Ground Red Pepper*

CHILI

*1 tablespoon olive oil*

*1 pound boneless, skinless chicken breasts, cut into ½-inch cubes*

*¼ cup chopped fresh onion*

*1 cup chicken broth*

*1 can (4 ounces) chopped green chilies, undrained*

*1 can (19 ounces) white kidney beans (cannellini), undrained*

✳   ✳   ✳

*Shredded Monterey Jack cheese to serve*

*Sliced scallions to garnish*

1. Place all ingredients for spice blend in small dish and stir until well blended. Set aside.

2. Heat oil in 2 to 3-quart saucepan over medium-high heat. Add chicken cubes and cook 4 to 5 minutes, stirring. Remove chicken with slotted spoon, cover, set aside, and keep warm.

3. Add chopped onion to saucepan and cook 2 minutes. Stir in chicken broth, chilies, and reserved spice blend. Simmer over low heat 20 minutes.

4. Stir in reserved chicken and beans and simmer, uncovered, 10 minutes.

5. Spoon into serving dish and sprinkle with cheese and scallions.

*Makes 4 servings, 1 cup each*

# Mexican Chicken Stew

*1 tablespoon olive oil*

*1 pound boneless, skinless chicken breasts, cut into ½-inch cubes*

*1 can (16 ounces) whole-kernel corn, drained*

*1 can (15 ounces) red kidney beans, undrained*

*1 can (15 ounces) black beans, drained and rinsed*

*1 can (4 ounces) chopped green chilies, undrained*

*1 cup chicken broth*

*1½ teaspoons California Style Garlic Powder*

*1½ teaspoons Ground Cumin*

*1 teaspoon Oregano Leaves*

*1 teaspoon Chili Powder*

*½ cup sliced scallions*

*Red bell pepper cut into flower shapes to garnish, if desired*

1. Heat oil in large skillet over medium-high heat. Add chicken cubes and cook 5 minutes, stirring often. Remove chicken from skillet and set aside.

2. Add remaining ingredients except scallions to skillet and stir to mix well. Heat to boil, reduce heat to medium, cover, and cook 10 minutes.

3. Stir in reserved chicken and scallions. Cover and simmer 5 to 10 minutes.

4. Spoon into serving bowl and garnish with red bell pepper flowers.

*Makes 6 servings*

**OREGANO**

# Oriental Chicken

¼ cup soy sauce

3 tablespoons orange juice

2 tablespoons honey

1 tablespoon vegetable oil

1 teaspoon Cilantro Leaves

1 clove garlic, minced, or
   ¼ teaspoon Garlic Powder

½ teaspoon sesame oil

¼ teaspoon Ground Ginger

1 pound boneless, skinless chicken
   breasts, cut into ¾-inch strips

1. Place soy sauce, orange juice, honey, vegetable oil, cilantro, garlic, sesame oil, and ginger in 1-cup glass measure and beat with fork until well combined. Pour into self-closing plastic bag or shallow glass or stainless steel dish.

2. Add chicken strips and toss or stir to coat.

3. Cover if using dish and refrigerate at least 30 minutes or up to 2 hours.

4. Preheat broiler or grill.

5. Remove chicken from marinade and discard marinade.

6. Weave chicken strips onto metal skewers and broil or grill 8 minutes or until chicken is cooked, turning halfway through cooking.

*Makes 4 servings, 3 ounces each*

# Chicken Wrap-Ups

1 can (10¾ ounces) chicken broth

½ cup lime juice

1 teaspoon Onion Powder

1 teaspoon Garlic Powder

½ teaspoon Ground Cumin

⅛ teaspoon Ground Red Pepper

1½ pounds boneless, skinless
   chicken breasts

6 flour tortillas to serve

Fresh Tomato Salsa to serve (page 66)

1. Place chicken broth, lime juice, onion powder, garlic powder, cumin, and red pepper in 2-cup glass measure and stir to combine. Pour into self-closing plastic bag or glass or stainless steel dish. Add chicken and toss or turn to coat. Cover if using dish and refrigerate at least 30 minutes.

2. Preheat broiler or grill.

3. Remove chicken from marinade and discard marinade. Place chicken on lightly greased broiler pan or grill and cook 5 to 6 minutes. Turn over and cook 5 to 6 minutes or until chicken is no longer pink in center.

4. Warm tortillas. Cut chicken into strips and serve on tortillas with salsa.

*Makes 6 servings, 4 ounces each*

# Chicken and Vegetable Stir-Fry

*2 teaspoons vegetable oil, divided*

*1 pound boneless, skinless chicken breasts, cut into thin strips*

*4 cups assorted chopped fresh vegetables such as broccoli, green or red bell peppers, carrots, and/or snow peas*

*1 tablespoon cornstarch*

*¾ cup chicken broth*

*2 tablespoons dry white wine or white cooking wine*

*1 tablespoon soy sauce*

*1 teaspoon California Style Garlic Powder*

*Hot cooked rice to serve, if desired*

1. Heat 1 teaspoon oil in large nonstick skillet over medium-high heat. Add chicken strips and cook 4 to 5 minutes, stirring constantly. Remove chicken with slotted spoon, cover, set aside, and keep warm.

2. Add remaining 1 teaspoon oil to skillet. Add vegetables and sauté 3 to 4 minutes or until crisp-tender, stirring.

3. Place cornstarch in small bowl. Add small amount of chicken broth and stir to smooth paste. Stir in remaining chicken broth, wine, soy sauce, and garlic powder.

4. Pour mixture over vegetables in skillet and cook 1 to 2 minutes or until sauce thickens. Add reserved chicken and toss to coat.

5. Serve over hot cooked rice.

*Makes 4 servings, 1½ cups each*

# Chicken Caesar Salad

1 pound boneless, skinless chicken
   breasts, cut into wide strips

1½ teaspoons Lemon & Pepper
   Seasoning

1 teaspoon Garlic Powder

¼ cup olive oil

2 tablespoons white wine vinegar

1 teaspoon Dijon-style mustard

½ teaspoon Worcestershire sauce

1 head romaine lettuce, torn into
   bite-size pieces

1 cup garlic-flavored croutons

¼ cup grated Parmesan cheese

1. Toss chicken with seasoning and garlic powder.

2. Heat oil in nonstick skillet over medium-high heat. Add seasoned chicken
   to skillet and cook 4 to 5 minutes or until thoroughly cooked, stirring
   frequently. Remove from heat and set aside. Do not drain off oil!

3. Place vinegar, mustard, and Worcestershire in small bowl and beat with fork
   to combine. Stir into reserved chicken.

4. Place lettuce in large salad bowl. Add chicken, croutons, and cheese. Toss
   gently and sprinkle with additional grated cheese, if desired.

*Makes 4 servings*

# Lemon-Herb Chicken

1 egg

½ cup dry bread crumbs

1½ teaspoons Lemon & Pepper
   Seasoning

½ teaspoon Dill Weed

1 pound boneless, skinless
   chicken breasts
   (4 half breasts)

2 tablespoons vegetable oil

1. Place egg in pie plate and beat lightly. Place bread crumbs on large piece of
   wax paper. Add seasoning and dill. Stir with fork until well combined.

2. Dip chicken breasts, 1 at a time, in beaten egg. Allow excess egg to drip off.
   Coat chicken evenly in bread crumb mixture.

3. Heat oil in skillet. Add coated chicken and sauté 5 to 6 minutes. Turn chicken
   over and cook 5 to 6 minutes or until no longer pink in center. Drain on
   paper towels.

*Makes 4 servings, 3 ounces each*

*Chicken Caesar Salad*

# Honey-Mustard Glazed Chicken

2 tablespoons Dijon-style mustard

2 tablespoons honey

1 tablespoon butter or margarine, melted

1 teaspoon Basil Leaves

½ teaspoon California Style Garlic Powder

1 pound boneless, skinless chicken breasts (4 half breasts)

1. Preheat broiler or grill.

2. Combine mustard, honey, butter, basil, and garlic powder in small bowl and beat until well mixed.

3. Arrange chicken on lightly greased broiler pan or grill and cook 3 to 4 minutes. Brush half of mustard-honey mixture on cooked side and cook 2 minutes.

4. Turn chicken over and cook 3 to 4 minutes. Brush second side with remaining mustard-honey mixture. Cook second side 2 minutes or until chicken is thoroughly cooked.

*Makes 4 servings, 3 ounces each*

# Snappy Chicken and Vegetables

1 tablespoon vegetable oil

3 teaspoons Chicken & Fish Seasoning, divided

1 pound boneless, skinless chicken breasts (4 half breasts)

4 cups assorted sliced fresh vegetables such as onion, zucchini, yellow squash, broccoli, and/or tomato

Juice from ½ lemon (optional)

1. Heat oil in nonstick skillet over medium-high heat. Stir in 2 teaspoons seasoning.

2. Add chicken to skillet and cook 4 to 5 minutes. Turn chicken over. Cover, reduce heat to medium, and cook 5 minutes or until chicken is no longer pink in center. Remove chicken with slotted spoon, cover, set aside, and keep warm.

3. Add vegetables to skillet, sprinkle with remaining 1 teaspoon seasoning, and sauté about 4 minutes or until vegetables are crisp-tender, stirring.

4. Place chicken breasts on warm serving platter, surround with vegetables, and sprinkle chicken with lemon juice.

*Makes 4 servings, 1½ cups each*

# Italian Chicken and Peppers

*1 pound boneless, skinless chicken breasts (4 half breasts)*

*¾ teaspoon Italian Seasoning*

*¼ teaspoon Ground Black Pepper*

*3 teaspoons olive oil, divided*

*½ red bell pepper, cut into strips*

*½ green bell pepper, cut into strips*

*¼ teaspoon Garlic Powder*

*3 tablespoons balsamic or red wine vinegar*

*2 teaspoons honey*

1. Place chicken breasts between 2 pieces of wax paper or plastic wrap and pound to ½-inch thickness. Sprinkle on both sides with Italian seasoning and pepper.

2. Heat 2 teaspoons oil in large nonstick skillet over medium heat. Add chicken breasts and cook 4 minutes on each side or until no longer pink in center. Remove to serving dish, cover, set aside, and keep warm.

3. Heat remaining 1 teaspoon oil in skillet. Add red and green bell peppers and garlic powder. Cook 3 to 4 minutes, stirring constantly, or until bell peppers are tender. Spoon over chicken.

4. Add vinegar and honey to skillet. Cook 1 minute, stirring constantly. Spoon over chicken and bell peppers.

*Makes 4 servings, 4 ounces each*

# Chicken Parmigiana

1 egg

⅓ cup dry bread crumbs

2 tablespoons grated Parmesan cheese

¾ teaspoon Italian Seasoning

½ teaspoon Garlic Powder

1 pound boneless, skinless chicken breasts (4 half breasts)

1 can (8 ounces) tomato sauce

¾ cup shredded mozzarella cheese

1. Preheat oven to 375°F.

2. Place egg in pie plate and beat lightly. Place bread crumbs on large piece of wax paper. Add Parmesan cheese, Italian seasoning, and garlic powder. Stir with fork until well combined.

3. Dip chicken breasts, 1 at a time, in beaten egg. Allow excess egg to drip off. Coat evenly with bread crumb mixture.

4. Place chicken on ungreased cookie sheet or jelly-roll pan. Bake in preheated 375°F oven 10 minutes or until chicken is thoroughly cooked.

5. Spoon tomato sauce over chicken breasts and sprinkle with mozzarella cheese. Bake 3 minutes or until cheese has melted.

*Makes 4 servings*

# Quick Turkey Breast

2-pound fully cooked boneless turkey breast

2 tablespoons butter or margarine, melted

Garlic Powder

Ground Black Pepper

Oregano Leaves

1. Preheat oven to 350°F.

2. Brush turkey breast with melted butter and sprinkle with garlic powder, pepper, and oregano.

3. Place on rack in baking pan and bake in preheated 350°F oven 20 to 30 minutes or until heated through.

*Makes 8 servings, 3 ounces each*

# Smoked Turkey and Black-eyed Peas

2 cans (16 ounces each) black-eyed peas, undrained

1 can (14½ ounces) stewed tomatoes, broken up

1 medium-size onion, sliced

2 teaspoons Season-All Seasoned Salt

1½ teaspoons Basil Leaves

½ teaspoon Oregano Leaves

½ teaspoon Thyme Leaves

½ teaspoon Ground Black Pepper

¼ teaspoon Ground Red Pepper

3 pounds smoked turkey drumsticks

Hot cooked rice to serve, if desired

1. Place all ingredients except turkey and rice in 6-quart stockpot and stir to combine.
2. Add turkey and heat to boil. Cover, reduce heat to low, and simmer 30 minutes. Uncover and simmer 30 minutes.
3. Remove turkey from stockpot and slice meat, discarding skin and bones. Return sliced turkey meat to stockpot and stir into black-eyed pea mixture. Serve over hot cooked rice.

*Makes 6 servings, 1½ cups each*

# Mustard-Tarragon Burgers

1 pound ground turkey or lean ground beef

2 tablespoons applesauce

1½ tablespoons Instant Minced Onion

2 teaspoons Ground Mustard

½ teaspoon Tarragon Leaves

½ teaspoon Ground Black Pepper

1. Preheat broiler or grill.
2. Combine turkey or ground beef, applesauce, minced onion, mustard, tarragon, and pepper in large bowl. Mix well and shape into 4 patties.
3. Place patties on lightly greased broiler pan or grill and cook 5 minutes on each side or until turkey burgers are no longer pink in center. (Cook beef patties to desired doneness.)

*Makes 4 servings, 3 ounces each*

# Italian Turkey Burgers

1½ pounds ground turkey
1 tablespoon Instant Minced Onion
1¼ teaspoons Oregano Leaves

1 teaspoon Basil Leaves
¼ teaspoon Garlic Powder

1. Preheat broiler or grill.
2. Combine all ingredients in large bowl, mix well, and shape into 6 patties.
3. Place patties on lightly greased broiler pan or grill and cook 5 minutes on each side or until no longer pink in center.

*Makes 6 servings, 3 ounces each*

# Turkey Scallopine Two Ways

½ cup all-purpose flour
½ teaspoon Garlic Salt
½ teaspoon Rosemary Leaves, crushed
1 pound turkey cutlets

2 tablespoons butter, margarine, or vegetable oil
Lemon juice to serve

1. Combine flour, garlic salt, and rosemary and dredge cutlets in flour mixture.
2. Heat butter in large skillet. Add cutlets and panfry 3 to 5 minutes. Turn cutlets over and cook 3 to 5 minutes or until no longer pink in center.
3. Remove to serving platter and sprinkle with lemon juice.

*Makes 4 servings, 3 ounces each*

VARIATION:

Eliminate flour, garlic salt, rosemary, and lemon juice. Sprinkle cutlets on both sides with Garlic Powder, Ground Black Pepper, and Oregano Leaves instead. Proceed as above.

## *FISH / SEAFOOD*

# *Crispy Lemon and Pepper Fish*

*1 pound firm white fish fillets such as
    flounder, sole, cod, or pollack (4 fillets)*
*½ cup all-purpose flour*
*1 tablespoon Lemon & Pepper Seasoning*

*1 egg*
*1 cup dry bread crumbs*
*Vegetable oil for frying*

1. Rinse fish and pat dry with paper towels. Set aside.
2. Place flour on large piece of wax paper. Add seasoning and stir with fork until combined. Place egg in pie plate and beat lightly. Place bread crumbs on second piece of wax paper.
3. Dredge fillets in flour mixture and dip, 1 at a time, in beaten egg. Allow excess egg to drip off. Coat with bread crumbs.
4. Heat ¼ inch oil in large skillet.
5. Add fillets to skillet, 2 at a time, and cook about 2 minutes or until lightly browned on bottom. Turn carefully and cook about 2 minutes or until browned on second side.
6. Place on paper towel-lined platter and keep warm. Repeat with remaining 2 fillets. Drain, discard paper towels, and serve immediately.

*Makes 4 servings, 3 ounces each*

**PEPPER**

# Seasoned Paprika Fish

3 tablespoons butter or margarine, melted

2 teaspoons lemon juice

1 teaspoon Dijon-style mustard

1 teaspoon Paprika

½ teaspoon Seasoned Pepper

1 pound firm white fish fillets (4 fillets)

Tomato slices and lettuce to serve, if desired

1. Preheat broiler.
2. Place melted butter, lemon juice, mustard, paprika, and seasoned pepper in small bowl and stir to combine. Brush on both sides of fish.
3. Place fish fillets on lightly greased broiler pan and broil 5 minutes or until fish flakes easily with fork.
4. Place on serving dish with tomato slices and lettuce.

*Makes 4 servings, 3 ounces each*

# Catfish Fry

⅓ cup cornmeal

4 teaspoons Old Bay Seasoning

¾ teaspoon Parsley Flakes

¼ teaspoon Garlic Salt

4 catfish fillets, about 1 pound

1 egg, beaten

3 tablespoons vegetable oil

1. Place cornmeal on large piece of wax paper. Add Old Bay Seasoning, parsley, and garlic salt. Stir with fork until well combined.
2. Dip fish fillets, 1 at a time, in beaten egg. Allow excess egg to drip off. Coat with cornmeal mixture.
3. Heat oil in large skillet. Panfry fillets 5 to 6 minutes on each side or until fish flakes easily with fork.

*Makes 4 servings, 3 ounces each*

# Rosemary Fish Bundles for Two

*2 carrots, cut into julienne strips*

*10 to 12 ounces firm white fish fillets such as orange roughy, flounder, or pollack (2 fillets)*

*Garlic Powder to taste*

*Rosemary Leaves to taste*

*Season-All Seasoned Salt to taste*

*2 scallions, cut into julienne strips*

*½ red bell pepper, cut into rings*

*2 tablespoons dry white wine or white cooking wine*

1. Preheat oven to 350°F.
2. Cut 2 pieces of aluminum foil into 12 x 16-inch rectangles.
3. Arrange half of carrots in center of 1 piece of foil. Place 1 fish fillet on top of carrots. Sprinkle lightly with garlic powder, rosemary, and seasoned salt. Arrange half of scallions and red bell pepper on top of fillet. Bring sides of foil up around fish and sprinkle fish in each bundle with 1 tablespoon wine. Bring sides of foil together over fish and fold tightly to encase fish completely.
4. Repeat with remaining ingredients on second piece of foil.
5. Place bundles on cookie sheet and bake in preheated 350°F oven 15 to 20 minutes or until fish flakes easily with fork.

*Makes 2 servings, 5 ounces each*

# Baked Fish Dijon

*1½ pounds firm white fish fillets such as flounder, sole, cod, or pollack (6 fillets)*

*Juice from 1 lemon*

*1 tablespoon olive oil*

*1 tablespoon Dijon-style mustard*

*1 teaspoon Dill Weed*

*½ teaspoon Ground Black Pepper*

*¼ teaspoon Garlic Powder*

*1 carrot, shredded*

*3 tablespoons grated Parmesan cheese*

1. Preheat oven to 350°F.
2. Rinse fish and pat dry with paper towels. Set aside.
3. Place lemon juice, oil, mustard, dill, pepper, and garlic powder in 1-cup glass measure and beat with fork until well combined.

4. Brush lemon dressing on both sides of fillets. Arrange in 13 x 9 x 2-inch baking pan, overlapping thinnest portions. Drizzle remaining dressing over fish, cover with shredded carrot, and sprinkle with cheese.

5. Bake in preheated 350°F oven about 12 minutes or until fish flakes easily with fork.

*Makes 6 servings, 4 ounces each*

# Grilled Tuna with Basil Butter

*¼ cup butter or margarine, softened*

*1 teaspoon lemon juice*

*1 teaspoon Basil Leaves*

*½ teaspoon Parsley Flakes*

*4 tuna steaks, 5 to 6 ounces each*

*Ground Black Pepper*

1. Preheat grill or broiler.

2. Combine butter, lemon juice, basil, and parsley in small bowl and mix until well blended.

3. Place tuna steaks on lightly greased grill or broiler pan and spread half of butter mixture on top of steaks. Sprinkle with pepper.

4. Grill or broil about 5 minutes per inch of thickness of steaks. Turn fish over, spread with remaining butter mixture, and sprinkle with pepper.

5. Cook about 5 minutes per inch of thickness or until fish flakes easily with fork.

*Makes 4 servings, 5 ounces each*

**BASIL**

# Salmon Cakes

*½ cup fine dry bread crumbs*

*1 stalk celery, very finely chopped*

*2 tablespoons mayonnaise*

*1 tablespoon Parsley Flakes*

*2 teaspoons Instant Minced Onion*

*1 teaspoon Lemon & Pepper Seasoning*

*1 teaspoon baking powder*

*1 egg, beaten*

*1 can (16 ounces) red or pink salmon, drained and bones removed*

1. Preheat broiler.
2. Place all ingredients except salmon in medium-size bowl and stir until well combined.
3. Add salmon and mix lightly but thoroughly. Shape into 4 patties.
4. Place patties on lightly greased broiler pan and broil, 8 inches from source of heat, 4 minutes on each side.

*Makes 4 servings, 4 ounces each*

# Easy Shrimp Scampi

*1 pound shrimp, peeled and deveined, tails left on*

*3 tablespoons butter or margarine*

*1 teaspoon Lemon & Pepper Seasoning*

*¼ teaspoon Garlic Powder*

*¼ teaspoon salt*

*Hot cooked rice to serve, if desired*

*Celery flutes and radish accordion to garnish, if desired*

1. Rinse shrimp and pat dry with paper towels. Set aside.
2. Melt butter in large skillet and stir in seasonings.
3. Add shrimp to skillet and sauté until pink, stirring occasionally.
4. Serve over hot cooked rice and garnish with celery flutes and radish accordion.

*Makes 4 servings, 3 ounces each*

# Lime Shrimp in Tortillas

1 pound medium-size shrimp, peeled and
   deveined

¼ cup lime juice

2 tablespoons plus 2 teaspoons vegetable
   oil, divided

1 teaspoon California Style Garlic Pepper

½ teaspoon Parsley Flakes

1 medium-size onion, sliced

½ green bell pepper, cut into strips

6 warm flour tortillas
   (each 6 inches round)
   to serve

Mild or hot salsa, dairy sour
   cream, and/or shredded
   Cheddar cheese to serve

Chili peppers, lime wedges,
   and sprigs of Italian
   parsley to garnish

1. Rinse shrimp and pat dry with paper towels. Set aside.
2. Place lime juice, 2 tablespoons oil, garlic pepper, and parsley in 1-cup glass measure and beat with fork until well combined.
3. Pour into self-closing plastic bag. Add shrimp and marinate 15 minutes.
4. Heat remaining 2 teaspoons oil in large skillet. Add onion and green bell pepper and sauté 3 to 4 minutes.
5. Add shrimp and marinade to skillet and cook 4 to 5 minutes or until shrimp are pink.
6. Spoon onto tortillas and top with salsa, sour cream, and/or cheese. Garnish with chili peppers, lime wedges, and sprigs of parsley.

*Makes 6 servings, 4 ounces each*

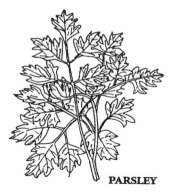

**PARSLEY**

*Lime Shrimp in Tortillas*

# Scallops in Lemon Herb Pasta

*1 pound bay or sea scallops*

*3 tablespoons butter or margarine, divided*

*2 tablespoons lemon juice*

*½ teaspoon Dill Weed*

*½ teaspoon Garlic Salt*

*8 ounces linguine, cooked and drained*

1. Rinse scallops and pat dry with paper towels.
2. Melt 1 tablespoon butter in skillet, add scallops, and cook 5 minutes. Drain off liquid.
3. Melt remaining 2 tablespoons butter in small saucepan. Stir in lemon juice, dill, and garlic salt.
4. Toss lemon-butter sauce with hot cooked linguine, add scallops, and serve immediately.

*Makes 4 servings, 1 cup each*

# VEGETABLES

# Tomato-Zucchini Sauté

*2 tablespoons butter or margarine*

*1 large zucchini, sliced*

*1 tablespoon Instant Minced Onion*

*2 medium-size tomatoes, chopped*

*½ teaspoon Garlic Salt*

*¼ teaspoon Oregano Leaves*

*¼ teaspoon Ground Black Pepper*

1. Melt butter in medium-size skillet. Add zucchini and minced onion. Sauté 2 minutes, stirring.
2. Add tomatoes, garlic salt, oregano, and pepper. Sauté 5 minutes, stirring.

*Makes 4 servings, 1 cup each*

# Zucchini and Tomato Frittata

*1 medium-size zucchini*

*1 teaspoon olive oil*

*1 tomato, chopped*

*2 teaspoons Instant Minced Onion*

*½ teaspoon Garlic Powder*

*¼ teaspoon Thyme Leaves*

*¼ teaspoon Season-All Seasoned Salt*

*⅛ teaspoon Ground Black Pepper*

*1 large egg*

*3 large egg whites*

*½ cup shredded Cheddar cheese*

1. Cut zucchini in half lengthwise. Cut each half into ¼-inch slices.
2. Heat oil in nonstick skillet over medium-high heat. Add zucchini and sauté 2 minutes.
3. Add tomato, minced onion, garlic powder, thyme, seasoned salt, and pepper. Sauté 1 minute.
4. Beat egg and egg whites until well combined. Pour over vegetables in skillet. Cover, reduce heat to medium-low, and cook 7 minutes.
5. Sprinkle with cheese, cover, and cook 2 minutes or until cheese has melted.

*Makes 4 servings, 3 ounces each*

# Gourmet Carrots

*3 cups sliced carrots*

*4 slices bacon, cooked and crumbled*

*3 tablespoons butter or margarine, melted*

*3 tablespoons brown sugar*

*3 tablespoons minced fresh onion*

*½ teaspoon Dill Weed*

*½ teaspoon salt*

*¼ teaspoon Ground Black Pepper*

1. Preheat oven to 350°F.
2. Heat lightly salted water to boil. Add carrots, cover, reduce heat, and cook 5 minutes. Drain thoroughly and place in ovenproof dish.
3. Combine remaining ingredients and stir into carrots.
4. Cover and bake in preheated 350°F oven 20 to 25 minutes or until carrots are fork tender.

*Makes 6 servings, ½ cup each*

# Black Bean and Corn Sauté

*1 tablespoon vegetable oil*

*½ cup chopped red or green bell pepper*

*1 can (16 ounces) whole-kernel corn, drained*

*2 scallions, sliced*

*1 teaspoon Cilantro Leaves or Dill Weed*

*⅛ teaspoon Ground Red Pepper*

*1 can (15 ounces) black beans, drained and rinsed*

1. Heat oil in medium-size skillet. Add red or green bell pepper and sauté over medium-high heat 1 minute.

2. Add corn, scallions, cilantro, and red pepper. Sauté 1 minute.

3. Add black beans and cook until heated through.

*Makes 6 servings, ½ cup each*

# Cowboy Beans

*2 cans (15 ounces each) pinto beans, drained*

*1 can (14½ ounces) whole tomatoes, broken up*

*4 slices bacon, chopped*

*1 tablespoon Instant Minced Onion*

*1 tablespoon Chili Powder*

1. Place all ingredients in 4-quart saucepan. Heat to boil, reduce heat, cover, and simmer 30 minutes, stirring occasionally.

*Makes 6 servings, ½ cup each*

**RED PEPPER**

*Cowboy Beans*

# Sesame Green Beans and Pepper Strips

½ pound green beans, trimmed

½ red bell pepper, cut into strips

2 teaspoons Sesame Seed

1 tablespoon butter or margarine

1 teaspoon lemon juice

¼ teaspoon Garlic Powder

¼ teaspoon Ground Black Pepper

¼ teaspoon Tarragon Leaves

¼ teaspoon Marjoram Leaves

1. Steam beans in 2-quart saucepan 4 to 5 minutes. Add bell pepper strips and steam 2 minutes. Remove vegetables from steamer, drain saucepan, and return vegetables to pan.

2. Place sesame seed in small nonstick skillet and cook over medium-high heat, stirring constantly, until lightly browned.

3. Add sesame seed to saucepan with remaining ingredients and stir gently.

*Makes 4 servings, 3 ounces each*

# Rosemary-Parmesan Potatoes

4 medium-size baking potatoes, unpeeled

1 tablespoon olive oil

½ cup grated Parmesan cheese

1 tablespoon Parsley Flakes

1 tablespoon Freeze-Dried Chives

2 teaspoons Paprika

¾ teaspoon Rosemary Leaves

½ teaspoon Garlic Powder

1. Preheat oven to 400°F. Coat 13 x 9 x 2-inch baking pan with no-stick cooking spray and set aside.

2. Scrub potatoes and cut each into 12 to 16 wedges. Place in large bowl and toss with oil.

3. Place remaining ingredients in small bowl and stir to combine. Add to potatoes and toss to coat evenly.

4. Spread potatoes in single layer in prepared pan. Bake in preheated 400°F oven 35 to 40 minutes or until fork tender.

*Makes 6 servings, 1 cup each*

# Vanilla Stir-Fry of Summer Vegetables

½ cup olive oil

1 medium-size onion, sliced

1 Bay Leaf

1 tablespoon Bon Appétit

½ teaspoon Pure Vanilla Extract

¼ teaspoon Ground Black Pepper

2 small zucchini, sliced

2 small yellow squash, sliced

4 plum tomatoes, quartered

1 can (2 ¼ ounces) sliced ripe olives, drained

2 tablespoons grated Parmesan cheese to serve

1. Heat oil in large skillet or wok. Add onion, bay leaf, Bon Appétit, vanilla, and pepper. Stir well.

2. Add vegetables and olives. Cook, stirring, 5 minutes.

3. Remove and discard bay leaf. Spoon into serving dish and sprinkle with cheese.

*Makes 6 servings, 1/2 cup each*

# Summer Squash Cakes

3 medium-size yellow squash

½ cup all-purpose flour

1 egg, beaten

2 tablespoons grated fresh onion

1 teaspoon Lemon & Pepper Seasoning

1 tablespoon vegetable oil

1. Grate squash into medium-size bowl. Squeeze out excess moisture and return squash to dry bowl.

2. Add flour, egg, onion, and seasoning. Stir to combine. Form mixture into sixteen 2-inch patties.

3. Heat oil in nonstick skillet. Cook patties, a few at a time, 2 to 3 minutes on each side or until lightly browned. Remove from skillet and keep warm while cooking remaining patties.

*Makes 16 patties*

# Herbed Asparagus

*1 pound asparagus, ends trimmed*

*1 teaspoon Parsley Flakes*

*½ teaspoon Basil Leaves*

*⅛ teaspoon Ground Black Pepper*

*¼ cup butter or margarine, melted*

*Pimiento strips to garnish, optional*

1. Steam asparagus 8 to 10 minutes or until crisp-tender.
2. Stir parsley, basil, and pepper into melted butter.
3. Place asparagus in serving dish and pour seasoned butter over. Garnish with pimiento strips.

*Makes 4 servings, 4 ounces each*

## PASTA / RICE

# Spinach Fettuccine

*½ pound spinach*

*8 ounces fettuccine*

*8 cups rapidly boiling, lightly salted water*

*1 cup heavy cream*

*¼ cup grated Parmesan cheese*

*1 teaspoon Garlic Salt*

1. Remove and discard tough stems from spinach and wash spinach thoroughly to remove sand. Pat dry and finely chop.
2. Place fettuccine and chopped spinach in boiling water and cook, uncovered, 10 minutes or until pasta is cooked.
3. Drain well and return to saucepan. Add remaining ingredients and toss gently to combine.

*Makes 6 servings, 1 cup each*

# Rice Is Nice

BASIC INGREDIENTS
(see specifics below)
2½ cups liquid
Seasoning

*1 cup long grain rice*

*1 tablespoon butter or margarine*

*Stir-in food, below*

1. Heat liquid and seasoning to boil in 2-quart saucepan. Add rice and butter and stir gently.

2. Cover saucepan tightly, reduce heat, and simmer 20 minutes or until all liquid has been absorbed. Do not stir rice during cooking; it will make rice gummy.

3. Fluff cooked rice with fork, add food to be stirred in, and toss gently. Serve immediately.

*Makes 6 servings, ½ cup each*

| 1 tablespoon butter or margarine and 1 cup long grain rice PLUS | | | |
|---|---|---|---|
| | LIQUID | SEASONING | STIR-INS |
| Rice à l'Orange | 1¼ cups orange juice<br><br>1¼ cups water | ½ teaspoon Ground Ginger | ⅓ cup chopped scallion |
| Oriental Rice | 2½ cups beef broth<br><br>1 tablespoon soy sauce | ½ teaspoon Ground Ginger<br><br>¼ teaspoon Chili Powder<br><br>¼ teaspoon Garlic Powder | 1 package (4 ounces) frozen snow peas, thawed<br><br>⅓ cup chopped scallion |
| Mexican Rice | 2 cups water<br><br>½ cup tomato sauce | ½ teaspoon Onion Salt<br><br>¼ teaspoon Ground Cumin | 2 tablespoons chopped pimiento |
| Herb and Mushroom Rice | 2½ cups chicken broth | 2 teaspoons Parsley Flakes<br><br>2 teaspoons Instant Minced Onion<br><br>½ teaspoon Oregano Leaves | 1 can (4 ounces) sliced mushrooms, drained<br>OR<br>¼ cup slivered almonds, toasted (optional) |

# Fresh Vegetable Pasta Sauce

1 tablespoon olive oil

½ pound zucchini, sliced

½ pound yellow squash, sliced

½ pound mushrooms, quartered

1 can (28 ounces) whole tomatoes, drained and broken up

1 can (8 ounces) tomato sauce

1 teaspoon sugar (optional)

¾ teaspoon Oregano Leaves

¾ teaspoon Basil Leaves

¾ teaspoon Garlic Powder

¾ teaspoon Onion Salt

8 ounces pasta, cooked, to serve

1. Heat oil in large saucepan or Dutch oven. Add zucchini, yellow squash, and mushrooms and cook just until tender, stirring occasionally. Set aside.

2. Combine remaining ingredients except pasta in 2-quart saucepan, and heat to boil.

3. Reduce heat, cover, and simmer 20 minutes. Stir in cooked vegetables and cook just until heated through. Serve over hot cooked pasta.

MICROWAVE METHOD

1. Place oil in 3-quart microwave-safe casserole. Stir in zucchini, yellow squash, and mushrooms.

2. Cover and microcook on high 5 minutes, stirring once.

3. Stir in remaining ingredients except pasta. Cover and microcook on high 10 minutes, stirring once.

4. Serve over hot cooked pasta.

*Makes 6 servings, 1 cup each*

BASIL

# Lemon-Basil Pasta

8 ounces linguine or other pasta

2 tablespoons butter or margarine, melted

1 tablespoon lemon juice

1½ teaspoons Basil Leaves

¾ teaspoon Garlic Salt

¼ teaspoon Ground Black Pepper

¼ cup grated Parmesan cheese

Lemon slices and fresh basil leaves to garnish

Sautéed chicken cutlets to serve (optional)

1. Cook pasta in unsalted water according to package directions. Drain pasta and return to pot.
2. Combine melted butter, lemon juice, basil, garlic salt, and pepper in small bowl. Add to cooked pasta and toss gently.
3. Spoon into serving dish and sprinkle with cheese. Garnish with lemon slices and fresh basil leaves. Serve immediately with sautéed chicken cutlets, if desired.

*Makes 4 servings*

VARIATIONS:

Add 2 cups cooked, cubed chicken or 1 pound cooked, peeled, and deveined large shrimp with seasonings and toss gently. Eliminate chicken cutlets.

# Supreme Pasta Salad

16 ounces rotini, fusilli, or shell pasta

1 bottle (8 ounces) Italian or ranch-style salad dressing

4 tablespoons Salad Supreme Seasoning

4 to 6 cups assorted raw vegetables such as tomato wedges, sliced carrots, broccoli florets, and/or red onion rings

1. Cook pasta according to package directions. Rinse under cold water to stop cooking and drain well.
2. Place pasta in large salad bowl, add dressing and seasoning, and toss gently to coat.
3. Add vegetables and mix gently.
4. Cover and refrigerate at least 4 hours.

*Makes 10 servings, 1 cup each*

Lemon-Basil Pasta

Supreme Pasta Salad (see photo on page 132)

# BREAD

## Herbed French Bread

1 loaf French bread
½ cup butter or margarine, softened
1 teaspoon Parsley Flakes

½ teaspoon Onion Powder
⅛ teaspoon Thyme Leaves

1.  Preheat oven to 400°F.
2.  Cut bread diagonally into 1-inch slices, but do not cut through bottom of loaf. Place cut bread on piece of aluminum foil large enough to enclose entire loaf.
3.  Combine remaining ingredients and spread on both sides of bread slices.
4.  Bring foil up around bread and close tightly. Bake in preheated 400°F oven 10 minutes or until bread is heated through.

*Makes 12 servings*

## Parmesan Garlic Bread

1 loaf Italian bread
¼ cup butter or margarine, softened
2 tablespoons grated Parmesan cheese

1 teaspoon Garlic Powder
¼ teaspoon Italian Seasoning

1.  Preheat broiler.
2.  Split bread in half horizontally and place, cut sides up, on work surface.
3.  Combine remaining ingredients and spread on bread.
4.  Place on broiler pan and brown lightly in broiler.

*Makes 12 servings*

*Supreme Pasta Salad (see recipe on page 131)*

# Onion-Garlic Bread

*½ cup butter or margarine, softened*

*1 teaspoon Garlic Powder*

*½ teaspoon Onion Powder*

*½ teaspoon Parsley Flakes*

*1 loaf Italian bread, sliced*

*2 to 3 tablespoons grated Parmesan cheese*

1. Preheat broiler.
2. Place butter, garlic powder, onion powder, and parsley in small bowl and mix well.
3. Arrange bread slices on broiler pan and spread butter mixture on bread. Sprinkle with cheese.
4. Broil 2 to 3 minutes or until golden brown.

*Makes 12 servings*

# Herb Bubble Bread

*1 loaf (16 ounces) frozen bread dough*

*¼ cup butter or margarine, melted*

*1 egg, lightly beaten*

*½ teaspoon Parsley Flakes*

*¼ teaspoon Marjoram Leaves*

*¼ teaspoon Thyme Leaves*

1. Thaw bread dough according to package directions.
2. Lightly grease 9 x 5 x 3-inch loaf pan and set aside.
3. Place remaining ingredients in small bowl and beat to combine.
4. Cut thawed dough into 1-inch pieces, dip each piece in butter mixture, and layer pieces one over the other in prepared pan.
5. Cover pan and let rise in warm, draft-free place until dough doubles in size, at least 1 hour.
6. Preheat oven to 375°F.
7. Bake in preheated 375°F oven 25 to 30 minutes. Remove from pan immediately and cool on wire rack.

*Makes 12 servings*

# Muffins Plain and Fancy

BASIC MUFFIN BATTER

*2 cups sifted all-purpose flour*

*3 tablespoons sugar*

*3 teaspoons baking powder*

*½ teaspoon salt*

*1 egg*

*1 cup milk*

*3 tablespoons vegetable shortening, melted*

*1 teaspoon Pure Vanilla Extract*

1. Preheat oven to 425°F. Grease 12-cup muffin pan or line cups with paper baking cups and set aside.

2. Combine sifted flour, sugar, baking powder, and salt. Sift into large bowl and set aside.

3. Place egg in separate bowl and beat lightly. Add milk, shortening, and vanilla and beat until well combined.

4. Make well in center of dry ingredients and stir in egg mixture with spoon just until dry ingredients are moistened.

5. Spoon into prepared muffin cups, filling cups no more than two-thirds full.

6. Bake in preheated 425°F oven 20 to 25 minutes or until toothpick inserted in center of muffin comes out clean. Remove from pan immediately and serve hot.

*Makes 12 muffins*

VARIATIONS:

**Blueberry-Nutmeg Muffins:** Add ⅛ teaspoon Ground Nutmeg to dry ingredients. Reduce milk to ¾ cup and add 1 cup blueberries with milk. Bake as directed above.

**Orange Muffins:** Add 2 teaspoons Orange Peel to dry ingredients. Bake as directed above. Combine ½ cup confectioners sugar, 2 teaspoons water, ½ teaspoon Orange Peel, and ½ teaspoon Pure Orange Extract. Mix well and drizzle over tops of hot baked muffins.

**Spice Muffins:** Add 1 teaspoon Pumpkin Pie Spice to dry ingredients. (As an alternative, make your own spice mixture by combining ¼ teaspoon Ground Cinnamon, ¼ teaspoon Ground Ginger, ¼ teaspoon Ground Nutmeg, and ¼ teaspoon Ground Cardamom.) Bake as directed above.

**Cinnamon-Streusel Muffins:** Combine 1 tablespoon butter or margarine with ¼ cup Cinnamon Sugar. Sprinkle over top of muffin batter just before baking. Bake as directed above.

# Chunky Apple-Bran Muffins

1 cup chunky applesauce

2 egg whites

1 teaspoon Ground Cinnamon

1 teaspoon Pure Vanilla Extract

1 package (7 ounces) bran muffin mix

1. Preheat oven to 400°F. Grease 10 cups of 12-cup muffin pan or line 10 cups with paper baking cups and set aside.
2. Place all ingredients in medium-size bowl and stir until well combined.
3. Spoon batter into 10 prepared muffin cups, filling cups no more than two-thirds full. Half-fill 2 empty cups with water.
4. Bake in preheated 400°F oven 15 to 20 minutes or until toothpick inserted in center of muffin comes out clean. Remove from pan immediately and serve hot.

*Makes 10 muffins*

# Herb Butter for Fresh Baked Rolls

½ cup butter or margarine, softened

½ teaspoon Parsley Flakes

¼ teaspoon Tarragon Leaves

⅛ teaspoon Thyme Leaves

1. Combine all ingredients.
2. Serve with freshly baked dinner rolls.

*Makes ½ cup*

TIP:

Just before baking homemade rolls or ready-to-bake rolls, brush tops of rolls with beaten egg and sprinkle with Poppy Seed, Sesame Seed, or Caraway Seed.

# Herb Biscuits

2 cups biscuit mix

½ teaspoon Thyme Leaves

¼ teaspoon Marjoram Leaves

¼ teaspoon Oregano Leaves

¼ teaspoon Onion Powder

1 cup milk

1. Preheat oven to 425°F. Lightly grease cookie sheet and set aside.

2. Place biscuit mix in large bowl and stir in seasonings. Add milk and stir with spoon just until biscuit mix is moistened.

3. Drop 10 equal-size biscuits from spoon onto prepared cookie sheet. Bake in preheated 425°F oven 12 to 15 minutes or until biscuits are lightly browned. Serve hot.

*Makes 10 biscuits*

# Cinnamon-Raisin Quick Bread

2 cups all-purpose flour

1 tablespoon Ground Cinnamon

2 teaspoons baking powder

1 teaspoon salt

1 cup firmly packed dark brown sugar

¼ cup butter or margarine

2 eggs

1 cup milk

1 tablespoon Pure Vanilla Extract

1 cup raisins

1. Preheat oven to 350°F. Lightly grease and flour 9 x 5 x 3-inch loaf pan and set aside.

2. Place flour, cinnamon, baking powder, and salt in medium-size bowl and stir until well combined. Set aside.

3. Place sugar and butter in mixer bowl and beat until creamy. Add eggs, milk, and vanilla and beat well.

4. Add reserved flour mixture and stir well. Stir in raisins.

5. Pour batter into prepared pan and bake in preheated 350°F oven 55 to 60 minutes or until toothpick inserted in center comes out clean.

6. Cool in pan on wire rack 10 minutes. Remove from pan and cool completely on wire rack.

*Makes 12 servings*

# Banana Bread

1 package (16 ounces)
  pound cake mix
1 cup mashed ripe banana

1 teaspoon Pure Vanilla Extract
½ teaspoon Ground Cinnamon

1. Preheat oven to 350°F. Lightly grease and flour 9 x 5 x 3-inch loaf pan and set aside.
2. Prepare cake mix according to package directions.
3. Add banana, vanilla, and cinnamon to batter and fold in gently.
4. Pour batter into prepared pan and bake in preheated 350°F oven 1 hour and 10 minutes or until toothpick inserted in center comes out clean.
5. Cool in pan on wire rack 10 minutes. Remove from pan and cool completely on rack.

*Makes 12 servings*

# Whole-Wheat, Carrot and Zucchini Mini-Loaves

1½ cups sifted all-purpose flour
1½ cups sifted whole-wheat flour
1½ teaspoons baking powder
1 teaspoon baking soda
1 teaspoon Ground Cinnamon
1 teaspoon Ground Nutmeg
¼ teaspoon Ground Cloves

1 cup sugar
1 cup shredded carrot
1 cup shredded zucchini
2 eggs, lightly beaten or 2 egg whites
1 cup water
⅓ cup corn oil
1 teaspoon Pure Vanilla Extract

1. Preheat oven to 400°F. Lightly grease seven 4 x 2½-inch mini-loaf pans and set aside.
2. Combine sifted flours, baking powder, baking soda, cinnamon, nutmeg, and cloves. Sift into large bowl and set aside.
3. Combine sugar, carrot, zucchini, eggs, water, oil, and vanilla in separate mixer bowl and beat with electric mixer at low speed 1 minute.

4. Stir reserved flour mixture into carrot mixture with spoon just until dry ingredients are moistened.

5. Spoon into prepared pans and bake in preheated 400°F oven 25 to 30 minutes or until toothpick inserted in center comes out clean.

6. Cool in pans on wire racks 10 minutes. Remove from pans and cool completely on racks.

*Makes 7 mini-loaves*

TIP:

If you don't own 7 mini-pans, fill as many pans as you have and bake loaves in 2 or more batches.

# Sweet Potato Corn Bread

*2 cups cooked, mashed sweet potatoes*
*½ cup butter or margarine, softened*
*½ cup firmly packed light brown sugar*
*4 eggs*
*1 cup plain yogurt*
*1½ cups yellow cornmeal*

*¾ cup all-purpose flour*
*1 teaspoon Ground Cinnamon*
*1 teaspoon Ground Allspice*
*1 teaspoon salt*
*½ teaspoon baking soda*

1. Preheat oven to 350°F. Lightly grease 9-inch square baking pan and set aside.

2. Place mashed sweet potatoes in mixer bowl. Add butter and sugar and beat with electric mixer until creamy. Add eggs, 1 at a time, beating after each addition. Blend in yogurt.

3. Place remaining ingredients in medium-size bowl and stir until well combined. Add to sweet potato mixture and stir with spoon just until dry ingredients are well moistened.

4. Pour batter into prepared pan and bake in preheated 350°F oven 45 to 50 minutes or until toothpick inserted in center comes out clean.

5. Cut into squares and serve immediately or cool in pan on wire rack 10 minutes, remove from pan, and cool completely on rack. Reheat before serving.

*Makes nine 3-inch squares*

# Cayenne Corn Bread

*2 eggs*

*1 can (8 ounces) cream-style corn*

*1 cup dairy sour cream*

*1 cup shredded Cheddar cheese*

*1 cup yellow cornmeal*

*2 tablespoons sugar*

*1 teaspoon baking soda*

*½ teaspoon Ground Red Pepper*

*3 tablespoons butter or margarine, divided*

1. Preheat oven to 400°F.
2. Place eggs in medium-size bowl and beat lightly.
3. Add remaining ingredients except butter and mix well.
4. Melt 1 tablespoon butter and stir into batter.
5. Place remaining 2 tablespoons butter in 10-inch cast-iron skillet or 9-inch square baking pan. Place in preheated 400°F oven to melt butter, and distribute butter evenly over bottom surface of pan.
6. Pour batter into pan immediately and bake in preheated 400°F oven 25 minutes or until bread is firm in center and golden brown on top.
7. Cut into wedges or squares and serve immediately.

*Makes 6 to 8 wedges or nine 3-inch squares*

# Holiday Quick Breads

BASIC BREAD BATTER

*1 cup sugar*

*¼ cup vegetable shortening*

*1 cup milk*

*1 egg, lightly beaten*

*1 teaspoon Pure Vanilla Extract*

*2 cups all-purpose flour*

*3 teaspoons baking powder*

*1 teaspoon salt*

1. Preheat oven to 350°F. Lightly grease and flour 9 x 5 x 3-inch loaf pan and set aside.
2. Cream sugar and shortening in large bowl. Add milk, egg, and vanilla and beat until well combined.
3. Combine flour, baking powder, and salt in separate bowl. Stir into sugar mixture until well mixed.

4. Pour batter into prepared pan and bake in preheated 350°F oven 45 to 50 minutes or until toothpick inserted in center comes out clean.

5. Cool in pan on wire rack 10 minutes. Remove from pan and cool completely on rack.

*Makes 12 servings*

VARIATIONS:

Cranberry Bread: Add 1 teaspoon Pure Orange Extract and 1 teaspoon Ground Cinnamon to batter with egg. Stir 1½ cups chopped cranberries into flour mixture. Bake as directed above.

Fresh Apple Bread: Combine 2 cups peeled, chopped apples with ¼ cup sugar and 1½ teaspoons Apple Pie Spice. Pour half of Basic Bread Batter into prepared pan and cover with half of apple mixture. Repeat layers and bake as directed above.

Pumpkin Bread: Increase milk to 1¼ cups. Add 1 tablespoon Pumpkin Pie Spice to Basic Bread Batter. Stir in 1 cup canned pumpkin. Bake as directed above.

# DESSERTS

# Cannoli

*1 container (15 ounces) ricotta cheese*
*½ cup confectioners sugar*
*½ teaspoon Pure Vanilla Extract*
*½ teaspoon Rum Extract and ½ cup semisweet chocolate morsels*

OR

*¼ teaspoon Pure Almond Extract and ¼ cup chopped candied fruit*
*6 cannoli shells*

1. Place cheese, sugar, and vanilla in bowl and stir until smooth and well combined.

2. Stir in either rum extract and chocolate morsels OR almond extract and candied fruit.

3. Spoon mixture into cannoli shells and refrigerate until ready to serve.

*Makes 6 servings*

# Sautéed Apple Rings

*3 large apples*

*2 tablespoons butter*
  *or margarine*

*2 tablespoons brown sugar*

*¾ teaspoon Ground Cinnamon*

1. Peel, core, and slice each apple into four ½-inch rings.
2. Heat butter in medium-size skillet. Stir in sugar and cinnamon.
3. Add apple rings to skillet and toss gently to coat. Cover and cook over low heat 10 to 15 minutes, stirring occasionally. Serve warm.

*Makes 12 apple rings*

# Vanilla-Rum Party Pineapple

*8 cups assorted fresh fruit such as whole strawberries, pineapple wedges, peeled and sliced kiwi, honeydew and cantaloupe balls, seedless grapes, and/or star fruit, peeled, if desired, and sliced*

*¼ cup honey*

*1 bottle (1 ounce) Pure Vanilla Extract*

*1 tablespoon Rum Extract*

*1 whole pineapple*

1. Prepare 8 cups assorted fruit and place in large bowl.
2. Place honey, vanilla extract, and rum extract in small bowl and stir until well combined.
3. Pour honey mixture over fruit and toss thoroughly to coat. Cover and refrigerate at least 2 hours.
4. Slice ½ inch off bottom of pineapple so it will stand firmly upright and place in center of serving dish.
5. Toss fruit again. Spear several pieces of fruit with frilled toothpicks and attach fruit pieces to pineapple. Spoon remaining fruit around bottom of pineapple. Serve with additional toothpicks.

*Makes 16 servings*

# Cinnamon Peaches

*2 tablespoons light corn syrup*

*¼ teaspoon Ground Cinnamon*

*¼ teaspoon lemon juice*

*6 peaches, peeled and sliced, or 2 cans (16 ounces each) sliced peaches, drained*

1. Place corn syrup, cinnamon, and lemon juice in saucepan.
2. Add peaches and simmer, uncovered, 10 minutes.
3. Spoon into serving dishes and serve hot or cold.

*Makes 4 servings*

# Bananas Foster

*½ cup butter or margarine*

*½ cup firmly packed brown sugar*

*1 teaspoon Rum Extract*

*½ teaspoon Ground Cinnamon*

*4 bananas, sliced*

*Ice cream to serve*

1. Heat butter in large skillet. Add sugar and stir until sugar has melted. Stir in rum extract and cinnamon.
2. Add bananas to skillet and cook 2 minutes, stirring gently to coat banana slices.
3. Place 1 or 2 scoops ice cream in each serving dish and spoon banana slices and sauce over. Serve immediately.

*Makes 4 servings*

**CINNAMON**

# Fresh Fruit with Two Dipping Sauces

SOUR CREAM DIP

2 tablespoons sugar

⅛ teaspoon Ground Cinnamon

⅛ teaspoon Ground Nutmeg

⅛ teaspoon Ground Allspice

⅛ teaspoon salt

1 cup dairy sour cream

OR

½ cup dairy sour cream and
½ cup plain yogurt

½ teaspoon Pure Vanilla Extract

⅛ teaspoon Rum Extract

CHOCOLATE DIPPING SAUCE

1 package (12 ounces) semisweet
chocolate morsels

2 tablespoons vegetable shortening

½ teaspoon Pure Orange Extract,
½ teaspoon Rum Extract

OR

⅛ teaspoon Pure Almond Extract

\*   \*   \*

Assorted fresh fruit such as strawberries, banana chunks, seedless
grapes, cubed melon, pineapple
wedges, and/or apple wedges

1. *To make Sour Cream Dip:* place sugar, cinnamon, nutmeg, allspice, and salt in small bowl and stir until well combined. Place sour cream in separate bowl and stir sugar mixture into sour cream. Add vanilla and rum extracts and stir. Spoon into serving dish, cover, and refrigerate at least 2 hours.

2. *To make Chocolate Dipping Sauce:* place chocolate morsels and shortening in top of double boiler over (not in) simmering water. Stir until chocolate has melted and combined with shortening. Stir in orange and rum extracts. Spoon into serving dish and keep warm.

3. Arrange fruit on large serving platter and serve with Sour Cream Dip and Chocolate Dipping Sauce.

*Makes 1 cup Sour Cream Dip and 1 cup Chocolate Dipping Sauce*

# Gingerbread Boys

1 cup molasses

½ cup vegetable shortening

½ cup sugar

1 egg, beaten

1½ teaspoons Ground Cinnamon

1½ teaspoons Ground Ginger

1 teaspoon baking soda

¼ teaspoon salt

3½ cups sifted all-purpose flour

Cake Mate® Icings, Gels, and
  Décors to decorate

1. Place molasses, shortening, and sugar in large saucepan and heat until shortening has melted, stirring frequently. Set aside to cool.

2. Add egg and mix well.

3. Add cinnamon, ginger, baking soda, and salt to sifted flour and sift again. Gradually add to molasses mixture, stirring well.

4. Cover and refrigerate to chill until very firm.

5. Preheat oven to 350°F. Lightly grease cookie sheets and set aside.

6. Lightly flour work surface and roll out chilled dough to ¼-inch thickness. Cut dough with 3 to 4-inch gingerbread boy cutter. Pick up gingerbread boys carefully with wide spatula and place on prepared cookie sheets.

7. Bake in preheated 350°F oven 10 minutes.

8. Remove from cookie sheets with wide spatula and place on wire racks to cool. Decorate as desired, using Cake Mate Icings, Gels, and Décors.

*Makes 2 dozen Gingerbread Boys*

GINGER

# Apple-Walnut Bread Pudding

PUDDING

½ loaf French bread

2 large eggs, lightly beaten

1¼ cups milk

2 teaspoons Pure Vanilla Extract

1 teaspoon Black Walnut Extract

½ cup sugar

1 teaspoon Ground Cinnamon

½ teaspoon Ground Nutmeg

1 cup peeled, diced tart apples

¾ cup chopped walnuts, toasted

⅓ cup raisins

2 tablespoons butter or margarine

EGGNOG SAUCE

4 egg yolks

½ cup sugar

¼ teaspoon salt

2½ cups milk, scalded

2 teaspoons Rum Extract

1 teaspoon Pure Vanilla Extract

1 cup heavy cream, whipped

Ground Nutmeg

1. Preheat oven to 325°F. Grease 11 x 7 x 2-inch baking pan and set aside.

2. Trim crust from bread and cut enough bread into ¾-inch cubes to make 3 cups. Set aside.

3. Place remaining pudding ingredients except butter in large bowl and stir until well mixed. Add bread cubes and toss to combine.

4. Spread mixture in prepared pan and dot with butter. Bake in preheated 325°F oven 35 minutes or until firm.

5. To make Eggnog Sauce, place egg yolks in top of double boiler and beat lightly. Beat in sugar and salt. Stir in scalded milk gradually.

6. Place pan over (not in) simmering water. Cook, stirring constantly, until mixture thickens and coats back of metal spoon. Remove from heat and set aside to cool.

7. Stir rum and vanilla extracts into cooled sauce and fold in whipped cream. Spoon into serving dish, sprinkle with nutmeg, and refrigerate until ready to serve.

8. Warm pudding, if necessary, and top with Eggnog Sauce.

*Makes 4 to 6 servings*

# Refrigerator Cookies with Five Variations

*¾ cup butter or margarine, softened*
*1 cup sugar*
*1 egg*

*1 teaspoon Pure Vanilla Extract*
*⅛ teaspoon salt*
*2 cups all-purpose flour*

1. Place butter and sugar in mixer bowl. Beat with electric mixer to cream. Add egg, vanilla, and salt. Beat until well combined. Stir in flour to make smooth dough.

2. Divide dough in half and form each half into cylinder about 1½ inches wide and 9 inches long. Wrap each half tightly in wax paper and refrigerate at least 5 hours or overnight. (Wrapped dough may be frozen up to 3 weeks.)

3. Preheat oven to 350°F.

4. Cut dough into ¼-inch-thick slices. Arrange slices 1½ inches apart on ungreased cookie sheets. Bake in preheated 350°F oven 12 to 15 minutes or until golden brown. Remove from cookie sheets and cool completely on wire racks.

*Makes 36 cookies*

VARIATIONS:

(Arrange variations on cookie sheets and bake according to directions in Step 4.)

**Poppy Seed Cookies:** Add ½ cup Poppy Seed and ½ teaspoon Ground Cinnamon to dough before adding flour.

**Gingersnaps:** Reduce butter to ½ cup and add ¼ cup molasses to butter-sugar mixture. Add 2 teaspoons Ground Ginger, ½ teaspoon Ground Cinnamon, and ¼ teaspoon Ground Cloves before adding flour.

**Lemon-Clove Cookies:** Eliminate vanilla and substitute ½ teaspoon Pure Lemon Extract. Add ¼ teaspoon Ground Cloves before adding flour. Stir 2 tablespoons lemon juice into 1¼ cups confectioners sugar. Spread or drizzle over cooled cookies.

**Almond Crescents:** Reduce butter to ½ cup. Eliminate vanilla and substitute ½ teaspoon Pure Almond Extract. Add ½ cup finely ground unblanched almonds before adding flour. Roll each ¼-inch slice into 2-inch cylinder. Bend cylinders to form crescents. Roll baked and cooled cookies in confectioners sugar.

**Thumbprint Cookies:** Reduce butter to ½ cup. Add ¼ teaspoon Ground Cardamom and 1 teaspoon Orange Peel before adding flour. Roll each ¼-inch slice into small ball. Press thumb into center of ball and fill indentation with ⅛ teaspoon raspberry preserves.

# Fruit Cobbler Four Ways

PEACH COBBLER:

1 cup all-purpose flour

1 cup sugar

1 tablespoon baking powder

⅛ teaspoon salt

⅔ cup milk

¼ cup butter or margarine, diced

1 can (29 ounces) sliced peaches, drained with juice reserved

½ teaspoon Lemon Peel

¼ teaspoon Ground Nutmeg

¼ teaspoon Ground Cinnamon

Cream, whipped cream, or ice cream to serve

1. Preheat oven to 350°F.
2. Combine flour, sugar, baking powder, and salt in 8 x 8 x 2-inch glass baking dish. Stir until well combined. Add milk and stir well. Dot surface of batter with butter.
3. Arrange peaches over batter and pour reserved peach juice over. Sprinkle with lemon peel, nutmeg, and cinnamon. Do not stir.
4. Bake in preheated 350°F oven 55 to 60 minutes or until golden crust has formed on top of cobbler.
5. Serve warm with cream, whipped cream, or ice cream.

*Makes 9 servings*

VARIATIONS:

**Apple Cobbler:** Prepare batter through Step 2 as directed above. Replace peaches and peach juice with 1 can (21 ounces) apple pie filling and 1 cup water. Do not stir. Proceed as directed above.

**Cherry Cobbler:** Prepare batter through Step 2 as directed above. Replace peaches and peach juice with 1 can (21 ounces) cherry pie filling and 1 cup water. Do not stir. Proceed as directed above.

**Pineapple Cobbler:** Prepare batter through Step 2 as directed above. Replace peaches and peach juice with 1 can (20 ounces) crushed pineapple in juice and 1 cup water. Do not stir. Proceed as directed above.

# Apple-Pumpkin Pie

¾ *cup granulated sugar*

*2 tablespoons all-purpose flour*

⅛ *teaspoon salt*

*1 cup canned pumpkin*

*1 large egg, lightly beaten*

*1 tablespoon Pure Vanilla Extract*

½ *teaspoon Ground Cinnamon*

¼ *teaspoon Ground Nutmeg*

¼ *teaspoon Ground Allspice*

⅛ *teaspoon Ground Cloves*

*2 cups peeled, chopped Granny Smith apples*

*Pastry for 9-inch 1-crust pie*

CRUMB TOPPING

⅓ *cup all-purpose flour*

⅓ *cup firmly packed brown sugar*

¼ *teaspoon Ground Cinnamon*

*2 tablespoons butter or margarine, softened*

*Whipped cream or ice cream to serve, if desired*

1. Preheat oven to 375°F.

2. To make pie filling, place granulated sugar, 2 tablespoons flour, and salt in large mixer bowl and stir to combine. Add pumpkin, egg, and seasonings. Beat with electric mixer until smooth. Add apples and stir gently.

3. Pour mixture into pie crust. Cover edges of crust with aluminum foil and bake in preheated 375°F oven 45 minutes.

4. To make topping, place 1/3 cup flour, brown sugar, and cinnamon in small bowl and stir to combine. Add butter and stir with fork until mixture resembles coarse crumbs.

5. Remove foil from edge of crust and sprinkle topping over pie. Return pie to oven and bake 15 minutes.

6. Serve warm with whipped cream or ice cream.

*Makes 8 servings*

**CLOVES**

# Black Forest Cake

1 package (18¼ ounces) chocolate
   cake mix

2 eggs

1 can (21 ounces) cherry pie filling

1 teaspoon Pure Almond Extract

1 teaspoon Pure Vanilla Extract

1 package (6 ounces) semisweet
   chocolate morsels

1. Preheat oven to 350°F. Grease and flour 13 x 9 x 2-inch baking pan and set aside.

2. Pour cake mix into mixer bowl. Add eggs, pie filling, and almond and vanilla extracts. Stir until well combined.

3. Beat with electric mixer at medium speed 2 minutes. Fold in chocolate morsels.

4. Pour batter into prepared pan. Bake in preheated 350°F oven 35 to 40 minutes or until toothpick inserted in center of cake comes out clean.

5. Cool in pan on wire rack 15 minutes. Remove from pan and cool completely on rack. Place on flat surface and cut into bars.

*Makes 18 bars, 2⅛ x 3 inches each*

# Peanut Butter Freezer Candy

2 cups chunky peanut
   butter

1 cup vanilla cookie crumbs

1 milk chocolate candy bar
   (8 ounces), melted

1 tablespoon Pure Vanilla Extract

1. Line 8-inch square pan with wax paper and set aside.

2. Combine all ingredients and stir until well combined. Spread mixture in prepared pan and place in freezer.

3. When frozen, remove from freezer, invert onto cutting surface, and remove wax paper. Cut into 1-inch squares and serve very cold.

*Makes 64 squares, 1 x 1 inch each*

# Cinnamon Toffee Bars

½ cup butter or margarine

2 cups firmly packed dark brown sugar

2 eggs, lightly beaten

2 teaspoons Pure Vanilla Extract

2 cups all-purpose flour

2 teaspoons baking powder

1 teaspoon Ground Cinnamon

¼ teaspoon salt

1 cup chopped pecans

1 package (12 ounces) semisweet chocolate morsels

1. Preheat oven to 350°F. Grease 15½ x 10½ x 1-inch jelly-roll pan and set aside.

2. Place butter and sugar in saucepan over low heat and cook, stirring frequently, until sugar has melted and mixture bubbles. Pour into large mixer bowl and set aside to cool slightly.

3. Beat eggs and vanilla into butter-sugar mixture. Sift flour, baking powder, cinnamon, and salt together. Add to butter mixture and stir until well blended. Stir in pecans.

4. Spread in prepared pan and bake in preheated 350°F oven 25 minutes.

5. Remove from oven and pour chocolate morsels over top immediately. Let stand 5 minutes to cool slightly. Spread melted chocolate evenly over surface. Cut into 2-inch squares and remove from pan while bars are still warm.

*Makes about 40 squares, 2 x 2 inches each*

# Spiced Cider

1 gallon apple cider

1 cup orange juice

½ teaspoon Pure Orange Extract

½ teaspoon Pure Lemon Extract

4 Cinnamon Sticks, each 3 inches long

2 teaspoons Whole Cloves

1 teaspoon Whole Allspice

1. Place all ingredients in very large saucepan or Dutch oven.

2. Cover pan, heat to boil, reduce heat, and simmer 45 minutes. Strain into large punch bowl. Serve hot or cold.

*Makes 8 to 10 servings*

# Vanilla-Almond Coffee

1 can (13 ounces) ground coffee, regular or decaffeinated

1 bottle (1 ounce) Pure Vanilla Extract

1 bottle (1 ounce) Pure Almond Extract

1. Pour ground coffee into large self-closing plastic bag or large bowl. Add vanilla and almond extracts to coffee and stir until thoroughly blended.
2. Close plastic bag or if using bowl instead, pour into airtight container and store in refrigerator or freezer until ready to use.
3. Brew coffee as usual.

VARIATION:

To make Vanilla-Orange Coffee, substitute 1 bottle (1 ounce) Pure Orange Extract for almond extract.

# Microwave Truffles

2 packages (12 ounces each) semi-sweet chocolate morsels

2 tablespoons butter or margarine

2 tablespoons dairy sour cream

½ teaspoon Brandy Extract

½ teaspoon Rum Extract

½ teaspoon Pure Vanilla Extract

Unsweetened cocoa powder

Flaked coconut

Finely chopped pecans

1. Place chocolate morsels, butter, and sour cream in 3-quart microwave safe dish. Cover and microcook on high 2 minutes. Stir well, cover, and microcook on high 1 minute. Stir.
2. Divide chocolate mixture into 3 portions and place each portion in separate bowl. Add 1 extract to each portion and stir well.
3. Place 3 pieces of wax paper on flat work surface. Place cocoa powder on 1 piece of wax paper, coconut on second piece of paper, and pecans on third piece of paper.
4. Shape chocolate mixture into 1-inch balls and roll balls in cocoa, coconut, or pecans. Store truffles in airtight containers.

*Makes about 50 truffles*

# FINE DINING

～

**FINE DINING ALWAYS INCLUDES** moments of surprise, an unexpected taste, an elegant combination of flavors, and a sense of style in the presentation of special dishes.

For this section, we have deliberately chosen recipes that demonstrate how the proper use of spices can make the difference in taste. Some of these recipes require a little more time and detail in preparation than those in Easy Family Recipes, but you will find the time well spent.

Many of these dishes can be prepared a day ahead of time, so you can enjoy both elegance and ease in serving a carefree meal.

*Bon appétit!*

## APPETIZERS

# *Chili Cheese Roll*

*2 cups (8 ounces) grated American cheese*

*1 package (3 ounces) cream cheese, softened*

*⅛ teaspoon Garlic Powder*

*¼ cup finely chopped pecans*

*2 tablespoons Chili Powder*

*Assorted crackers to serve*

1. Place American cheese and cream cheese in medium-size bowl. Add garlic powder and pecans and mix well.
2. Place mixture on piece of wax paper about 12 inches long and shape into log about 10 inches long.
3. Sprinkle chili powder on clean piece of wax paper and roll log in chili powder to coat evenly on all sides.
4. Wrap in wax paper or plastic wrap and refrigerate to chill.
5. When ready to serve, thinly slice and serve on crackers.

*Makes 40 slices, about ¼ inch thick each*

# Crab Meat Dunk

1 cup crab meat, picked over*

¼ cup lime juice or lemon juice

1 package (3 ounces) cream cheese, softened

2 tablespoons milk

2 tablespoons mayonnaise

1 teaspoon Worcestershire sauce

1 teaspoon Instant Minced Onion

½ teaspoon salt

⅛ teaspoon Garlic Powder

⅛ teaspoon Ground Red Pepper

French bread and/or raw vegetables to serve

1. Place crab meat in small bowl, add lime juice, and mix. Set aside to marinate 30 minutes.

2. Place cream cheese in medium-size bowl and add milk, mayonnaise, Worcestershire, minced onion, salt, garlic powder, and red pepper. Mix until smooth.

3. Fold in marinated crab meat, cover, and refrigerate at least 1 hour.

4. Spoon into serving dish and serve with pieces of French bread and/or raw vegetables.

*Makes about 1½ cups*

*(See page 47)

---

# Dilly of a Dip

1 cup dairy sour cream or plain yogurt

1 teaspoon Dill Weed

1 teaspoon Bon Appétit

⅛ teaspoon Onion Powder

Assorted crackers, chips, and/or raw vegetables to serve

1. Place sour cream in small bowl and add seasonings. Mix thoroughly.

2. Cover and refrigerate at least 1½ hours to blend flavors.

3. Serve with crackers, chips, and/or raw vegetables.

*Makes 1 cup*

TIP:

This dip is delicious when served as topping on baked potatoes.

# Guacamole Dip

1 large or 2 small ripe avocados, peeled and pit removed

½ ripe tomato, peeled and finely chopped

½ green bell pepper, finely chopped

1 teaspoon lime juice

½ teaspoon olive oil

1 teaspoon Onion Salt

½ teaspoon Chili Powder

½ teaspoon salt

¼ teaspoon Ground Black Pepper

¼ cup mayonnaise

Corn chips or sliced tomatoes to serve, if desired

1. Place avocado in medium-size bowl and mash with fork.

2. Add remaining ingredients except mayonnaise and corn chips. Mix well.

3. Spread mayonnaise over top of dip to prevent darkening. Cover and refrigerate until ready to serve.

4. When ready to serve, blend in mayonnaise and serve with corn chips or use as topping for sliced tomatoes.

*Makes 1½ to 2 cups*

# Fennel Cheese Spread

2 packages (8 ounces each) cream cheese, softened

1 teaspoon Fennel Seed

¼ teaspoon Bon Appétit

¼ teaspoon Basil Leaves

⅛ teaspoon Ground Savory

⅛ teaspoon Garlic Powder

⅛ teaspoon Onion Powder

Plain or toasted almonds to garnish, if desired

Assorted crackers and/or raw vegetables to serve

1. Place cream cheese in medium-size mixer bowl and beat with electric mixer until fluffy. Add seasonings and mix well.

2. Cover and refrigerate 4 hours or overnight.

3. When ready to serve, shape into ball or place in small crock.

4. Garnish with almonds and serve at room temperature with crackers and/or raw vegetables.

*Makes about 2 cups*

# Bon Appétit Dip aux Herbes

1 package (8 ounces) cream cheese,
    softened

6 tablespoons milk

1 teaspoon Chicken Flavor Base

1 tablespoon hot water

1 tablespoon Instant Minced Onion

½ teaspoon Bon Appétit

½ teaspoon Marjoram Leaves

½ teaspoon Tarragon Leaves

½ cup cooked, finely minced
    chicken, shrimp, or clams

Assorted crackers and chips,
    baked miniature tart shells,
    or marinated mushroom caps
    to serve

1. Place cream cheese in small bowl and beat until creamy. Stir in milk gradually.

2. Dissolve flavor base in hot water. Add to cheese mixture with seasonings and mix well. Stir in chicken. Cover and refrigerate to chill.

3. Serve with crackers and chips, or use to fill baked miniature tart shells or marinated mushroom caps.

*Makes about 1¼ cups*

TIP:

Crab meat, picked over, can also be used. *(See page 47)*

# Sesame Cheese Ball

¼ cup Sesame Seed

2 tablespoons lemon juice

2 tablespoons Instant Minced Onion

1 teaspoon Beef Flavor Base

8 ounces medium-sharp Cheddar
    cheese, grated and softened at
    room temperature

2 tablespoons mayonnaise

1 tablespoon ketchup

Melba toast and/or assorted
    crackers to serve

1. Preheat oven to 350°F.

2. Place sesame seed in shallow baking pan and toast in preheated 350°F oven 15 minutes.

3. Place lemon juice, minced onion, and flavor base in medium-size bowl and stir to combine.

4. Add cheese, mayonnaise, and ketchup to onion mixture. Beat with electric mixer at medium speed until smooth. Shape into ball.

5. Spread toasted sesame seed on wax paper. Roll cheese ball in sesame seed until well coated on all sides. Wrap in plastic wrap and refrigerate at least 2 hours.

6. Serve with melba toast and/or crackers.

*Makes about 2 cups*

TIP:

To make cheese ball, cheese must be at room temperature.

# *Spicy Shrimp*

*1 quart water*

*¼ cup cider vinegar*

*3 tablespoons Pickling Spice*

*2 tablespoons Season-All Seasoned Salt*

*1 teaspoon Crushed Red Pepper*

*1 pound shrimp in shells, about 24 shrimp*

*Cocktail sauce to serve*

1. Place water, vinegar, pickling spice, seasoned salt, and red pepper in large saucepan and stir. Cover, heat to boil, and boil 10 minutes.

2. Add shrimp and boil 5 minutes or until shrimp turn pink. Do not overcook.

3. Remove from heat. Let stand 20 minutes. Drain and set aside to cool. Peel and devein shrimp, place in bowl, cover, and refrigerate to chill.

4. Arrange on platter of cracked ice or place around bowl of cocktail sauce.

*Makes about 24 shrimp*

# Oysters Rockefeller

Rock salt

⅓ cup butter or margarine

1 package (10 ounces) frozen chopped spinach, thawed and squeezed dry

1 tablespoon Instant Minced Onion

1 teaspoon Parsley Flakes

½ teaspoon Bon Appétit

⅛ teaspoon Tarragon Leaves

⅛ teaspoon Ground Red Pepper

⅛ teaspoon Ground White Pepper

Dash Garlic Powder

2 tablespoons dry bread crumbs

BACON AND CHEESE TOPPING

¼ cup crumbled crisp-cooked bacon

¼ cup grated Parmesan cheese

OR

HOLLANDAISE SAUCE

1 package (1¼ ounces) Hollandaise Sauce Mix

1 tablespoon olive oil

⅛ teaspoon Tarragon Leaves

⅛ teaspoon Ground Mustard

¾ cup water

★ ★ ★

24 oysters on the half shell

1. Spread layer of rock salt in shallow roasting pan large enough to hold oysters in single layer. Set aside.

2. Melt butter in medium-size saucepan and stir in spinach.

3. Add minced onion, parsley, Bon Appétit, tarragon, red pepper, white pepper, and garlic powder. Stir well and simmer 15 minutes. Remove from heat and stir in bread crumbs. Set aside.

4. Prepare bacon and cheese for Bacon and Cheese Topping, if using, OR prepare Hollandaise Sauce:

   To make Hollandaise Sauce, place Hollandaise Sauce Mix in small saucepan. Add oil, tarragon, and mustard. Combine well. Stir in water gradually, mixing well. Cook over medium heat, stirring constantly, until sauce thickens.

5. Preheat broiler.

6. Arrange oysters in shells on rock salt in pan.

7. Spread 1 tablespoon reserved spinach mixture over each oyster and top each with ½ teaspoon bacon and ½ teaspoon Parmesan cheese OR 1½ teaspoons Hollandaise Sauce.

8. Broil, 4 to 5 inches from source of heat, 4 minutes. Serve immediately.

*Makes 24 Oysters Rockefeller*

# *Crab Stuffed Mushrooms*

24 large firm mushrooms

2 quarts water

1 teaspoon salt

2 tablespoons butter or margarine

1 tablespoon Instant Minced Onion

2 tablespoons all-purpose flour

¼ cup light cream or milk

¼ cup dry sherry

3 tablespoons lemon juice

1 tablespoon Worcestershire sauce

1 tablespoon prepared mustard

1½ teaspoons Bon Appétit

Dash Ground Red Pepper

1 pound crab meat, picked over*

1. Preheat oven to 450°F.
2. Rinse mushrooms, remove stems, and set caps and stems aside.
3. Heat water and salt to boil in 3-quart saucepan. Add mushroom caps and cook 2 to 3 minutes. Drain on paper towels and set aside.
4. Thinly slice tender part of mushroom stems. Heat butter in large skillet and add sliced stems and minced onion. Sauté quickly, but do not brown.
5. Reduce heat, sprinkle flour into skillet, and stir well. Add remaining ingredients except crab meat and mix thoroughly. Stir in crab meat gently and cook over low heat 5 minutes, stirring occasionally.
6. Fill mushroom caps with crab meat mixture and place, filled side up, in ungreased 15 x 10 x 1-inch baking pan.
7. Bake in preheated 450°F oven 15 minutes or until tops are delicately browned.

*Makes 24 stuffed mushrooms*

*(See page 47)

**MUSTARD**

# Meatballs in Almond Sauce

**SAUCE**

2 tablespoons vegetable oil

1 slice white bread, crust trimmed, cut into ½-inch cubes

½ cup slivered blanched almonds

⅛ teaspoon Instant Minced Garlic

2 teaspoons Chicken Flavor Base

1½ cups hot water

½ cup tomato sauce

1 tablespoon Instant Minced Onion

⅛ teaspoon Ground Black Pepper

**MEATBALLS**

2 slices white bread, crusts trimmed, torn into small pieces

½ cup hot milk

1 pound lean ground beef

1 pound lean ground pork

1 egg, beaten

1½ teaspoons Season-All Seasoned Salt

¼ teaspoon Ground Cumin

⅛ teaspoon Ground Black Pepper

⅛ teaspoon Ground Oregano

1. To make sauce, heat oil in skillet. Add bread cubes, almonds, and minced garlic. Cook until bread cubes are browned.

2. Add flavor base to hot water and stir. Pour ½ cup into blender and add bread mixture. Blend at high speed to make paste. Set aside.

3. Add remaining 1 cup water with flavor base, tomato sauce, minced onion, and pepper to skillet. Cover and simmer 5 minutes. Set aside.

4. To make meatballs, soak torn bread in milk. Drain and place in large bowl. Add meat and mix well. Add remaining ingredients to meat mixture and stir to combine.

5. Moisten hands and shape mixture into 84 meatballs, each 1 to 1¼ inches.

6. Add meatballs to sauce in skillet and stir to coat. Cover and simmer 20 minutes.

7. Add reserved almond mixture to skillet and stir. Cover and simmer 15 minutes. Skim off any excess fat.

*Makes 12 servings, 7 meatballs each*

# Quiche Lorraine

Pastry for 10-inch pie crust

2½ ounces thinly sliced Smithfield ham, diced

1 cup (4 ounces) shredded Swiss cheese

5 eggs

1½ cups milk

1 cup light cream

½ teaspoon Bon Appétit

⅛ teaspoon Ground Red Pepper

Dash Ground Nutmeg

1. Preheat oven to 350°F.
2. Line 10-inch pie plate or quiche pan with pastry and sprinkle ham and cheese over pastry.
3. Place eggs in medium-size bowl and beat lightly. Stir in milk, cream, Bon Appétit, red pepper, and nutmeg. Mix well and pour over cheese and ham.
4. Bake in preheated 350°F oven 45 to 50 minutes.

*Makes 8 wedges, 3½ inches each*

VARIATIONS:

Crab Meat Quiche: Follow recipe above but eliminate ham and substitute 2 cups crab meat, picked over. *(See page 47)*

Vegetable Quiche: Follow recipe above but eliminate ham and substitute 2 cups chopped, cooked vegetables of your choice. Add ¼ teaspoon salt.

Bacon Quiche: Follow recipe above but eliminate ham and substitute 12 slices crisp-cooked, finely crumbled bacon.

# Best Ever Stuffed Eggs

6 hard-cooked eggs*

¼ cup mayonnaise

2 teaspoons lemon juice or vinegar

½ teaspoon Chicken Flavor Base

½ teaspoon Bon Appétit

⅛ teaspoon Onion Powder

⅛ teaspoon Ground Turmeric

⅛ teaspoon Ground White Pepper

Paprika, Parsley Flakes, capers, olive slices, or pimiento strips to garnish

1. Cut eggs in half lengthwise and carefully remove yolks. Place yolks in small bowl and mash.

2. Add mayonnaise, lemon juice, flavor base, Bon Appétit, onion powder, turmeric, and white pepper. Mix thoroughly.

3. Spoon egg yolk mixture into egg whites, piling mixture high. Arrange on platter and garnish as desired with paprika, parsley, capers, olive slices, or pimiento strips.

*Makes 12 stuffed egg halves*

VARIATIONS:

**Dill Stuffed Eggs:** In place of Bon Appétit and turmeric, use ¾ teaspoon Celery Salt, ½ teaspoon Dill Weed, and dash Ground Red Pepper.

**Curry Stuffed Eggs:** Add ½ teaspoon Curry Powder.

**Chicken, Shrimp, or Bacon Stuffed Eggs:** Stir in ½ cup finely minced home-cooked or canned chicken; ¼ cup canned, drained shrimp; or 3 slices crisp-cooked, finely crumbled bacon.

*(To hard-cook eggs, see page 48)

# *Herby Cheese Bites*

*1 package (8 ounces) cream cheese, softened*

*2 tablespoons butter or margarine, softened*

*1 tablespoon Freeze-Dried Chives*

*1 tablespoon Parsley Flakes*

*½ teaspoon California Style Garlic Pepper*

*¼ teaspoon Dill Weed*

*⅛ teaspoon Thyme Leaves*

*5 flour tortillas (each 6 inches round)*

*5 slices cooked ham, smoked turkey, or roast beef*

*3 scallions, green part only*

1. Place cream cheese and butter in medium-size bowl and beat until well combined and fluffy. Add chives, parsley, garlic pepper, dill, and thyme. Beat well. Cover and refrigerate 3 to 4 hours or overnight.

2. Remove mixture from refrigerator and let stand until soft enough to spread.

3. Place tortillas on work surface. Set aside 1 tablespoon cheese mixture in small bowl. Spread remaining cheese mixture on tortillas and top with slice of meat.

4. Cut ten 6-inch pieces of scallion and place 2 pieces at 1 edge of each tortilla.

5. Starting at edge of tortillas where scallion is placed, roll tortillas and seal edges of rolls with reserved cheese mixture.

6. Cut each tortilla roll into ¾-inch slices and arrange on serving dish.

7. Serve immediately or cover and refrigerate until ready to serve.

*Makes about 36 appetizers*

## SOUP

# Maryland Crab Soup

1 can (28 ounces) whole tomatoes,
   cut into small pieces

3 cups water

1 cup frozen lima beans

1 cup frozen baby carrots or sliced carrots

1 cup frozen yellow sweet corn

2 tablespoons Instant Chopped
   Onions

1 tablespoon Old Bay Seasoning

2 teaspoons Beef Flavor Base

1 pound backfin blue crab meat,
   picked over*

1. Place all ingredients except crab meat in 4-quart saucepan.
2. Heat to boil, cover, and boil 5 minutes.
3. Reduce heat to low, add crab meat, cover, and simmer 10 minutes.

*Makes 10 servings, 1 cup each*

*(See page 47)

---

# Gazpacho

2 cups tomato juice

1 tablespoon red wine vinegar

1 tablespoon lemon juice

1 tablespoon olive oil

1 tablespoon Instant Minced Onion

1 teaspoon Freeze-Dried Chives

½ teaspoon California Style Garlic Salt

¼ teaspoon Parsley Flakes

⅛ teaspoon Marjoram Leaves

1 cucumber, peeled

1 green bell pepper

1 ripe tomato, seeded

1 cup croutons to serve

1. Place tomato juice, vinegar, lemon juice, oil, and seasonings in food processor and process 5 seconds.
2. Set aside ¼ cucumber and ½ green bell pepper. Cut remaining ¾ cucumber, ½ green bell pepper, and tomato into chunks. Add to food processor and process 10 seconds. Scrape down and process 5 seconds. Pour into large serving dish.

3. Coarsely chop reserved ¼ cucumber and ½ green bell pepper. Sprinkle over Gazpacho, cover, and refrigerate at least 2 hours or until ready to serve.

4. When ready to serve, garnish each portion with croutons.

*Makes 8 servings, ½ cup each*

# Lobster Bisque Élégante

*11 cups water, divided*

*2½ teaspoons salt, divided*

*4 frozen rock lobster tails, 8 ounces each*

*1 tablespoon Chicken Flavor Base*

*1 tablespoon Instant Minced Onion*

*6 Coriander Seeds*

*3 Whole Black Peppercorns*

*1 Bay Leaf*

*⅓ cup butter or margarine*

*½ cup all-purpose flour*

*1 teaspoon Bon Appétit*

*3 cups milk*

*1 cup light cream*

*Paprika to garnish*

1. Place 8 cups water in 4-quart saucepan and heat to boil. Add 2 teaspoons salt and lobster tails. Cover and boil 10 minutes.

2. Remove lobster tails and discard water. Remove meat from shells and set meat aside. Crush shells and return shells to saucepan.

3. Chop lobster meat and set aside.

4. Add remaining 3 cups water, flavor base, minced onion, coriander seeds, peppercorns, and bay leaf to saucepan. Heat to boil, reduce heat to low, cover, and simmer 30 minutes. Pour through sieve into large bowl and set broth aside. Discard shells and spices.

5. Melt butter in saucepan. Stir in flour, Bon Appétit, and remaining ½ teaspoon salt. Cook just until bubbly. Remove from heat.

6. Stir in milk gradually, return to low heat, and simmer, stirring constantly, until thickened.

7. Stir in reserved lobster broth, reserved lobster meat, and cream. Cook over low heat just until heated through. Do not boil.

8. Ladle into soup bowls and garnish with paprika.

*Makes 8 servings, 1 cup each*

# Tortilla Soup with Meatballs

### MEATBALLS

½ pound lean ground beef

½ pound lean ground pork

½ cup chopped blanched
  almonds

¼ cup milk

¼ cup dry bread crumbs

1 egg, beaten

1 tablespoon Instant Minced
  Onion

1 teaspoon Parsley Flakes

¾ teaspoon Bon Appétit

⅛ teaspoon Ground Cumin

⅛ teaspoon Ground Oregano

⅛ teaspoon Ground Black Pepper

1 tablespoon olive oil

### SOUP

10 cups hot water

1½ cups tomato juice

¾ cup thinly sliced carrots

¾ cup coarsely chopped celery

1 can (4 ounces) green chilies,
  drained and cut into strips

2 small whole hot chilies

2 Whole Black Peppercorns

1 Bay Leaf

3 tablespoons Beef Flavor Base

1 tablespoon Instant Minced Onion

¼ teaspoon Garlic Powder

\* \* \*

48 tortilla chips and 1½ cups shredded
  Monterey Jack cheese to serve

1. To make meatballs, place all ingredients except oil in large bowl and mix well. Moisten hands with cold water and shape meat into seventy-two 1-inch balls.

2. Heat oil in large skillet.

3. Add meatballs in batches (do not overcrowd pan) and cook 5 minutes over medium heat, turning to brown on all sides. Remove from skillet with slotted spoon and drain on paper towels, if desired. Set aside and keep warm.

4. To make soup, place water, tomato juice, carrots, celery, green and hot chilies, peppercorns, bay leaf, flavor base, minced onion, and garlic powder in large saucepan. Stir to combine and heat to boil. Reduce heat, cover, and simmer 20 minutes.

5. Remove and discard whole hot chilies and bay leaf.

6. When ready to serve, place 6 meatballs in large soup plate. Ladle 1 cup broth over meatballs, add 4 tortilla chips, and sprinkle with 2 tablespoons cheese.

*Makes 12 servings: 1 cup broth, 6 meatballs,
4 tortilla chips, and 2 tablespoons cheese each*

# Mixed Bean Soup

½ cup dry kidney beans

½ cup dry lima beans

½ cup dry pinto beans

4 quarts cold water, divided

1 can (14½ ounces) whole tomatoes, cut into small pieces

¼ cup Instant Chopped Onions

1 tablespoon Beef Flavor Base

1 teaspoon Bon Appétit

½ teaspoon Ground Savory

¼ teaspoon Hot Shot! Pepper Blend

⅛ teaspoon Ground Cumin

1. Pick over beans to remove stones and empty shells. Place in 4-quart bowl, add 2 quarts water, and soak overnight. Drain and rinse thoroughly. If preferred, follow instructions for quick-soaking method on package of beans.

2. Place 2 quarts fresh water and beans in Dutch oven or large saucepan. Heat to boil, reduce heat, cover, and simmer 2½ to 3 hours or until beans are tender.

3. Add remaining ingredients to beans. Stir well, cover, and simmer 30 minutes.

*Makes 10 servings, 1 cup each*

# Chicken-Corn Soup

3 to 4-pound chicken, cut up

6 cups water

1 tablespoon Chicken Flavor Base

10 Saffron threads

2 cups egg noodles

1 can (16 ounces) whole-kernel corn or 2 cups frozen whole-kernel corn

1 teaspoon Instant Minced Onion

½ teaspoon Parsley Flakes

½ teaspoon Ground Black Pepper

¼ teaspoon Celery Salt

2 hard-cooked eggs, chopped*

1. Place chicken in Dutch oven or large saucepan. Add water, flavor base, and saffron. Heat to simmering, cover, and cook 1½ hours over low heat, adding additional water as necessary.

2. Remove chicken from stock and set aside to cool slightly. Skim fat off stock.

3. When cool enough to handle, remove meat from bones of chicken. Discard skin and bones and cut meat into small pieces. Add meat to stock and heat to boil.

4. Add noodles, corn, minced onion, parsley, pepper, and celery salt to stock. Stir gently, cover, reduce heat, and simmer 15 minutes.

5. Ladle into soup bowls and sprinkle with chopped egg.

*Makes 8 servings, 1 cup each*

*(To hard-cook eggs, see page 48)*

# Show Stopper Soup

3½ cups milk, divided

1 package (10 ounces) frozen chopped spinach, thawed and squeezed dry

½ cup drained oysters

¼ cup butter or margarine

¼ cup all-purpose flour

2 teaspoons Instant Minced Onion

1 teaspoon Chicken Flavor Base

¾ teaspoon Bon Appétit

½ teaspoon Ground White Pepper

¼ teaspoon Ground Nutmeg

1 cup heavy cream

Unsweetened whipped cream and Crushed Red Pepper to garnish

1. Pour 1½ cups milk into blender or food processor.

2. Add spinach in small amounts, blending until smooth after each addition. Pour into bowl.

3. Purée oysters in blender, add to spinach mixture, and set aside.

4. Melt butter in 3-quart saucepan. Stir in flour, minced onion, flavor base, Bon Appétit, white pepper, and nutmeg. Cook, stirring constantly, until bubbly.

5. Stir in reserved spinach-oyster mixture.

6. Add remaining 2 cups milk and 1 cup cream to saucepan. Cook, stirring constantly, over medium heat until mixture begins to boil. Reduce heat and simmer 2 minutes.

7. Garnish with dollops of unsweetened whipped cream and sprinkle lightly with crushed red pepper.

*Makes 6 servings, 1 cup each*

*Show Stopper Soup (see photo on page 176)*

# *Minestrone*

1 cup dry beans (Great Northern, kidney, pinto, lima, or mixture)

4 quarts plus 4 to 6 cups water, divided

¼ cup olive oil

¼ cup chopped celery

¼ cup chopped green bell pepper

¼ cup Instant Chopped Onions

1 tablespoon Parsley Flakes

⅛ teaspoon Instant Minced Garlic

1 can (28 ounces) whole tomatoes, cut into small pieces

½ pound spinach, washed, stems removed, and torn into bite-size pieces

1 cup peeled, diced potato

1 cup chopped cabbage

1 cup chopped zucchini

½ cup elbow macaroni

1 tablespoon Beef Flavor Base

1 tablespoon Season-All Seasoned Salt

1 teaspoon Ground Thyme

¼ teaspoon Italian Seasoning

¼ teaspoon Ground Black Pepper

⅛ teaspoon Rubbed Sage

Grated Parmesan cheese to serve

1. Pick over beans to remove stones and empty shells. Place in 4-quart bowl, add 2 quarts water, and soak overnight. Drain and rinse thoroughly. If preferred, follow instructions for quick-soaking method on package of beans.

2. Place 2 quarts fresh water and beans in Dutch oven or large saucepan. Heat to boil, reduce heat, cover, and simmer 2½ to 3 hours or until beans are tender.

3. Heat oil in skillet. Add celery, green bell pepper, chopped onions, parsley, and minced garlic. Sauté but do not brown. Add to beans.

4. Add remaining ingredients except water and cheese to beans. Cover and simmer 30 minutes.

5. Add 4 to 6 additional cups water, depending on consistency desired. Cook until heated through.

6. Ladle into soup bowls and sprinkle with Parmesan cheese.

*Makes 12 to 16 servings, 1 cup each*

TIP:

This is a thick soup. If desired, thin with additional boiling water to desired consistency.

*Show Stopper Soup (see recipe on page 175)*

# Golden Cream of Carrot Soup

2 cups thinly sliced fresh or frozen carrots

½ cup water

1 tablespoon lemon juice

1 teaspoon Bon Appétit, divided

3 teaspoons Chicken Flavor Base, divided

¼ cup butter or margarine

2 tablespoons all-purpose flour

¼ teaspoon Ground Ginger

⅛ teaspoon Onion Powder

2 cups milk

¼ cup light cream (optional)

1. Place carrots, water, lemon juice, ½ teaspoon Bon Appétit, and 1 teaspoon flavor base in 2-quart saucepan. Stir to combine. Cook until carrots are very soft and liquid is reduced to about 1 tablespoon.

2. Purée carrots and liquid in blender or food processor. Set aside.

3. Melt butter in medium-size saucepan. Stir in flour, remaining ½ teaspoon Bon Appétit and 2 teaspoons flavor base, ginger, and onion powder. Mix well.

4. Add milk to saucepan gradually and cook over low heat, stirring constantly, until mixture is smooth and thickened.

5. Add reserved carrot purée and stir to mix well. Cook just until heated through. Stir in cream and serve immediately.

*Makes 4 servings, 1 cup each*

GINGER

## SALADS / SALAD DRESSINGS

# Chicken Salad

2 cups cooked, cubed chicken

1 cup chopped celery

¼ cup chopped pickle

1 hard-cooked egg, chopped*

DRESSING

½ cup mayonnaise

1 tablespoon lemon juice

½ teaspoon Season-All Seasoned Salt

½ teaspoon Ground Mustard

Dash Nutmeg

⅛ teaspoon Ground White Pepper

\*  \*  \*

Lettuce, tomato cups, or avocado
halves to serve

Paprika and capers to garnish,
if desired

1. Place chicken, celery, pickle, and egg in medium-size bowl and stir to combine.

2. Place dressing ingredients in small bowl and mix well.

3. Add dressing to chicken mixture and toss lightly to coat chicken.

4. Refrigerate several hours or serve immediately. Serve on crisp lettuce or use to fill tomato cups or avocado halves.

5. Garnish with paprika and a few capers.

*Makes 6 servings, ½ cup each*

*(To hard-cook eggs, see page 48 )

TIP:

May also be used to make delicious sandwiches.

# Cajun Salad with Six-Season Dressing

1 pound medium-size or large shrimp, cooked, peeled, and deveined

1 can (15 ounces) pinto beans, drained

1 can (11 ounces) whole-kernel corn, drained

1 can (2¼ ounces) sliced ripe olives, drained

1 green bell pepper, chopped

DRESSING

½ cup olive oil

½ cup ketchup

1 tablespoon cider vinegar

2 tablespoons Parsley Flakes

1½ teaspoons Creole Seasoning

½ teaspoon Garlic Powder

½ teaspoon Ground Cumin

½ teaspoon Lemon Peel

¼ teaspoon Ground Red Pepper

\* \* \*

12 cherry tomatoes, halved

Lettuce to serve

1. Place shrimp, beans, corn, olives, and green bell pepper in large salad bowl and toss gently.

2. Place dressing ingredients in 2-cup glass measure. Beat with fork until well combined.

3. Pour dressing over shrimp mixture, add tomatoes, and toss gently.

4. Cover and refrigerate at least 2 hours.

5. Toss salad just before serving and serve on bed of lettuce.

*Makes 6 servings*

**RED PEPPER**

# Island Chicken Salad with Citrus-Rum Dressing

MARINADE

3 tablespoons soy sauce

2 tablespoons olive oil

1 tablespoon cider vinegar

1 tablespoon Instant Minced Onion

2 teaspoons sugar

2 teaspoons Thyme Leaves

1 teaspoon Ground Black Pepper

1 teaspoon Ground Allspice

½ teaspoon Ground Cinnamon

½ teaspoon Ground Nutmeg

¼ teaspoon Ground Red Pepper

＊　＊　＊

1½ pounds boneless, skinless
   chicken breasts

DRESSING

¼ cup vegetable oil

3 tablespoons orange juice

1 tablespoon lime juice

1 tablespoon honey

¼ teaspoon Rum Extract

¼ teaspoon Ground Ginger

¼ teaspoon Ground Nutmeg

¼ teaspoon Garlic Salt

＊　＊　＊

Lettuce and assorted raw vegetables
   to serve

1. Place marinade ingredients in 1-cup glass measure and beat with fork until well combined. Pour into large self-closing plastic bag or shallow glass or stainless steel dish.

2. Rinse chicken and add to marinade. Seal plastic bag or cover if using dish and refrigerate at least 4 hours.

3. Place dressing ingredients in 1-cup glass measure and beat with fork until well combined. Set aside.

4. Preheat broiler or grill.

5. Remove chicken from marinade and discard marinade. Place chicken on lightly greased broiler pan or grill rack and broil or grill 5 to 6 minutes on each side, or until lightly browned.

6. Cut cooked chicken into strips and arrange on bed of lettuce. Surround with assorted vegetables and sprinkle with reserved dressing.

*Makes 4 to 6 servings*

# Crab Salad

DRESSING

½ cup mayonnaise

2 teaspoons lemon juice

1 teaspoon Bon Appétit

¼ teaspoon Ground Mustard

¼ teaspoon Ground White Pepper

⅛ teaspoon Ground Red Pepper

⅛ teaspoon Ground Ginger

✳   ✳   ✳

1 pound backfin blue crab meat,
  picked over*

1 cup chopped celery

¼ cup chopped stuffed green olives

Paprika to garnish

1. Place dressing ingredients in small bowl and mix well.
2. Place crab meat in serving dish and add celery and chopped olives. Mix gently.
3. Add dressing to crab meat mixture and mix gently but thoroughly. Cover and refrigerate to chill.
4. Garnish with paprika when ready to serve.

*Makes 8 servings, ½ cup each*

*(See page 47)

---

# Shrimp Salad

1 pound shrimp, cooked, peeled,
  and deveined

2 hard-cooked eggs, chopped*

½ cup chopped celery

DRESSING

⅔ cup mayonnaise

1 teaspoon Bon Appétit

¼ teaspoon Ground White Pepper

⅛ teaspoon Tarragon Leaves

Dash Ground Red Pepper

1. Cut shrimp into bite-size pieces, saving a few whole shrimp to garnish. Set whole shrimp aside and place cut shrimp in serving dish.
2. Add eggs and celery to cut shrimp and mix lightly.
3. Place dressing ingredients in small bowl and mix well. Pour dressing over shrimp and mix gently.
4. Garnish with whole shrimp. Cover and refrigerate at least 1 hour.

*Makes 6 servings, ½ cup each*

*(To hard-cook eggs, see page 48)

# Waldorf Salad

3 cups cored, cubed, unpeeled apples

½ cup chopped celery

½ cup chopped walnuts or pecans

¼ cup raisins

DRESSING

½ cup mayonnaise

1 tablespoon light cream

2 teaspoons lemon juice

½ teaspoon Lemon Peel

¼ teaspoon Ground Mustard

¼ teaspoon Ground Ginger

⅛ teaspoon Ground Mace

Dash Ground Cardamom

＊　＊　＊

Lettuce cups to serve, if desired

1. Place apples, celery, nuts, and raisins in medium-size bowl.
2. Place dressing ingredients in small bowl and stir to combine.
3. Add to apple mixture and toss gently. Cover and refrigerate to chill several hours.
4. Serve in lettuce cups.

*Makes 9 servings, ½ cup each*

# Creamy Coleslaw

DRESSING

1 cup dairy sour cream

2 tablespoons vinegar

3 tablespoons sugar

2 teaspoons Season-All Seasoned Salt

1 teaspoon Ground Mustard

1 teaspoon Celery Seed

½ teaspoon Ground Ginger

Dash Ground White Pepper

＊　＊　＊

8 cups finely shredded cabbage

½ cup minced green bell pepper

Paprika to garnish

1. Place dressing ingredients in small bowl and mix well.
2. Place cabbage and green bell pepper in large bowl and toss.

3. Spoon dressing over cabbage mixture and mix well.

4. Spoon into serving dish, cover, and refrigerate to chill until ready to serve. Sprinkle lightly with paprika just before serving.

*Makes 8 servings, ¾ cup each*

VARIATION:

Use 1 cup mayonnaise, 2 tablespoons vinegar, 2 tablespoons light cream, 1 teaspoon sugar, 1 teaspoon Celery Seed, ½ teaspoon Bon Appétit, ½ teaspoon Ground Mustard, ¼ teaspoon Onion Salt, and dash Ground Red Pepper in place of dressing ingredients above.

# *Corn Salad in Pepper Shells*

*6 green bell peppers*

*⅓ cup vegetable oil*

*2 tablespoons vinegar*

*1 tablespoon Instant Minced Onion*

*½ teaspoon Ground Mustard*

*½ teaspoon Ground Black Pepper*

*⅛ teaspoon Ground Red Pepper*

*3 cups (2 cans, 11 ounces each) whole-kernel corn, undrained*

*1 can (8 ounces) water chestnuts, drained and thinly sliced*

*1 jar (6 ounces) pimientos, drained and cut into 1-inch squares*

*1 cup thinly sliced celery*

1. Cut tops off green bell peppers and remove seeds. Cut top edge of each bell pepper in petal shape, if desired. Place in large saucepan of boiling water and parboil 5 minutes. Drain and cool under cold running water. Place upside down on paper towels and set aside.

2. Place oil, vinegar, minced onion, mustard, and black and red pepper in 1-cup glass measure and beat with fork until well combined. Set aside.

3. Place corn, water chestnuts, pimientos, and celery in large bowl and stir to combine. Add dressing and toss to mix well.

4. Fill bell peppers with corn mixture. Cover lightly and refrigerate to chill.

*Makes 6 servings, 1 filled bell pepper each*

# Spinach Rotini Salad

1 package (16 ounces) spinach or
  tricolor rotini

1 cup sliced mushrooms

1 can (6 ounces) pitted ripe olives

1 package (3½ ounces) sliced pepperoni

1 medium-size red onion, thinly sliced

1 medium-size zucchini, sliced

1 green bell pepper, cut into bite-size
  strips

DRESSING

⅔ cup olive oil

½ cup malt vinegar

2 teaspoons sugar

2 teaspoons Italian
  Seasoning

1 teaspoon Lemon &
  Pepper Seasoning

1. Cook rotini according to package directions. Rinse with cold water to stop
   cooking and drain well.

2. Place cooked rotini, mushrooms, olives, pepperoni, onion, zucchini, and
   green bell pepper in large bowl and toss.

3. Place dressing ingredients in 2-cup glass measure and beat with fork until
   well combined.

4. Pour dressing over salad and toss to mix well. Cover and refrigerate to chill
   several hours.

*Makes 19 cups*

# Frozen Bing Cherry Salad

1 can (16½ ounces) pitted
  Bing cherries, about 2½ cups

1 can (8 ounces) pineapple chunks

1 package (3 ounces) cream
  cheese, room temperature

½ cup dairy sour cream

2 tablespoons sugar

1 teaspoon Lemon Peel

1 teaspoon Pure Vanilla Extract

½ teaspoon Ground Ginger

⅛ teaspoon Ground Mace

⅛ teaspoon salt

3 to 4 drops Red Food Color

1 cup miniature marshmallows

Lettuce to serve

1. Drain cherries and pineapple and set aside.

2. Place cream cheese in medium-size bowl and beat until fluffy. Add sour
   cream, sugar, lemon peel, vanilla, ginger, mace, salt, and food color. Mix well.

3. Carefully stir in marshmallows, reserved cherries, and reserved pineapple.

4. Pour into 9 x 5 x 3-inch loaf pan, cover, and place in freezer.

5. Remove from pan when frozen and place on cutting surface. Cut into 8 slices, each 1¼ inches wide. Serve on crisp lettuce.

*Makes 8 slices, 4 ½ x 1¼ x 1¼ inch each*

# Caesar Salad

DRESSING

*⅓ cup olive oil*

*2 tablespoons malt vinegar*

*1 tablespoon lemon juice*

*½ teaspoon Worcestershire sauce*

*1 teaspoon California Style Garlic Powder*

*½ teaspoon Season-All Seasoned Salt*

*¼ teaspoon Ground Mustard*

*⅛ teaspoon Ground Black Pepper*

*⅛ teaspoon sugar*

*3 anchovy fillets, mashed*

＊　＊　＊

*2 heads romaine lettuce*

*¾ cup grated Parmesan cheese*

*1 cup garlic-flavored croutons*

1. Place dressing ingredients in 1-cup glass measure and beat with fork until well combined.

2. Wash lettuce, remove and discard outside leaves, and break tender leaves crosswise into pieces about 1 inch wide. Store in plastic bag in refrigerator until ready to serve.

3. When ready to serve, place lettuce in large salad bowl. Pour dressing over lettuce and toss to coat leaves.

4. Sprinkle cheese and croutons over salad and toss to mix well. Serve immediately.

*Makes 8 servings, 2 cups each*

# Piquant Tomato Aspic

¼ cup cold water

2 envelopes unflavored gelatin

4 cups tomato juice

3 tablespoons lemon juice

¼ cup Instant Chopped Onions

2 tablespoons light brown sugar

1 teaspoon Season-All Seasoned Salt

½ teaspoon Basil Leaves

6 Whole Black Peppercorns

4 Whole Allspice

3 Bay Leaves

3 Whole Cloves

Salad greens to serve

1. Place water in small dish and sprinkle gelatin over water. Set aside to soften.

2. Place remaining ingredients except salad greens in 2-quart saucepan and stir to combine. Heat to boil, reduce heat, cover, and simmer 15 minutes.

3. Strain through fine sieve into bowl to remove spices and discard spices.

4. Add softened gelatin to liquid in bowl and stir to dissolve.

5. Pour into 1½-quart mold or 8-inch square pan and refrigerate to chill until firm.

6. When ready to serve, unmold aspic and serve on bed of salad greens.

*Makes 6 servings, ½ cup each*

# Green Goddess Dressing

3 cups mayonnaise

¼ cup white wine vinegar

1 can (2 ounces) anchovy fillets, mashed

1 tablespoon Instant Minced Onion

1 tablespoon Parsley Flakes

1 tablespoon Tarragon Leaves

1 tablespoon Freeze-Dried Chives

⅛ teaspoon Onion Powder

Dash Garlic Powder

1. Place all ingredients in medium-size bowl and stir until well blended.

2. Let stand 30 minutes or longer to blend flavors.

3. Serve with tossed salads.

*Makes 3½ cups*

# Cardamom Cream Dressing

4 egg yolks

¼ cup vinegar

1 tablespoon sugar

1 tablespoon butter or margarine

½ teaspoon Ground Mustard

½ teaspoon salt

¼ teaspoon Ground Cardamom

Dash Ground White Pepper

1 cup heavy cream, whipped

1 cup miniature marshmallows

½ cup chopped pecans

1. Place egg yolks in saucepan or top of double boiler and beat until light. Stir in vinegar, sugar, butter, and seasonings.
2. Cook over low heat, stirring constantly, until mixture thickens, about 3 minutes.
3. Remove from heat and set aside to cool.
4. When ready to serve, fold in whipped cream, marshmallows, and pecans. Serve with fruit salads.

*Makes 3⅓ cups*

# Vanilla Vinaigrette

¾ cup olive oil

½ cup white wine vinegar

1 tablespoon water

1 tablespoon Pure Vanilla Extract

1 teaspoon Tarragon Leaves

1 teaspoon salt

½ teaspoon sugar

¼ teaspoon Ground Black Pepper

1. Place all ingredients in 2-cup glass measure and beat with fork until well combined.
2. Refrigerate until well chilled.
3. Beat again just before serving. Serve on salad greens.

*Makes 1¼ cups*

# Honey Spice Dressing

1 cup French dressing

2 tablespoons honey

1 teaspoon Ground Cinnamon

½ teaspoon Ground Cloves

¼ teaspoon Ground Ginger

1. Place all ingredients in 2-cup glass measure and mix well.
2. Cover and refrigerate until ready to use.
3. Serve on fruit or mixed salad greens.

*Makes 1 cup*

# Skinny Dip

DRESSING

¼ cup corn oil or olive oil

¼ cup malt vinegar

2 tablespoons water

1 teaspoon sugar

1 teaspoon Italian Seasoning

½ teaspoon Instant Minced Garlic

¼ teaspoon Ground Black Pepper

* * *

Assorted bite-size vegetables to serve such as yellow pear tomatoes, baby carrots, baby corn, enoki mushrooms, cauliflowerets, broccoli florets, snow peas, cooked and sliced new potatoes, or salad greens

Salad burnet to garnish, if desired

1. Place all dressing ingredients in screw-top jar and shake vigorously, or place in 1-cup glass measure and beat with fork until well blended.
2. Store in refrigerator in covered container until ready to use. Shake well before serving.
3. Place small dish of dressing in center of each individual serving plate and arrange vegetables around dressing. Garnish with salad burnet.

*Makes 4 servings, 2½ tablespoons each*

# Creamy Roquefort Dressing

½ cup mayonnaise

½ cup light cream

2 teaspoons lemon juice

¼ teaspoon Ground Mustard

Dash Ground White Pepper

Dash Garlic Salt

8 ounces Roquefort cheese, crumbled

1. Place all ingredients except cheese in bowl and stir to combine. Add cheese and mix well.
2. Cover and refrigerate to chill.
3. Serve on salad greens.

*Makes 2 cups*

## MEAT

# Sesame Steaks

1-pound boneless sirloin steak, cut ½ inch thick

¼ cup soy sauce

1 tablespoon vegetable oil

1 teaspoon lemon juice

1 tablespoon brown sugar

1 tablespoon Sesame Seed

1 teaspoon Onion Powder

¼ teaspoon Ground Black Pepper

¼ teaspoon Garlic Salt

¼ teaspoon Ground Ginger

1. Cut steak into 4 equal-size pieces, place in shallow glass or stainless steel dish.
2. Place remaining ingredients in 1-cup glass measure and beat with fork until well combined. Pour over steak.
3. Cover and refrigerate at least 1 hour, turning once or twice.
4. Preheat broiler.
5. Discard marinade. Broil meat 4 to 6 minutes each side or to desired doneness. Serve immediately.

*Makes 4 servings, 4 ounces each*

# Peppered Tenderloin

6 beef tenderloin steaks, cut 1 inch thick

1 tablespoon Coarse Ground
 Black Pepper

½ teaspoon Garlic Salt

3 tablespoons butter or margarine

1 teaspoon all-purpose flour

½ teaspoon Beef Flavor Base

¼ cup hot water

2 tablespoons Cognac

1. Season steaks on both sides with pepper and garlic salt. Press pepper into meat.

2. Melt butter in 10-inch skillet. Sauté steaks 4 to 5 minutes on each side. Remove from skillet and keep warm on platter.

3. Add flour and flavor base to skillet and stir to mix well. Add hot water and Cognac and stir.

4. Heat to boil, spoon over steaks, and serve immediately.

*Makes 6 servings, 1 steak each*

# Steak Teriyaki

MARINADE

1 bottle or can (12 ounces) beer

½ cup soy sauce

2 tablespoons vegetable oil

2 teaspoons lemon juice

3 tablespoons dark brown sugar

1 teaspoon Ground Ginger

½ teaspoon Ground Mustard

½ teaspoon Coarse Ground Black Pepper

⅛ teaspoon Garlic Powder

\* \* \*

3-pound sirloin steak, cut 1 inch thick

1. Place marinade ingredients in bowl or 4-cup glass measure and beat with fork until well combined.

2. Place meat in shallow glass dish. Pour marinade over steak and pierce surface of meat all over with tines of fork. Cover and refrigerate 12 to 24 hours, turning once.

3. Preheat broiler or grill.

4. Remove meat from marinade, reserving marinade. Broil or grill steak 10 minutes on each side or to desired doneness, basting frequently with marinade.

5. Slice steak thinly on the diagonal.

*Makes 8 servings, 6 ounces each*

# Beef Stroganoff

2 tablespoons butter or margarine

2-pound beef tenderloin steak,
    cut into bite-size strips

¼ cup dry sherry

1 tablespoon Instant Minced Onion

1 teaspoon Season-All Seasoned Salt

Dash Ground Nutmeg

1 cup dairy sour cream,
    room temperature

Hot cooked wild rice or buttered
    noodles to serve, if desired

1. Melt butter in 10-inch skillet. Add meat and cook 5 minutes, stirring, over medium heat.

2. Add sherry, minced onion, seasoned salt, and nutmeg to skillet and stir. Cover and cook 5 minutes. Remove from heat.

3. Stir in sour cream and cook over low heat just until heated through. (Be careful not to let sauce boil. Boiling will make sauce look curdled.)

4. Serve over hot cooked wild rice or noodles.

*Makes 6 servings, ½ cup each*

TIP:

Beef is easier to slice if partially frozen. Cut across grain into bite-size strips.

# Pot Roast with Vegetables

2 tablespoons vegetable oil

4-pound beef bottom round roast

1 can (28 ounces) whole tomatoes,
    undrained

2 cups water

2 tablespoons Instant Chopped Onions

1 tablespoon Beef Flavor Base

1½ teaspoons Season-All Seasoned Salt

¼ teaspoon Ground Black Pepper

¼ teaspoon Oregano Leaves

¼ teaspoon Basil Leaves

3 carrots, quartered

3 stalks celery, cut into 2-inch
    pieces

3 medium-size potatoes, peeled
    and quartered

1. Heat oil in Dutch oven or large saucepan and brown meat on all sides over high heat.

2. Add tomatoes, water, chopped onions, flavor base, seasoned salt, pepper, oregano, and basil. Stir well and heat to boil. Reduce heat until liquid is barely simmering. Cover and cook 1 hour.

3. Add remaining vegetables to pan and simmer 1 hour or until vegetables and meat are tender. Add additional water during cooking as necessary.

*Makes 8 servings, 5 ounces each*

# Pot Roast aux Herbes

*2 tablespoons all-purpose flour*

*1 teaspoon Bon Appétit*

*1 teaspoon Cracked Black Pepper*

*½ teaspoon Ground Mustard*

*4-pound boneless beef rump or chuck roast*

*2 tablespoons vegetable oil*

*1 cup water*

*2 teaspoons Beef Flavor Base*

*1 teaspoon Oregano Leaves*

*½ teaspoon Marjoram Leaves*

*3 Whole Allspice*

*2 Bay Leaves*

*1 piece Whole Ginger*

1. Place flour, Bon Appétit, pepper, and mustard in shallow dish and stir to combine. Coat meat on all sides in flour mixture.

2. Heat oil in Dutch oven or large saucepan and brown meat on all sides over high heat.

3. Add remaining ingredients to pan and stir. Cover, reduce heat, and simmer over very low heat 2½ hours or until meat is tender. (Be sure surface of liquid does not bubble.) Add additional water as necessary.

4. Remove and discard bay leaves before serving.

*Makes 8 servings, 5 ounces meat each*

# Sunday Dinner Pot Roast

*3-pound boneless beef chuck roast, cut about 2 inches thick*

*2 teaspoons Montreal Steak Seasoning*

*1 cup beef broth*

*½ teaspoon Basil Leaves*

*¼ teaspoon Oregano Leaves*

*¼ teaspoon Thyme Leaves*

*4 small potatoes, peeled and halved*

*4 carrots, cut into 1-inch pieces*

*1 medium-size onion, cut into wedges*

*All-purpose flour for thickening (optional)*

1. Preheat oven to 350°F.
2. Place meat in 4-quart baking pan and sprinkle with steak seasoning.
3. Combine beef broth with basil, oregano, and thyme and add to pan.
4. Cover and bake in preheated 350°F oven 1½ hours.
5. Uncover meat and scatter potatoes, carrots, and onion around roast. Cover and bake 1½ hours or until meat is tender.
6. Remove meat from pan and slice. Arrange on serving dish and surround with vegetables. If desired, thicken pan juices with flour and serve with meat and vegetables.

*Makes 8 servings*

**BAY LEAVES**

# Old-Fashioned Sauerbraten

2 cups cider vinegar

2 cups water

12 Whole Black Peppercorns

6 Whole Cloves

3 Bay Leaves

½ cup Instant Chopped Onions

¼ cup sugar

1 teaspoon Mustard Seed

¼ teaspoon Thyme Leaves

1 large carrot, sliced

4-pound beef top round roast

2 teaspoons salt

¼ teaspoon Ground Black Pepper

¼ cup all-purpose flour

2 tablespoons vegetable oil

18 gingersnaps, crushed

¼ cup raisins

Potato Dumplings (page 254) to serve, if desired

1. Place vinegar, water, peppercorns, cloves, bay leaves, chopped onions, sugar, mustard seed, thyme, and carrot in large glass or stainless steel bowl. Stir to mix well.

2. Rub meat with salt and pepper and add to bowl. Turn meat to coat on all sides. Cover and refrigerate to marinate 3 days, turning meat occasionally.

3. When ready to cook, remove meat from marinade, reserving marinade. Pat meat dry with paper towels and dust with flour.

4. Heat oil in Dutch oven or large saucepan and brown meat on all sides over high heat. Add marinade, cover, reduce heat, and simmer 3 hours or until meat is tender.

5. Remove meat from pan, set aside, and keep warm.

6. Pour gravy through sieve into medium-size saucepan. Discard spices. Add crushed gingersnaps and raisins to pan and cook, stirring, until gravy thickens.

7. Slice meat and place on serving platter. Pour part of gravy over meat on platter and serve remaining gravy in small dish or gravy boat. Serve with Potato Dumplings.

*Makes 8 servings, 5 ounces meat and ⅓ cup gravy each*

# *Beef Stew*

*¼ cup vegetable oil*

*2 pounds beef for stew, cut into
1-inch cubes*

*1 Bay Leaf*

*1 tablespoon Season-All
Seasoned Salt*

*½ teaspoon Marjoram Leaves*

*½ teaspoon Parsley Flakes*

*¼ teaspoon Ground Black Pepper*

*⅛ teaspoon Tarragon Leaves*

*2 teaspoons Beef Flavor Base*

*2 cups plus 1 tablespoon water, divided*

*4 carrots, cut into 1-inch pieces*

*4 medium-size potatoes, peeled and
quartered*

*4 small onions*

*1 tablespoon all-purpose flour*

1. Heat oil in Dutch oven or large saucepan and brown cubes on all sides over high heat.

2. Add seasonings, flavor base, and 2 cups water. Stir well and heat to boil. Cover, reduce heat to very low, and simmer 1½ hours. (Be sure surface of liquid does not bubble.)

3. Add carrots, potatoes, and onions to stew. Cover and cook 30 minutes or until vegetables are fork tender. Add additional water as necessary.

4. Remove meat and vegetables with slotted spoon. Place in serving dish and keep warm. Remove and discard bay leaf.

5. Place flour in small dish. Add remaining 1 tablespoon water and stir until smooth. Stir into juices remaining in pan and cook over medium heat, stirring, just until thickened. Pour gravy over meat and vegetables.

*Makes 10 servings, 1 cup each*

# Hungarian Goulash

*3 tablespoons vegetable oil*

*¼ cup Instant Chopped Onions*

*3 pounds boneless beef shoulder, cut into 1½-inch cubes*

*1 tablespoon Paprika*

*2 teaspoons Season-All Seasoned Salt*

*½ teaspoon Coarse Ground Black Pepper*

*6 Anise Seeds*

*Dash Ground Red Pepper*

*2 medium-size tomatoes, peeled and cut into wedges*

*1 medium-size green bell pepper, cut into medium-size pieces*

*¼ cup tomato purée*

*1 cup water*

*3 slices bacon*

*Hot cooked noodles or spätzle to serve, if desired*

1. Heat oil in Dutch oven or large saucepan over medium heat. Add chopped onions and cook until browned. Remove onions and set aside.

2. Add beef to pan and brown on all sides. Drain off excess fat.

3. Place paprika, seasoned salt, black pepper, anise seed, and red pepper in small bowl and stir to combine. Sprinkle over meat. Add reserved onions, tomatoes, green bell pepper, tomato purée, and water to pan and stir.

4. Lay bacon strips over top of mixture. Cover and simmer over low heat 2 hours or until meat is tender. Add additional water as necessary. Serve over hot cooked noodles or spätzle.

*Makes 6 servings, 1 cup each*

**PAPRIKA**

# Texas Chili

5 pounds top round beef, cut into ½-inch cubes

3 cans (28 ounces each) whole tomatoes, undrained

2 cups chopped fresh onions

½ cup Texas Style Chili Powder or to taste

2 tablespoons Ground Cumin

2 teaspoons Crushed Red Pepper or to taste

1 teaspoon Season-All Seasoned Salt

½ teaspoon Ground Red Pepper or to taste

1 cup diced green bell peppers

1 cup diced red bell peppers

1. Brown meat in small batches in nonstick 6-quart pot over medium heat. Return all browned meat cubes to pot.

2. Add remaining ingredients except green and red bell peppers. Simmer 3 to 4 hours, uncovered, over very low heat, stirring occasionally.

3. Add green and red bell peppers. Stir to combine and simmer 15 minutes.

*Makes 12 servings, 1½ cups each*

TIP:

Texas Chili is hot! If you prefer a milder flavor, reduce amount of Chili Powder, Crushed Red Pepper, and/or Ground Red Pepper. On the other hand, Texans may want to make this chili even hotter!

# Bahamian Jerk Steak

12 rib eye steaks, cut 1 inch thick

1 cup Caribbean Jerk Paste (page 202)

1. Arrange steaks in single layer in shallow glass or stainless steel dishes and spread Caribbean Jerk Paste on both sides of steaks.

2. Cover and refrigerate at least 2 hours or overnight.

3. Preheat grill or broiler.

4. Grill or broil steaks 5 to 7 minutes each side or to desired doneness.

*Makes 12 servings, 1 steak each*

# Caribbean Shipwreck Marinade for Pork or Beef Roast

*5-pound pork loin roast or beef
    eye round roast*

MARINADE

*½ cup olive oil*

*½ cup orange juice*

*¼ cup malt vinegar*

*¼ cup lime juice*

*½ cup Caribbean Jerk Seasoning
    (page 202)*

1. Place meat in 13 x 9 x 2-inch glass dish.

2. Place marinade ingredients in small bowl or 4-cup glass measure and beat with fork until well combined. Pour over meat and turn meat to coat evenly.

3. Cover and refrigerate 3 hours or overnight.

4. Preheat oven to 350°F.

5. Place meat on rack in roasting pan. Insert meat thermometer into center of thickest part of meat.

6. Roast pork in preheated 350°F oven 2 hours to internal temperature of 170°F. Roast beef 1½ hours to internal temperature of 160°F (medium well-done), 170°F (well-done), or to desired doneness.

*Makes 16 servings, 4 ounces meat each*

**CUMIN**

# Caribbean Jerk Seasoning

¾ cup Onion Powder

6 tablespoons Thyme Leaves

3 tablespoons salt

1 tablespoon Freeze-Dried Chives

2 teaspoons Coarse Ground Black Pepper

1½ teaspoons Garlic Powder

1½ teaspoons Ground Red Pepper

1 teaspoon sugar

¾ teaspoon Ground Black Pepper

¼ teaspoon Ground Nutmeg

¼ teaspoon Ground Cinnamon

1. Place all ingredients in small electric spice mill or coffee grinder and grind 15 to 20 seconds. As an alternative, grind with mortar and pestle.

2. Store in airtight container.

*Makes 1 cup plus 2 tablespoons*

# Caribbean Jerk Paste

1 medium-size onion, quartered

4 scallions, trimmed

½ cup olive oil

½ cup Caribbean Jerk Seasoning (recipe above)

¼ cup cider vinegar

1 tablespoon soy sauce

1. Combine all ingredients in food processor. Process until smooth.

2. Store in covered container in refrigerator. Will keep 1 month.

3. Use Caribbean Jerk Paste to brush on steaks, chops, or hamburgers before broiling or grilling.

*Makes 1 cup paste*

# Sweet-Sour Pork

2 pounds boneless lean pork,
   cut into 1-inch cubes

1 cup water

6 Whole Cloves

SAUCE

¼ cup cornstarch

1½ cups pineapple juice

1 cup firmly packed brown sugar

¼ cup butter or margarine

¼ cup soy sauce

¼ cup cider vinegar

½ teaspoon Onion Powder

½ teaspoon Ground Ginger

*  *  *

2 tablespoons butter or margarine

1 medium-size green bell pepper, cubed

1 medium-size carrot, sliced

1 small onion, sliced

2 tablespoons cornstarch

2 tablespoons soy sauce

½ cup vegetable oil or shortening

Hot cooked rice to serve, if desired

1. Place meat in large saucepan with water and cloves. Heat to boil, reduce heat, cover, and simmer 25 minutes or until meat is tender. Drain and set aside to cool. Discard whole cloves.

2. While meat is cooking, prepare sauce. Place ¼ cup cornstarch in small bowl. Add small amount of pineapple juice and stir until smooth. Place remaining pineapple juice, cornstarch mixture, sugar, ¼ cup butter, ¼ cup soy sauce, vinegar, onion powder, and ginger in 3-quart saucepan and cook over low heat, stirring, until thickened. Set aside. (Steps 1 and 2 may be prepared 1 day ahead of time, covered, and refrigerated until ready to complete cooking.)

3. Melt 2 tablespoons butter in skillet. Sauté green bell pepper, carrot, and onion 2 to 3 minutes, stirring occasionally. Remove from skillet, set aside, and keep warm.

4. Mix 2 tablespoons cornstarch with 2 tablespoons soy sauce until smooth. Pour over cooled pork and toss to coat.

5. Heat oil in skillet over high heat and cook pork until crisp and browned.

6. Reheat sauce, if necessary. Combine meat, vegetables, and sauce. Serve over hot cooked rice.

*Makes 6 servings, ¾ cup each*

# Caribbean Grill

3 tablespoons soy sauce

2 tablespoons olive oil

1 tablespoon cider vinegar

1 tablespoon water

1 tablespoon Instant Minced Onion

2 teaspoons sugar

2 teaspoons Thyme Leaves

1 teaspoon Ground Allspice

1 teaspoon Hot Shot! Pepper Blend

½ teaspoon Ground Cinnamon

½ teaspoon Ground Nutmeg

3-pound boneless pork roast or bone-in turkey breast

Sautéed chunks of eggplant, zucchini, yellow squash, tomato wedges, onion rings, and scallions to serve

1. Place all ingredients except meat and vegetables in 2-cup glass measure and beat with fork until well combined. Pour into large self-closing plastic bag or glass or stainless steel dish.

2. Pierce pork roast with long-tined fork in 8 to 10 places and add to marinade, turning several times to coat meat well. Close bag, if using, or cover dish and refrigerate overnight, turning occasionally.

3. If using turkey, loosen skin from meat, leaving skin attached at breastbone. Pierce meat with fork and pull skin back over meat. Add to marinade and refrigerate as directed in Step 2.

4. Preheat covered grill for indirect-heat cooking by placing drip pan in center and arranging coals at outer edges of grill.

5. Remove meat from marinade and discard marinade. Place meat in center of preheated grill rack and close grill. Cook pork 20 to 22 minutes per pound or until meat thermometer inserted into center of meat registers 160°F. Cook turkey about 1½ hours or until meat thermometer registers 170°F.

6. Remove cooked meat to carving board and let stand 10 minutes. Slice and serve with sautéed vegetables.

*Makes 8 to 10 servings*

# Island Pork

12 thin slices onion, cut in half

12 thin slices orange, cut in half

24 slices boneless pork loin,
    cut 1 inch thick

1 cup orange juice

½ cup soy sauce

½ cup honey

2 Bay Leaves

2 teaspoons Season-All Seasoned
    Salt

1 teaspoon Ground Ginger

½ teaspoon Ground Black Pepper

1. Preheat oven to 325°F.

2. Place ½ onion slice and ½ orange slice on each slice of pork. Arrange, slightly overlapping, in 13 x 9 x 2-inch glass baking dish.

3. Place remaining ingredients in small saucepan and stir to combine. Heat to boil. Remove and discard bay leaves and pour sauce over meat, coating each slice.

4. Bake in preheated 325°F oven 1 hour, basting with pan liquid 3 times during cooking.

5. Remove meat slices with onion and orange slices to heated platter. Spoon some of pan liquid over meat. Serve with remaining sauce in small dish or gravy boat on the side.

*Makes 12 servings, 2 slices meat each*

# Polynesian Pork with Almonds

4 tablespoons sesame or vegetable oil

6 pounds boneless lean pork loin,
    cut into ½-inch cubes

24 scallions, trimmed and chopped

4 zucchini, each 6 inches long, diced

8 teaspoons Thai Seasoning

2 tablespoons cornstarch

2 tablespoons cold water

⅔ cup sake (rice wine) or
    dry sherry

½ cup soy sauce

¾ cup (2 ounces) toasted sliced
    almonds to serve

1. Heat oil over high heat in 2 large skillets or prepare half of recipe at a time. Use 2 tablespoons oil per skillet.

2. Add half of pork to each skillet and stir-fry 4 to 5 minutes.

3. Add half of scallions, zucchini, and Thai seasoning to each skillet and cook, stirring, 1 minute.

4. Place cornstarch in 2-cup glass measure. Add water and stir to smooth paste. Stir in sake and soy sauce and pour half of mixture over ingredients in each skillet. Stir and cook 2 to 3 minutes.

5. Spoon into serving dish and sprinkle with almonds.

*Makes 12 servings, 1 cup each*

TIP:

To toast almonds, spread in shallow baking pan and bake in preheated 350°F oven 10 to 12 minutes or until lightly browned.

# *Pork Mandarin*

| | |
|---|---|
| *2 teaspoons Bon Appétit* | *¼ teaspoon Ground Thyme* |
| *1 teaspoon Orange Peel* | *¼ teaspoon Ground Black Pepper* |
| *½ teaspoon Ground Mustard* | *5-pound boneless pork loin roast* |
| *½ teaspoon Ground Ginger* | *½ cup honey* |
| *½ teaspoon Onion Salt* | *½ cup orange juice* |

1. Preheat oven to 350°F.

2. Place Bon Appétit, orange peel, mustard, ginger, onion salt, thyme, and pepper in small bowl and stir to combine. Rub all of seasoning on surface of meat.

3. Place meat on rack in roasting pan. Roast in preheated 350°F oven 1 hour.

4. Mix honey with orange juice and baste roast with half of honey-orange juice mixture. Roast 1 hour.

5. Baste with remaining half of honey-orange juice mixture and roast 15 minutes or to internal temperature of 160°F. Cut in very thin slices and spoon pan juices over meat.

*Makes 12 servings, 6 ounces each*

# Golden Clove-Glazed Ham

8-pound ready-to-eat ham

½ cup firmly packed brown sugar

1 tablespoon honey

⅛ teaspoon Ground Cloves

Whole Cloves

1. Preheat oven to 325°F.

2. Place ham, fat side up, on rack in roasting pan. Bake in preheated 325°F oven 1½ hours.

3. Remove ham from oven and remove skin carefully, leaving covering of fat about ¼ inch thick. Score fat in diamond pattern.

4. Place sugar, honey, and ground cloves in small bowl and mix well. Spread over ham. Insert whole clove in center of each diamond shape.

5. Increase oven temperature to 375°F and bake ham 30 minutes or until well glazed.

*Makes 18 servings, 6 ounces each*

# Lone Star Barbecued Ribs

1 cup strong black coffee

1 cup Worcestershire sauce

1 cup ketchup

½ cup vinegar

½ cup firmly packed light brown sugar

½ cup Instant Minced Onion

¼ cup butter or margarine

2 tablespoons Chili Powder

2 teaspoons Season-All Seasoned Salt

2 teaspoons Instant Minced Garlic

1 teaspoon Ground Mustard

½ teaspoon Ground Red Pepper

10 pounds spareribs
 (4 racks if large, meaty ribs)

1. Combine all ingredients except ribs in 2-quart saucepan. Stir to mix well. Heat and simmer 30 minutes, stirring occasionally.

2. Half-fill large stockpot with water and heat to boil. Add ribs, cover, and boil 10 minutes. Drain thoroughly.

3. Preheat oven to 350°F.

4. Arrange ribs in single layer on racks in roasting pans. Brush both sides of ribs with sauce.

5. Cook in preheated 350°F oven 1½ hours, turning and brushing with sauce every 15 to 20 minutes.

6. As an alternative, ribs may be cooked on grill over low fire. Place ribs on grill rack and brush with sauce. Cook, turning occasionally and brushing frequently with sauce, until meat is thoroughly cooked. Time will depend on heat and distance of meat from coals.

*Makes 12 servings, 4 to 6 ribs each*

# Veal Marsala

*4 tablespoons butter or margarine, divided*

*2 cups sliced mushrooms*

*2 slices bacon, chopped*

*¼ cup all-purpose flour*

*½ teaspoon Garlic Powder*

*½ teaspoon Season-All Seasoned Salt*

*¼ teaspoon Ground Black Pepper*

*1½ pounds veal cutlets, 12 pieces cut ¼ inch thick*

*1 teaspoon cornstarch*

*¼ cup cold water*

*½ cup dry Marsala wine*

*½ teaspoon Marjoram Leaves*

*¼ teaspoon Onion Powder*

*¼ teaspoon Basil Leaves*

*¼ teaspoon Bon Appétit*

1. Melt 1 tablespoon butter in 10-inch skillet. Add mushrooms and sauté. Remove mushrooms from skillet and set aside.

2. Add chopped bacon to skillet and cook over low heat until cooked but not crisp. Add 2 tablespoons butter to skillet.

3. Place flour, garlic powder, seasoned salt, and pepper on plate and stir to combine.

4. Dust veal with flour mixture. Add veal to skillet and sauté, a few pieces at a time, 2 minutes on each side over medium heat. Add remaining 1 tablespoon butter to skillet as needed.

5. Place veal on serving platter and keep warm.

6. Place cornstarch in 1-cup glass measure. Add water and stir until smooth. Stir in remaining ingredients and pour into skillet.

7. Add reserved mushrooms and cook, stirring, over low heat just until mixture begins to boil. Pour over veal. Serve immediately.

*Makes 6 servings, 2 veal cutlets each*

# Veal Parmigiana

SAUCE

1 can (6 ounces) tomato paste

¾ cup (1 tomato paste can) water

1 tablespoon brown sugar

1 teaspoon Worcestershire sauce

1 teaspoon Season-All Seasoned Salt

½ teaspoon Italian Seasoning

¼ teaspoon Oregano Leaves

⅛ teaspoon Garlic Powder

\* \* \*

2 eggs

1 teaspoon Season-All Seasoned Salt

¼ teaspoon Ground Black Pepper

1 cup dry bread crumbs

2 pounds veal cutlets, 16 pieces cut ½ inch thick

½ cup olive oil

¼ cup grated Parmesan cheese

½ pound mozzarella cheese, sliced

1. Place sauce ingredients in small saucepan and stir to mix. Cook over medium heat, stirring, until slightly thickened. Set aside.

2. Preheat oven to 350°F.

3. Place eggs in shallow dish, add seasoned salt and pepper, and beat lightly.

4. Place bread crumbs in separate shallow dish or on large piece of wax paper.

5. Dip cutlets into egg mixture and allow excess egg to drip off. Coat on all sides in bread crumbs.

6. Heat oil in large skillet over medium heat and brown cutlets, a few at a time, on both sides.

7. Place cutlets in 13 x 8 x 2-inch baking pan and pour reserved sauce over. Sprinkle with Parmesan cheese.

8. Cover and bake in preheated 350°F oven 30 minutes or until meat is tender.

9. Uncover meat and place slices of mozzarella cheese over cutlets. Bake, uncovered, just until cheese melts, about 5 minutes.

*Makes 8 servings, 2 cutlets each*

# Osso Buco
# (Braised Veal Shanks)

¼ cup butter or margarine

½ cup finely chopped carrot

½ cup finely chopped celery

⅓ cup Instant Minced Onion

½ teaspoon Instant Minced Garlic

⅓ cup all-purpose flour

1 teaspoon Season-All Seasoned Salt

¼ teaspoon Ground Black Pepper

10 veal shanks, cut 2 inches thick
 (about 6 pounds)

½ cup olive oil

1 cup dry vermouth

¾ cup hot water

1 teaspoon Beef Flavor Base

2 cans (28 ounces each) whole
 tomatoes, drained and cut
 in half

1 cup tomato juice

2 Bay Leaves

2 teaspoons Parsley Flakes

½ teaspoon Basil Leaves

½ teaspoon Thyme Leaves

1½ teaspoons cornstarch

2 tablespoons water

1. Melt butter in ovenproof Dutch oven over medium heat. Add carrot, celery, minced onion, and minced garlic. Cook 10 minutes, stirring occasionally. Remove from heat and set aside.

2. Place flour, seasoned salt, and pepper in shallow dish and stir to combine. Roll veal shanks in seasoned flour.

3. Heat oil in large skillet over medium heat. Add meat, a few pieces at a time, and brown on all sides. Remove from skillet and add to vegetables in Dutch oven.

4. Preheat oven to 350°F.

5. Discard oil in skillet, add vermouth, and simmer 5 minutes.

6. Place hot water in 1-cup glass measure, add flavor base, and stir well. Add to skillet. Stir in tomatoes, tomato juice, bay leaves, parsley, basil, and thyme.

7. Place cornstarch in small dish, add water, and stir until smooth. Add to skillet, stirring, and heat to boil. Pour sauce over veal and vegetables.

8. Cover and bake in preheated 350°F oven 1 hour and 15 minutes, basting occasionally. Remove and discard bay leaves before serving.

*Makes 10 braised veal shanks*

# Lamb Chops with Horseradish-Pecan Sauce

HORSERADISH-PECAN SAUCE

1 tablespoon olive oil

1 tablespoon all-purpose flour

1 teaspoon Bon Appétit

⅛ teaspoon Instant Minced Garlic

⅛ teaspoon Ground White Pepper

1 cup half and half

1 tablespoon prepared horseradish

¼ cup chopped pecans

\* \* \*

6 slices bacon

6 boneless lamb loin double chops,
   cut 1½ inches thick

1 tablespoon olive oil

1 tablespoon soy sauce

1 tablespoon lemon juice

⅛ teaspoon Garlic Powder

⅛ teaspoon Onion Powder

Fresh mint leaves to garnish

1. To make sauce, place oil and flour in small saucepan and stir to combine. Add Bon Appétit, minced garlic, and white pepper. Heat just until bubbly.

2. Add half and half gradually, stirring constantly. Stir in horseradish and pecans and cook over medium heat, stirring constantly, until sauce thickens slightly. (Do not overcook; sauce should be pourable.) Set aside and keep warm until ready to serve.

3. Cook bacon in skillet over low heat until cooked but not crisp. Flatten bacon on paper towel and let cool slightly.

4. Form chops into rounds and wrap each chop with 1 bacon slice. Secure bacon with wooden toothpicks.

5. Preheat broiler.

6. Place remaining ingredients in 1-cup glass measure and stir to combine. Brush chops on all sides with mixture. Set remaining mixture aside for basting.

7. Place chops on broiler pan and broil, 4 inches from source of heat, 10 minutes, turning once and brushing with seasoning mixture occasionally during cooking.

8. Serve immediately with hot Horseradish-Pecan Sauce and garnish with mint leaves.

*Makes 6 lamb chops and 1 cup sauce*

# East Indian Lamb Curry

¼ cup all-purpose flour

2 pounds boneless lean lamb for stew, cubed

3 tablespoons vegetable oil

1½ cups water

1 tart apple, peeled, cored, and diced

¼ cup Instant Chopped Onions

4 tablespoons Indian or Madras Curry Powder

2 tablespoons lemon juice

2 tablespoons flaked coconut

2 tablespoons raisins or currants

2 teaspoons salt

1 teaspoon sugar

¼ teaspoon Ground Mustard

Dash Ground Nutmeg

Hot cooked rice and assortment of condiments (see below) to serve

1. Place flour in plastic bag. Add meat and shake to coat.

2. Heat oil in 10-inch skillet over medium heat. Add meat and brown on all sides. Add remaining ingredients except rice and condiments and mix well.

3. Cover and simmer 1 hour or until meat is tender.

4. Serve with hot cooked rice and assortment of condiments such as chutney, toasted flaked coconut, pickle relish, chopped peanuts, spiced crab apples, chopped scallions, and/or chopped hard-cooked eggs. (To hard-cook eggs, see page 48)

*Makes 6 servings, ¾ cup each*

# Crown Roast of Lamb

1 teaspoon Bon Appétit

1 teaspoon salt

½ teaspoon Ground Marjoram

½ teaspoon Orange Peel

¼ teaspoon Ground Mustard

¼ teaspoon Ground Black Pepper

⅛ teaspoon Ground Cardamom

14-rib crown roast of lamb (about 3 pounds)

Basic Bread Stuffing (page 227) if desired

1. Preheat oven to 325°F.

2. Combine seasonings and rub over roast. Place meat on rack in shallow roasting pan.

3. Fill center with Basic Bread Stuffing. Extra stuffing can be placed in lightly greased baking pan, covered, and baked in oven during last 45 minutes meat is cooking.

4. Roast in preheated 325°F oven 2 hours or until meat thermometer registers 165°F to 170°F when tip is inserted into center of stuffing.

*Makes 6 servings, 2 to 3 rib chops each*

TIP:

Crown roast may be cooked without stuffing. Just before serving, fill center with cooked vegetables of your choice.

VARIATIONS:

Herbed Crown Roast: Eliminate Ground Marjoram and substitute ½ teaspoon Ground Thyme or Rosemary Leaves. Eliminate Bon Appétit and substitute 1 teaspoon Season-All Seasoned Salt.

Gingered Crown Roast: Add 1 teaspoon Ground Ginger to seasonings in recipe.

# Herb Roasted Rack of Lamb

*2 rib racks of lamb, 7 to 8 ribs each,
    fully trimmed*
*½ cup butter or margarine*
*1 teaspoon Ground Mustard*
*1 teaspoon Bon Appétit*
*½ teaspoon Ground Ginger*

*½ teaspoon Marjoram Leaves*
*½ teaspoon Basil Leaves*
*¼ teaspoon Garlic Powder*
*Fresh mint leaves to garnish*

1. Preheat oven to 350°F.

2. Arrange racks of lamb, ribs up and bones criss-crossed. Tie in place with kitchen string and place on rack in roasting pan.

3. Melt butter in small saucepan and add remaining ingredients. Stir to combine. Brush all surfaces of lamb with butter mixture.

4. Roast in preheated 350°F oven 40 to 50 minutes, brushing with seasoned butter every 10 minutes.

5. Place on serving platter and garnish with mint leaves.

*Makes 7 to 8 servings, 2 ribs each*

*Herb Roasted Rack of Lamb (see photo on page 216)*

# POULTRY

# *Game Hens Cardamom*

MARINADE

1 cup plain yogurt

1 teaspoon salt

1 teaspoon Fennel Seed

½ teaspoon Ground Ginger

½ teaspoon Ground Red Pepper

¼ teaspoon Garlic Powder

4 Cardamom Seeds

\* \* \*

6 Rock Cornish game hens,
   1½ pounds each

\* \* \*

¾ cup water

½ cup Instant Chopped Onions

¼ cup butter or margarine

2 Whole Cloves

1 Cinnamon Stick, 3 inches long,
   broken in half

1 teaspoon Chicken Flavor Base

1. Place all marinade ingredients in blender and blend 1½ minutes at highest speed. Set aside.

2. Rinse hens and pat dry. Place in large roasting pan, allowing 1 inch between hens. Use 2 pans if necessary.

3. Pour reserved marinade over hens, cover, and refrigerate to marinate 2 hours or overnight.

4. Preheat oven to 350°F.

5. Place remaining ingredients in 1-quart saucepan. Heat to boil, reduce heat, and simmer 5 minutes. Pour over hens and use pastry brush to baste hens with liquids in pan.

6. Bake in preheated 350°F oven 2 hours or until drumsticks twist easily and hens are browned. Baste with pan juices 3 or 4 times during baking.

7. Remove and discard cinnamon stick and cloves.

8. Cut hens in half and spoon pan juices over hens before serving.

*Makes 12 servings, ½ game hen each*

*Herb Roasted Rack of Lamb (see recipe on page 215)*

# Apricot Duckling

*2 Long Island ducklings, 4 pounds each*

*2 tablespoons Poultry Seasoning*

*2 stalks celery with leaves*

*1 onion, cut in half*

*¾ cup honey, divided*

*½ cup Grand Marnier, divided*

*¼ cup butter or margarine*

*1 can (12 ounces) apricot nectar*

*1 Bay Leaf*

*1 tablespoon grated fresh lemon peel*

*½ teaspoon Chicken Flavor Base*

*½ teaspoon Season-All Seasoned Salt*

*¼ teaspoon salt*

*⅛ teaspoon Ground Nutmeg*

*⅛ teaspoon Ground Cinnamon*

*⅛ teaspoon Rubbed Sage*

*⅛ teaspoon Ground White Pepper*

*1 tablespoon cornstarch*

*1 tablespoon cold water*

*1 can (17 ounces) apricot halves, drained*

1. Preheat oven to 325°F.

2. Wash ducklings and pat dry. Rub 1 tablespoon poultry seasoning inside each duckling and place 1 stalk celery and ½ onion inside each. Tie legs together with kitchen string.

3. Prick skin of ducklings with fork every ½ inch all over both ducklings and place on rack in roasting pan.

4. Roast in preheated 325°F oven 2½ hours.

5. Place ½ cup honey and ¼ cup Grand Marnier in 1-cup glass measure and mix well. Remove pan from oven and carefully drain off fat. Increase oven temperature to 400°F. Return pan to oven and roast ducklings 30 minutes, brushing every 10 minutes with honey mixture.

6. Melt butter in medium-size saucepan while ducklings are cooking. Stir in apricot nectar, bay leaf, lemon peel, flavor base, seasoned salt, salt, nutmeg, cinnamon, sage, white pepper, and remaining ¼ cup honey. Heat to boil, reduce heat, and simmer 5 minutes. Keep warm over very low heat until ducklings are cooked.

7. Remove and discard bay leaf.

8. Place cornstarch in small dish and stir in water until smooth. Stir into sauce and cook, stirring constantly, until mixture thickens. Stir in remaining ¼ cup Grand Marnier and add apricot halves.

9. Cut ducklings into quarters with poultry shears or heavy kitchen scissors and serve with sauce.

*Makes 8 servings, ¼ duckling with sauce each*

# Thai Lemon Chicken

*3 tablespoons olive oil*

*3 pounds boneless, skinless chicken breasts, cut into thin strips*

*¾ cup chopped fresh onion*

*3 cups chicken broth*

*⅓ cup firmly packed light brown sugar*

*⅓ cup lemon juice*

*3 tablespoons honey*

*3 tablespoons dry sherry*

*2 tablespoons soy sauce*

*1 tablespoon Thai Seasoning*

*¾ teaspoon Instant Minced Garlic*

*2 red bell peppers, cut into thin strips*

*3 tablespoons cornstarch*

*3 tablespoons cold water*

*1 tablespoon Freeze-Dried Chives*

*Hot cooked rice to serve, if desired*

1. Heat oil in large skillet over high heat. Add chicken strips and onion and stir-fry 5 minutes.

2. Place chicken broth, sugar, lemon juice, honey, sherry, soy sauce, Thai seasoning, and minced garlic in bowl or 4-cup glass measure and stir to combine. Pour over chicken in skillet and stir.

3. Add red bell pepper strips to skillet and simmer 5 minutes.

4. Place cornstarch in small dish, add water, and stir until smooth. Add to chicken mixture and stir. Cook until liquid in skillet is clear and has thickened.

5. Sprinkle with chives and serve over hot cooked rice.

*Makes 12 servings, ⅔ cup each*

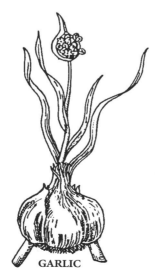

**GARLIC**

# Singapore Curry

½ cup vegetable oil

3 pounds boneless, skinless chicken breasts, cut into bite-size pieces

1½ cups chopped fresh onions

3 tablespoons Madras or Indian Curry Powder

1 can (16 ounces) pineapple chunks in juice, drained and juice reserved

2 cups milk

2 tablespoons tomato paste

1 teaspoon Bon Appétit

1 can (15 ounces) apricot halves, drained and chopped

1 cup cream of coconut

1 ripe banana, sliced

½ cup raisins

¼ cup sliced almonds, toasted

Hot cooked rice to serve, if desired

1. Heat oil in large skillet over medium heat. Add chicken pieces and onions. Cook, stirring occasionally, until lightly browned.

2. Sprinkle with curry powder and stir. Add reserved pineapple juice, milk, tomato paste, and Bon Appétit. Mix well and simmer, uncovered, 20 minutes.

3. Add pineapple chunks, apricots, cream of coconut, banana, and raisins. Stir gently and cook until heated through.

4. Sprinkle with toasted almonds and serve over hot cooked rice.

*Makes 12 servings, ¾ cup each*

# Chicken Tikka

1 cup plain yogurt

¼ cup tomato purée

4 tablespoons Madras Curry Powder

1 tablespoon Paprika

1 tablespoon lemon juice

¼ teaspoon salt

12 boneless, skinless chicken breast halves

12 lemon wedges

1. Combine yogurt, tomato purée, curry powder, paprika, lemon juice, and salt in small bowl and mix well.

2. Cut each chicken breast half crosswise into 4 equal-size strips and place in large glass bowl.

3. Pour yogurt mixture over chicken. Stir to coat chicken, cover, and refrigerate 1 to 2 hours.

4. Preheat grill.

5. Thread chicken onto skewers and grill 8 to 10 minutes, turning frequently, until chicken is tender and slightly charred on outside.

6. Squeeze lemon wedges over chicken just before serving.

*Makes 12 servings, 4 to 6 ounces each*

# Chicken Provençal

*9 pounds chicken parts, 24 pieces*

*1 cup all-purpose flour*

*2½ teaspoons Garlic Salt, divided*

*2 teaspoons Lemon & Pepper Seasoning*

*¼ to ½ cup olive oil*

*1 large onion, cut into eighths*

*1 cup halved, pitted ripe olives*

*1 tablespoon Parsley Flakes*

*1 teaspoon Thyme Leaves*

*½ teaspoon Mediterranean Oregano Leaves*

*½ teaspoon Rosemary Leaves, crushed*

*1 can (28 ounces) Italian-style tomatoes*

1. Rinse chicken and pat dry with paper towels.

2. Combine flour, 2 teaspoons garlic salt, and Lemon & Pepper seasoning in plastic bag.

3. Add chicken, a few pieces at a time, and shake to coat evenly.

4. Heat ¼ cup oil in large skillet. Brown chicken in hot oil, a few pieces at a time, cooking until chicken is well browned and skin is very crisp on all sides. Add additional oil as necessary. Place chicken in 15 x 11 x 2-inch roasting pan. Add onion and olives to chicken.

5. Preheat oven to 350°F.

6. Combine remaining ½ teaspoon garlic salt, parsley, thyme, oregano, and rosemary. Sprinkle evenly over chicken and pour tomatoes with liquid over all.

7. Cover with aluminum foil and bake in preheated 350°F oven 1 hour. Remove foil and bake 30 minutes.

*Makes 12 servings, 2 pieces chicken each*

# Coq au Vin

4 pounds chicken parts, 10 to 11 pieces

¼ cup all-purpose flour

2 teaspoons Season-All Seasoned Salt

½ teaspoon Paprika

¼ teaspoon Ground Black Pepper

⅛ teaspoon Ground Nutmeg

½ cup butter or margarine

¼ cup Cognac

12 small white onions

1 can (8 ounces) whole mushrooms, drained

1 cup dry red wine

1 teaspoon Parsley Flakes

½ teaspoon Rosemary Leaves

¼ teaspoon Thyme Leaves

⅛ teaspoon Garlic Powder

1. Rinse chicken and pat dry.

2. Place flour, seasoned salt, paprika, pepper, and nutmeg in plastic bag. Add chicken and shake to coat evenly.

3. Melt butter in Dutch oven. Add chicken and brown slowly.

4. Pour Cognac over chicken. Carefully light Cognac with match and allow flame to burn out.

5. Add remaining ingredients and stir. Cover and simmer 1 hour or until chicken is tender.

*Makes 10 to 11 chicken pieces with sauce*

# Chicken Paprika

3 pounds chicken parts, 6 to 8 pieces

½ cup plus 2 tablespoons all-purpose flour, divided

1 teaspoon Season-All Seasoned Salt

½ teaspoon Ground Thyme

¼ teaspoon Coarse Ground Black Pepper

¼ cup vegetable oil

2 tablespoons Paprika

½ teaspoon Garlic Salt

2 cups hot water

2 medium-size onions, sliced and separated into rings

½ cup milk

1. Rinse chicken and pat dry.

2. Place ½ cup flour, seasoned salt, thyme, and pepper in small bowl and stir to combine. Coat chicken on all sides with mixture.

3. Heat oil in large skillet or Dutch oven over high heat. Add chicken and fry, turning until crisp and browned on all sides. Drain off excess fat, if desired.

4. Combine paprika and garlic salt and sprinkle over chicken. Add hot water and simmer 30 minutes. (Do not boil.)

5. Place onion rings on top of chicken. Cover and simmer 30 minutes.

6. Remove chicken to warm serving platter and spoon onions on top.

7. Place remaining 2 tablespoons flour and milk in small bowl and stir until smooth. Stir into liquid remaining in pan. Cook just until thickened and pour over chicken.

*Makes 6 to 8 chicken pieces with sauce*

# Country Captain

*3 pounds chicken parts, 6 to 8 pieces*

*¼ cup all-purpose flour*

*1 teaspoon Bon Appétit*

*½ teaspoon Ground Black Pepper, divided*

*¼ cup butter or margarine*

*1 can (28 ounces) whole Italian plum tomatoes, undrained*

*2 tablespoons Instant Chopped Onions*

*2 teaspoons Madras Curry Powder*

*1 teaspoon Thyme Leaves*

*½ teaspoon Garlic Salt*

*¼ cup dried currants*

*¼ cup slivered almonds*

*Hot cooked rice to serve, if desired*

1. Preheat oven to 375°F.

2. Rinse chicken and pat dry.

3. Place flour, Bon Appétit, and ¼ teaspoon pepper in plastic bag. Add chicken and shake to coat evenly.

4. Melt butter in large skillet and brown chicken on all sides. Place chicken in 4-quart Dutch oven.

5. Place tomatoes, chopped onions, curry powder, thyme, garlic salt, and remaining ¼ teaspoon pepper in bowl and stir to combine. Pour over chicken.

6. Cover and bake in preheated 375°F oven 40 minutes.

7. Remove cover and sprinkle currants and almonds over chicken. Bake, uncovered, 15 minutes. Serve over hot cooked rice.

*Makes 6 to 8 chicken pieces with sauce*

# Stuffed Turkey Breasts

*2 boneless half turkey breasts*  
*Fruit Stuffing (recipe below)*

*Cooked carrots to serve*  
*Sprigs of parsley to garnish*

1. Preheat oven to 325°F. Lightly grease roasting pan.
2. Cut 3 parallel 1-inch-deep slits lengthwise in each half turkey breast and place, slit sides up, in prepared pan.
3. Spoon Fruit Stuffing into slits.
4. Cook in preheated 325°F oven 2 hours.
5. When ready to serve, slice each half turkey breast crosswise into 6 slices.
6. Arrange on serving platter with carrots and garnish with sprigs of parsley.

*Makes 6 servings, 2 slices each*

# Fruit Stuffing

*1 package (10 ounces) pitted dates*  
*1 package (6 ounces) dried apricot halves*  
*1 cup walnut pieces*  
*2 cups water*

*½ teaspoon Ground Cinnamon*  
*¼ teaspoon Ground Black Pepper*  
*¼ teaspoon Ground Ginger*  
*¼ teaspoon Ground Nutmeg*  
*¼ teaspoon Ground Cloves*

1. Cut dates in thirds and cut apricot halves in quarters with sharp knife or kitchen shears.
2. Place all ingredients in saucepan and stir to combine.
3. Heat to simmering and cook 2 minutes, stirring constantly. Set aside to cool slightly.

*Makes 4 cups*

TIP:

May also be used to stuff pork chops, veal chops, or boneless chicken breasts.

# Dijon Crusted Turkey

1 turkey, about 16 pounds

Basic Bread Stuffing (page 227), if desired

½ cup butter or margarine, melted

⅓ cup orange juice

¼ cup Dijon-style mustard

1 teaspoon Garlic Powder

½ teaspoon Rosemary Leaves

1. Preheat oven to 325°F.

2. Remove giblets from turkey and rinse turkey under cold running water. Pat dry and fill cavities of turkey with stuffing. (Do not, under any circumstances, place stuffing inside cavity of turkey ahead of time. Stuff turkey just before cooking and remove any leftover stuffing from cavity of cooked turkey before storing in refrigerator.) Truss* turkey to hold stuffing in place.

3. Place melted butter in 2-cup glass measure. Stir in orange juice, mustard, garlic powder, and rosemary. Place turkey, breast side up, on rack in roasting pan. Brush over surface of turkey.

4. Roast, uncovered, in preheated 325°F oven about 12 minutes per pound or until meat thermometer registers 180°F when tip is inserted into inner thigh, not touching bone. Center of stuffing must reach 165°F to be safe to eat and may require an additional 20 to 30 minutes roasting time. Baste frequently during roasting and cover loosely with aluminum foil if turkey browns too quickly.

5. Remove to carving board and let stand about 10 minutes before carving.

*Makes about 26 servings, 4 to 5 ounces turkey each*

TIP:

Cook turkey giblets in lightly salted boiling water until fork tender. Finely chop and add to stuffing or gravy, if desired. Stuffing also can be baked in casserole instead of inside turkey. Cover and bake in oven during last 45 minutes of roasting.

*To truss turkey, stuff neck cavity lightly, pull skin over stuffing, and attach skin to backbone with skewer. Tuck wing tips under shoulder joints and turn turkey over, breast side up. Put stuffing in body cavity, but don't pack tightly because stuffing expands during cooking. Close opening with skewers and tie legs together with kitchen string, if desired. If you prefer, you can close opening by sewing with trussing needle and kitchen string.

# Basic Bread Stuffing

1 cup butter or margarine

½ cup chopped fresh onion

1½ cups chopped celery

12 cups bread cubes, white and whole-wheat bread

2 tablespoons Parsley Flakes

1 tablespoon Bon Appétit

1½ teaspoons Poultry Seasoning

½ teaspoon Ground Black Pepper

1 teaspoon Chicken Flavor Base

½ cup hot water

1. Melt butter in large skillet or Dutch oven, add onion and celery, and sauté until onion is transparent.

2. Place bread cubes, parsley, Bon Appétit, poultry seasoning, and pepper in large bowl and toss to combine. Add to onion mixture and toss to brown bread cubes lightly.

3. Place flavor base in 1-cup glass measure, add water, and stir to dissolve. Sprinkle over bread mixture, stirring lightly.

4. Stuff loosely into neck and breast cavities of bird and truss bird *(page 226)*. As an alternative, place stuffing in casserole, cover, and bake with turkey or chicken during last 45 minutes of cooking.

*Makes 8 cups*

VARIATIONS:

Herb Stuffing: Add 1 of following to bread cubes: 2 teaspoons Rubbed Sage, 2 teaspoons Ground Thyme, or 2 teaspoons Ground Marjoram.

Chestnut Stuffing: Wash ½ pound chestnuts and cut slits on both sides of shells. Bake in 500°F oven 15 minutes. Cool. Remove shells and skin from nuts and place nuts in salted water. Cover and boil 20 minutes. Drain and finely chop. If preferred, use canned chestnuts, drained and chopped. Toss with bread cubes.

Oyster Stuffing: Cook ½ to 1 pint small or medium-size oysters in oyster liquor until the edges of oysters curl. Drain and chop or leave whole as preferred. Toss with bread cubes.

## FISH / SEAFOOD

# Broiled Salmon Tarragon

*½ cup melted butter or margarine*

*2 teaspoons lemon juice*

*1 teaspoon Season-All Seasoned Salt*

*1 teaspoon Tarragon Leaves*

*½ teaspoon Ground Marjoram*

*½ teaspoon Lemon Peel*

*¼ teaspoon Garlic Powder*

*Dash Ground Red Pepper*

*4 salmon steaks, cut 1 inch thick (about 2 pounds)*

1. Place melted butter, lemon juice, seasoned salt, tarragon, marjoram, lemon peel, garlic powder, and red pepper in small bowl and stir to combine.
2. Preheat broiler.
3. Place salmon steaks on lightly greased pan and brush with half of seasoned butter.
4. Broil, 5 inches from source of heat, 5 to 10 minutes.
5. Turn steaks carefully and brush with remaining butter mixture. Broil 5 to 7 minutes.

*Makes 4 servings, 1 salmon steak each*

VARIATION:

**Broiled Salmon with Dill:** In place of butter mixture above, combine ½ cup melted butter or margarine, 2 teaspoons lemon juice, 1 teaspoon Bon Appétit, 1 teaspoon Dill Weed, ½ teaspoon Lemon Peel, ¼ teaspoon Onion Powder, and ⅛ teaspoon White Pepper. Cook following directions above.

# Baked Fish with Herb Stuffing

*½ cup butter or margarine, divided*

*½ cup diced celery*

*2 tablespoons Instant Minced Onion*

*1½ teaspoons Bon Appétit, divided*

*1 teaspoon Parsley Flakes*

*½ teaspoon Tarragon Leaves*

*½ teaspoon Dill Weed*

*¼ teaspoon Marjoram Leaves*

*¼ teaspoon Lemon Peel*

*¼ teaspoon Ground Savory*

*3 cups soft bread crumbs, packed (crusts trimmed, if desired)*

*1 egg, beaten*

*4 to 5-pound whole fish (cod, red snapper, haddock, striped bass, halibut, or whitefish), cleaned and rinsed*

*1 tablespoon lemon juice*

*½ teaspoon Ground Mustard*

*½ teaspoon Fennel Seed, crushed*

1. Melt ¼ cup butter in small skillet. Add celery and minced onion and sauté. Stir in 1 teaspoon Bon Appétit, parsley, tarragon, dill, marjoram, lemon peel, and savory. Remove from heat and set aside.

2. Place bread crumbs in large bowl. Add egg and stir to combine. Add reserved onion-spice mixture and mix lightly.

3. Loosely fill cavity of fish with stuffing. Close cavity with toothpicks or thin skewers and draw edges of fish together over stuffing by lacing with kitchen string.

4. Preheat oven to 400°F.

5. Place fish on large piece of lightly oiled aluminum foil and place foil and fish in shallow baking pan large enough for fish to lie flat.

6. Melt remaining ¼ cup butter and add lemon juice, mustard, fennel seed, and remaining ½ teaspoon Bon Appétit. Stir to combine and brush part of butter mixture over fish.

7. Bake in preheated 400°F oven 30 to 35 minutes, basting occasionally with remaining seasoned butter.

*Makes 6 servings, about 4 ounces each*

# Sole Epicurean

2 pounds fillet of sole

1 teaspoon Season-All Seasoned Salt

1/4 teaspoon Ground White Pepper

1/8 teaspoon Paprika

1/2 cup butter or margarine

1 tablespoon lemon juice

8 Coriander Seeds, crushed

1/2 teaspoon Tarragon Leaves

1. Preheat broiler.
2. Place fish fillets, skin side down, on lightly greased broiler pan.
3. Mix seasoned salt, white pepper, and paprika. Sprinkle over fish.
4. Melt butter in small saucepan and heat until lightly browned. Add lemon juice slowly and stir in coriander seeds and tarragon. Brush half of mixture on fillets.
5. Broil, 4 to 6 inches from source of heat, 7 to 10 minutes or until fish flakes easily with fork.
6. Serve immediately with remaining butter mixture on the side.

*Makes 5 servings, 4 ounces each*

# Seafood Salad

1 cup dry white wine

1 cup water

1 pound sea scallops

1 pound shrimp, peeled and deveined

1 pound crab meat, picked over*

1 cucumber, peeled, seeded, and
   chopped

1/4 cup mayonnaise

1/4 cup dairy sour cream

1 teaspoon Parsley Flakes

1/2 teaspoon lemon juice

1/2 teaspoon Bon Appétit

1/2 teaspoon Freeze-Dried Chives

1/8 teaspoon Ground Black Pepper

1/8 teaspoon Tarragon Leaves

4 avocados

1. Combine wine and water in 4-quart saucepan. Heat to boil and reduce heat to low.
2. Add scallops and shrimp. Stir gently and simmer just until cooked through, about 4 minutes. Drain and cool slightly.
3. Place scallops, shrimp, crab meat, and cucumber in large bowl and toss gently.

4. Place remaining ingredients except avocados in small bowl and mix well. Spoon over seafood and toss lightly. Cover and refrigerate to chill.

5. When ready to serve, cut avocados in half lengthwise and remove pits. Spoon seafood salad into each avocado half.

*Makes 8 servings, ½ filled avocado each*

*(See page 47)

# Coquilles Saint Jacques

6 tablespoons butter or margarine, divided

3 tablespoons all-purpose flour

½ teaspoon Lemon Peel

½ teaspoon Bon Appétit

½ teaspoon prepared horseradish

¼ teaspoon Ground Mustard

2 cups light cream or milk

½ cup sliced mushrooms

2 teaspoons Instant Minced Onion

½ pound scallops, cut into bite-size pieces

½ pound cooked, peeled, and deveined shrimp, cut into small pieces

¼ pound crab meat, picked over*

2 tablespoons dry sherry

½ cup dry bread crumbs

1. Melt 4 tablespoons butter in medium-size saucepan. Stir in flour, lemon peel, Bon Appétit, horseradish, and mustard. Heat just until bubbly. Cook, stirring, 1 minute.

2. Add cream gradually, stirring until smooth. Cook, stirring constantly, until thickened. Set aside.

3. Melt remaining 2 tablespoons butter in skillet, add mushrooms and minced onion, and sauté. Remove mushrooms and set aside, leaving butter and onion in skillet. Add scallops to skillet and sauté 3 minutes.

4. Preheat oven to 400°F.

5. Add reserved mushrooms, scallops, onion, shrimp, crab meat, and sherry to saucepan and stir gently. Spoon mixture into scallop shells or small ramekins and sprinkle with bread crumbs.

6. Bake in preheated 400°F oven 10 minutes on top rack.

7. Change oven setting and broil 2 to 3 minutes or until tops are lightly browned.

*Makes 8 servings, ½ cup each*

*(See page 47)

# Shrimp Sautéed in Herb Butter

¼ cup butter or margarine

2 tablespoons lemon juice

1 teaspoon Parsley Flakes

1 teaspoon Freeze-Dried Chives

¾ teaspoon Season-All Seasoned Salt

½ teaspoon Tarragon Leaves

½ teaspoon Ground Mustard

⅛ teaspoon Ground Red Pepper

⅛ teaspoon Garlic Powder

1 pound shrimp, peeled and deveined (about 24 shrimp)

Hot cooked rice to serve, if desired

1. Place all ingredients except shrimp and rice in large skillet. Heat slowly until butter has melted and mix well.

2. Add shrimp and sauté over medium heat 8 minutes or until shrimp are pink. Turn once during cooking.

3. Serve with hot cooked rice.

*Makes 24 shrimp*

# Shrimp Creole

¼ cup butter or margarine

1 cup chopped celery

½ cup chopped green bell pepper

2 tablespoons Instant Minced Onion

2 tablespoons all-purpose flour

1 can (14½ ounces) stewed tomatoes

½ cup water

1 Bay Leaf

2 teaspoons Parsley Flakes

1½ teaspoons Season-All Seasoned Salt

⅛ teaspoon Ground Red Pepper

1 pound cooked, peeled, and deveined shrimp

1. Melt butter in large skillet. Add celery, green bell pepper, and minced onion. Sauté until onion is lightly browned.

2. Stir in flour and add tomatoes, water, bay leaf, parsley, seasoned salt, and red pepper. Mix well, heat, cover, and simmer 30 minutes.

3. Add shrimp and simmer just until shrimp are heated through.

4. Remove and discard bay leaf before serving.

*Makes 6 servings, ¾ cup each*

# Deviled Lobster Tails

4 quarts water

4 tablespoons salt

4 frozen rock lobster tails, 6 ounces each

¾ cup mayonnaise

½ cup dry bread crumbs

2 teaspoons Instant Minced Onion

¾ teaspoon Season-All Seasoned Salt

½ teaspoon Lemon Peel

½ teaspoon Ground Mustard

¼ teaspoon Ground White Pepper

Dash Ground Red Pepper

2 tablespoons butter, melted

Paprika

Vanilla Sauce (page 270)

1. Heat water to boil in 6-quart pot. Add salt and frozen lobster tails. Cover and boil 9 minutes. Drain and set aside to cool slightly.

2. Place mayonnaise and bread crumbs in medium-size bowl. Add seasonings and stir to mix well. Set aside.

3. Preheat broiler.

4. Cut away thin undershell of lobster tails and remove meat, being careful not to break shells. Set shells aside and cut lobster meat into bite-size pieces. Add lobster meat to reserved mayonnaise mixture and mix gently.

5. Spoon mixture into reserved lobster shells and brush tops with melted butter. Sprinkle with paprika.

6. Broil, 5 to 6 inches from source of heat, 5 to 8 minutes or until lightly browned.

7. Serve with Vanilla Sauce.

*Makes 4 stuffed lobster tails*

CHIVES

# Seafood Stew

¼ cup olive oil

1½ cups thinly sliced carrots

½ cup chopped green bell pepper

1 can (28 ounces) whole tomatoes, undrained

1 can (15 ounces) tomato sauce

3 cups water

1 Bay Leaf

1 tablespoon Instant Minced Onion

1 teaspoon Parsley Flakes

½ teaspoon Basil Leaves

¼ teaspoon Instant Minced Garlic

¼ teaspoon Coarse Ground Black Pepper

¼ teaspoon Season-All Seasoned Salt

¾ cup dry vermouth

¼ cup lemon juice

1 pound sea scallops, cut in half if very large

1 pound crab meat, picked over*

2 dozen cherrystone clams

1 dozen mussels

1 pound shrimp, peeled and deveined

1. Heat oil in 6-quart Dutch oven over medium heat. Add carrots and green bell pepper and cook until tender but not browned. Add tomatoes and tomato sauce and stir.

2. Add water and seasonings and stir. Heat to boil, reduce heat, cover, and simmer 20 minutes.

3. Add vermouth, lemon juice, and scallops. Simmer 10 minutes. Add crab meat to stew.

4. Scrub clams and mussels to clean shells. Discard any that are not tightly closed. Add to stew with shrimp and simmer 5 to 10 minutes or just until shells open. Remove and discard bay leaf. Discard any clams and mussels that do not open during cooking.

*Makes 12 servings, 1½ cups each*

*(See page 47)

**PEPPER**

# Bouillabaisse

1 pound tomatoes, peeled, seeded,
    and chopped

1 bottle (8 ounces) clam juice

1 carrot, diced

½ cup Instant Chopped Onions

⅓ cup olive oil

5 teaspoons Bon Appétit

1 tablespoon lemon juice

2 teaspoons Parsley Flakes

½ teaspoon Instant Minced Garlic

¼ teaspoon Thyme Leaves

¼ teaspoon Ground Black Pepper

⅛ teaspoon Fennel Seed

24 Saffron threads

1 Bay Leaf

4 rock lobster tails, 7 to 8 ounces each,
    cut into 2-inch pieces, shells still on

2 pounds fillet of sole, cut into 2-inch
    pieces

2 pounds red snapper fillets, cut into
    2-inch pieces

1 pound ocean perch fillets, cut into
    2-inch pieces

Water to cover

Warm French bread and tossed green
    salad to serve, if desired

1. Place tomatoes, clam juice, carrot, chopped onions, oil, Bon Appétit, lemon juice, parsley, minced garlic, thyme, pepper, fennel seed, saffron, bay leaf, and lobster tails in 8-quart pot. Heat to boil and boil 8 minutes.

2. Add remaining fish and just enough water to cover.

3. Heat to boil, cover, and boil 5 minutes.

4. Remove and discard bay leaf. Ladle into soup bowls and serve with warm French bread and large bowl of tossed green salad.

*Makes 9 servings, 2 cups each*

# *Paella*

¼ cup olive oil

3 to 4 pounds chicken parts or whole chicken, cut into pieces

¼ pound thinly sliced pepperoni

2 tomatoes, peeled and cut into sections

¼ cup Instant Chopped Onions

3 cups water

½ pound shrimp, peeled and deveined

12 whole clams or 1 can (6 ½ ounces) minced clams

1 cup lobster pieces

1½ cups long grain rice

10 Saffron threads

1 pimiento, sliced

1 tablespoon Parsley Flakes

2 teaspoons Chicken Flavor Base

1 teaspoon Paprika

1 teaspoon Season-All Seasoned Salt

1 teaspoon salt

¼ teaspoon Ground Black Pepper

⅛ teaspoon Garlic Powder

1 cup frozen peas

1. Heat oil in 15-inch skillet over medium heat, add chicken pieces, and cook until browned. Remove chicken from skillet and set aside.

2. Add pepperoni to skillet and cook until browned. Add tomatoes and chopped onions and cook until onions are lightly browned.

3. Return chicken to skillet and add remaining ingredients except peas. Stir gently, cover, and simmer 30 minutes.

4. Add peas to skillet and cook, uncovered, 5 minutes.

*Makes 12 servings, 1 cup each*

**SAFFRON**

# Superb Scalloped Oysters

*1 quart oysters (Selects)*

*½ cup butter or margarine*

*2 cups coarse saltine cracker crumbs*

*½ teaspoon Season-All Seasoned Salt*

*¼ teaspoon Celery Salt*

*¼ teaspoon Coarse Ground Black Pepper*

*Dash Onion Powder*

*¾ cup light cream*

*1 teaspoon Worcestershire sauce*

*1 teaspoon Parsley Flakes*

1. Preheat oven to 350°F. Lightly grease 10 x 6 x 2-inch baking pan and set aside.

2. Drain oysters, reserving ¼ cup liquor.

3. Melt butter in medium-size skillet over low heat. Add cracker crumbs, seasoned salt, celery salt, pepper, and onion powder.

4. Spread one-third of crumb mixture in prepared pan and cover with half of oysters.

5. Make second layer of each, saving one-third of crumb mixture.

6. Place cream, reserved ¼ cup oyster liquor, and Worcestershire in 2-cup glass measure and stir to combine. Pour over oysters.

7. Add parsley to remaining one-third of crumb mixture and sprinkle over oysters.

8. Bake in preheated 350°F oven 30 minutes.

*Makes 8 servings, ½ cup each*

CELERY SEED

# Crab Imperial

*1 cup plus 2 tablespoons milk, divided*

*1 tablespoon butter or margarine*

*2 tablespoons all-purpose flour*

*4 tablespoons mayonnaise, divided*

*1 egg, beaten*

*1 tablespoon lemon juice*

*1 teaspoon Season-All Seasoned Salt*

*1 teaspoon Ground Mustard*

*½ teaspoon Celery Salt*

*½ teaspoon Worcestershire sauce*

*¼ teaspoon Ground Red Pepper*

*¼ teaspoon Ground Black Pepper*

*2 pounds lump crab meat, picked over\**

*Paprika*

1. Preheat oven to 400°F.
2. Heat 1 cup milk to boil in small saucepan, remove from heat, and set aside.
3. Melt butter in separate small saucepan over low heat. Stir in flour and heat until bubbly. Gradually pour heated milk into flour-butter mixture, beating constantly until smooth and creamy. Set aside to cool.
4. Place 2 tablespoons mayonnaise, egg, lemon juice, seasoned salt, mustard, celery salt, Worcestershire, and red and black pepper in small bowl and mix well. Add to reserved milk mixture and stir to mix well.
5. Add crab meat and mix gently but thoroughly. Spoon into scallop shells or small ramekins.
6. Mix remaining 2 tablespoons milk into remaining 2 tablespoons mayonnaise and brush over top of crab meat. Sprinkle lightly with paprika.
7. Bake in preheated 400°F oven 8 minutes or until lightly browned.

*Makes 6 servings, ¾ cup each*

*\*(See page 47)*

# VEGETABLES

# Asparagus Oriental

1½ pounds fresh asparagus

2 tablespoons butter or margarine

½ teaspoon Chicken Flavor Base

½ teaspoon Season-All Seasoned Salt

⅛ teaspoon Ground Ginger

Dash Ground White Pepper

1 teaspoon soy sauce

1. Wash asparagus and break off stalks as far down as they snap easily. Cut asparagus diagonally into ¼-inch-thick slices.
2. Melt butter in skillet over low heat.
3. Add asparagus and remaining ingredients except soy sauce. Cover. Cook over high heat 2 minutes or until crisp-tender, stirring 2 or 3 times.
4. Add soy sauce and mix well.

*Makes 5 to 6 servings, ½ cup each*

# Hot Asparagus Vinaigrette

2 pounds fresh asparagus

½ cup olive oil

2 tablespoons malt vinegar

1 tablespoon lemon juice

1 teaspoon Bon Appétit

½ teaspoon sugar

¼ teaspoon Hot Shot! Pepper Blend

1 hard-cooked egg, chopped*

1. Wash asparagus and break stalks at point where they snap off easily. Trim ends.
2. Steam asparagus until crisp-tender. Remove from steamer, set aside in serving dish, and keep warm.
3. Place remaining ingredients except chopped egg in saucepan and heat to boil. Pour over asparagus and sprinkle with chopped egg.

*Makes 6 servings, 4 to 6 asparagus spears each*

*(To hard-cook eggs, see page 48)

# Old-Fashioned Baked Beans

*1 pound dry navy, pea, or pinto beans*

*¼ teaspoon baking soda*

*4 cups tomato juice*

*2 cups firmly packed dark brown sugar*

*2 tablespoons Instant Minced Onion*

*2 teaspoons Bon Appétit*

*1 teaspoon Pure Vanilla Extract*

*1 teaspoon prepared horseradish*

*½ teaspoon Ground Mustard*

*¼ teaspoon Ground Cloves*

*⅛ teaspoon Ground Cardamom*

*⅛ teaspoon Ground Black Pepper*

*8 slices bacon, cut into 1-inch pieces*

1. Pick over beans to remove stones and empty skins. Place in large bowl, cover with cold water, and soak overnight. Drain and rinse thoroughly. If preferred, follow instructions for quick-soaking method on package of beans.

2. Place in Dutch oven or large saucepan. Cover with fresh water and add baking soda.

3. Heat to boil, reduce heat, cover, and simmer 35 minutes. Drain and rinse under cold water. Place beans in 3-quart casserole or bean pot.

4. Preheat oven to 300°F.

5. Place remaining ingredients in large bowl and stir to combine. Pour over beans and stir.

6. Cover and bake in preheated 300°F oven 5 hours or until beans are tender. Add small amount of hot water if beans become dry on top during baking. Remove cover during last 30 minutes of baking.

*Makes 10 servings, ¾ cup each*

**CLOVES**

# Green Beans with Water Chestnuts

2 packages (9 ounces each) frozen
  French-style green beans or
  1 pound fresh green beans,
  sliced French-style

2 tablespoons butter or margarine

1 can (8 ounces) water chestnuts,
  drained and thinly sliced

2 teaspoons lemon juice

½ teaspoon salt

½ teaspoon Marjoram Leaves

½ teaspoon Tarragon Leaves

¼ teaspoon Ground Black Pepper

1. Cook frozen beans in 3-quart saucepan according to package directions. Drain and return to saucepan. If using fresh beans, cook in small amount of water until crisp-tender. Drain and return to saucepan.

2. Melt butter in small saucepan over low heat and stir in remaining ingredients. Simmer 1 minute.

3. Pour mixture over green beans and toss to mix. Cook just until heated through.

*Makes 6 servings, ½ cup each*

# Delectable Green Beans

1 package (16 ounces) frozen
  French-style green beans or
  1 pound fresh green beans,
  sliced French-style

½ cup water

½ teaspoon Instant Minced Onion

1 tablespoon butter or margarine

2 tablespoons all-purpose flour

1¼ teaspoons Bon Appétit

¼ teaspoon Ground Savory

⅛ teaspoon Ground Black Pepper

½ cup dairy sour cream

¼ cup shredded Swiss cheese

1. Lightly grease 1-quart casserole and set aside.

2. Place beans, water, and minced onion in saucepan. Cover and heat to boil. Reduce heat and simmer 8 minutes. Drain well and set aside.

3. Preheat broiler.

4. Melt butter in saucepan. Stir in flour, Bon Appétit, savory, and pepper. Add sour cream and cook over low heat, stirring constantly, until thickened. Do not boil. Add beans and mix well.

5. Pour into prepared casserole and sprinkle cheese over top.

6. Broil, 4 inches from source of heat, 4 minutes or until cheese has melted.

*Makes 4 servings, ½ cup each*

# *Harvard Beets*

*1 can (16 ounces) sliced or small whole beets, drained and liquid reserved*

*4 teaspoons cornstarch*

*¼ cup cider vinegar*

*¼ cup sugar*

*½ teaspoon Orange Peel*

*⅛ teaspoon Ground Cloves*

*1 tablespoon butter or margarine*

1. Set beets aside and place beet liquid in saucepan.

2. Place cornstarch in small dish and stir in vinegar until smooth. Add to saucepan with sugar, orange peel, and cloves.

3. Cook over medium heat, stirring, until sauce thickens. Stir in butter and add beets. Simmer 5 minutes.

*Makes 4 servings, ½ cup each*

**SAVORY**

# Oriental Cabbage

2 tablespoons vegetable oil

1 medium-size head cabbage, coarsely chopped, about 3 quarts

6 stalks celery, cut into ¼-inch slices

6 scallions, chopped

3 large yellow onions, sliced and slices cut in half

¼ cup lemon juice

2 tablespoons soy sauce

2 tablespoons brown sugar

1 teaspoon California Style Garlic Salt

½ teaspoon Ground Ginger

¼ teaspoon Hot Shot! Pepper Blend

1 large green bell pepper, cut into thin strips

1. Heat oil in wok or large skillet over high heat. Add cabbage, celery, scallions, and sliced onions. Stir to coat with oil.

2. Sprinkle lemon juice, soy sauce, sugar, garlic salt, ginger, and Hot Shot! over vegetables. Mix well.

3. Cook over high heat 7 minutes, stirring frequently, or until cabbage is crisp-tender.

4. Add green bell pepper strips and cook, stirring, 3 minutes.

*Makes 12 servings, ¾ cup each*

---

# Ginger Glazed Carrots

¾ cup water

2 tablespoons butter or margarine, divided

1 teaspoon Chicken Flavor Base

1 teaspoon Bon Appétit

1 teaspoon sugar

6 large carrots, sliced (2 cups)

3 tablespoons honey

1 tablespoon lemon juice

½ teaspoon Ground Ginger

¼ teaspoon Ground Nutmeg

Parsley Flakes

1. Place water, 1 tablespoon butter, flavor base, Bon Appétit, and sugar in 10-inch skillet and stir to mix well. Add carrots, cover, and cook over medium heat 12 minutes or until crisp-tender. Drain, leaving carrots in skillet.

2. Add remaining 1 tablespoon butter, honey, lemon juice, ginger, and nutmeg. Stir to mix well.

3. Cook, uncovered, over medium heat 3 to 4 minutes, tossing frequently to glaze carrots.

4. Sprinkle with parsley just before serving.

*Makes 4 servings, ½ cup each*

# Carrots with Rosemary

*¾ cup water*

*2 tablespoons butter or margarine*

*2 teaspoons sugar*

*½ teaspoon Onion Salt*

*⅛ teaspoon Hot Shot! Pepper Blend*

*1 pound carrots, cut into 2-inch pieces*

*½ teaspoon Rosemary Leaves, crushed*

1. Place water, butter, sugar, onion salt, and Hot Shot! in medium-size saucepan. Heat to boil.

2. Cut thicker pieces of cut carrots lengthwise and add carrots to saucepan with rosemary. Cover and cook until carrots are fork tender, about 7 minutes.

3. Remove carrots with slotted spoon to warm serving dish, leaving liquid in saucepan. Keep carrots warm.

4. Boil liquid in saucepan until reduced by half. Pour over carrots and stir to coat.

*Makes 8 servings, four 2-inch pieces each*

**ROSEMARY**

# Roasted Corn with Savory Butter

6 to 8 ears corn in husks

½ cup butter or margarine

½ teaspoon Ground Mustard

½ teaspoon salt

½ teaspoon Onion Powder

¼ teaspoon Ground Black Pepper

¼ teaspoon Madras Curry Powder

1. Preheat oven to 500°F.
2. Pull back husk on each ear of corn and remove silk. Replace husks and wrap each ear of corn in double thickness of aluminum foil.
3. Roast in preheated 500°F oven 35 minutes.
4. Melt butter in small saucepan over low heat and stir in remaining ingredients.
5. Peel back corn husks and brush corn with butter mixture.

*Makes 6 to 8 servings, 1 ear of corn each*

TIP:

To cook corn on grill, prepare corn as directed above. Place on preheated grill and cook wrapped corn 20 minutes, turning occasionally.

# Corn Pudding

4 eggs

½ cup milk

2 cans (17 ounces each) cream-style corn

1 can (12 ounces) whole-kernel corn, drained

¼ cup butter or margarine, melted

½ cup sugar

3 tablespoons Arrowroot or cornstarch

1½ teaspoons Season-All Seasoned Salt

1 teaspoon Instant Minced Onion

½ teaspoon Ground Mustard

Dash Ground Red Pepper

1. Preheat oven to 350°F. Lightly grease 12 x 8 x 2-inch baking pan and set aside.
2. Place eggs in mixer bowl and beat with electric mixer until light and fluffy. Add milk and beat well. Set aside.

3. Place cream-style corn and whole-kernel corn in large bowl and mix well. Add melted butter and stir.

4. Combine sugar, arrowroot, seasoned salt, minced onion, mustard, and red pepper in small bowl. Mix thoroughly and add to corn mixture. Stir to mix well.

5. Add reserved egg mixture and stir just until well blended. Pour into prepared pan.

6. Bake, uncovered, in preheated 350°F oven 30 minutes. Stir and bake 30 minutes more or until knife comes out clean when inserted near center.

*Makes 10 servings, 2 x 3½ x 1½-inch portions*

# Cucumber Sauté

4 slices bacon

2 large cucumbers

1 small yellow onion, cut into ⅛-inch slices

1 medium-size red bell pepper, cut into thin strips

½ teaspoon cornstarch

3 tablespoons water

2 tablespoons red wine vinegar

¼ teaspoon sugar

¼ teaspoon Celery Seed

¼ teaspoon Season-All Seasoned Salt

¼ teaspoon Parsley Flakes

⅛ teaspoon Ground White Pepper

Sprigs of fresh parsley to garnish

1. Fry bacon until crisp. Drain on paper towels, reserving 2 tablespoons bacon fat in skillet. Set aside.

2. Peel cucumbers. Cut in half lengthwise and remove seeds and cut in half crosswise. Thinly slice lengthwise to make julienne strips.

3. Separate onion slices into rings. Heat bacon fat in skillet over medium heat. Add cucumbers, onion rings, and red bell pepper strips. Stir-fry 3 minutes. Remove vegetables from skillet with slotted spoon and set aside.

4. Place cornstarch in small bowl and stir in water until smooth. Add remaining ingredients to cornstarch mixture and mix well. Pour into skillet and cook, stirring constantly, until mixture thickens. Add reserved vegetables and mix well. Cook just until vegetables are heated through.

5. Arrange vegetables on 6 salad plates. Crumble reserved bacon and sprinkle over each serving. Garnish with sprigs of parsley.

*Makes 6 servings, ½ cup each*

*Cucumber Sauté (see photo on page 248)*

# Eggplant Italian

1 medium-size eggplant, about
    1½ pounds

¼ to ½ cup butter or margarine

1 pound lean ground beef

1 tablespoon Instant Minced Onion

1 teaspoon Bon Appétit

1 teaspoon sugar

¼ teaspoon Basil Leaves

¼ teaspoon Ground Oregano

⅛ teaspoon Ground Black Pepper

1 can (8 ounces) tomato sauce

¼ cup grated Parmesan cheese

½ pound mozzarella cheese, sliced

1. Wash but do not peel eggplant. Cut into twelve ½-inch-thick slices.

2. Melt ¼ cup butter in 10-inch skillet over low heat. Add eggplant slices and brown lightly on both sides, adding extra butter if needed. Arrange in shallow 2-quart baking pan and set aside.

3. Add ground beef, minced onion, Bon Appétit, sugar, basil, oregano, and pepper to skillet. Mix well and cook until meat is no longer pink. Drain off excess fat, if desired.

4. Preheat oven to 350°F.

5. Spoon meat mixture over eggplant. Pour tomato sauce over meat and sprinkle with Parmesan cheese.

6. Bake, uncovered, in preheated 350°F oven 20 minutes.

7. Place mozzarella cheese slices on top of casserole and bake 10 minutes or until cheese has melted. Serve hot.

*Makes 6 servings, 2 eggplant slices each*

**OREGANO**

*Cucumber Sauté (see recipe on page 247)*

# Eggplant Parmigiana

2 medium-size eggplant, 1 pound each

2 tablespoons olive oil

1 can (16 ounces) whole tomatoes, broken up

1 can (6 ounces) tomato paste

1 Bay Leaf

1 tablespoon Parsley Flakes

1½ teaspoons Season-All Seasoned Salt

¼ teaspoon Garlic Powder

⅛ teaspoon Ground Black Pepper

½ cup grated Parmesan cheese

2 cups soft bread crumbs

½ pound mozzarella cheese, sliced

1. Peel eggplant and cut each crosswise into twelve ½-inch slices.

2. Heat oil in large skillet over low heat and sauté eggplant slices 5 minutes or until tender and lightly browned. Remove from skillet, set aside, and keep warm.

3. Place tomatoes, tomato paste, bay leaf, parsley, seasoned salt, garlic powder, and pepper in skillet. Stir to combine, cover, and simmer 15 minutes. Remove and discard bay leaf. Stir in Parmesan cheese and bread crumbs.

4. Preheat oven to 350°F. Lightly grease 12 x 8 x 2-inch baking pan.

5. Arrange layer of 12 eggplant slices in prepared pan. Cover with half of tomato sauce and half of mozzarella cheese slices. Repeat layers ending with cheese.

6. Bake, uncovered, in preheated 350°F oven 20 minutes or until cheese has melted and top is lightly browned. Serve immediately.

*Makes 8 servings, 3 eggplant slices each*

# Creamed Onions

1 tablespoon butter or margarine

1 tablespoon all-purpose flour

1 teaspoon Bon Appétit

¼ teaspoon Ground Mustard

⅛ teaspoon Ground White Pepper

1½ cups milk

1 package (16 ounces) frozen pearl onions

1. Melt butter in 1-quart saucepan over low heat. Stir in flour and seasonings. Cook 1 minute, allowing mixture to bubble slightly. Do not brown.

2. Remove from heat and gradually stir in milk. Return to heat and cook, stirring, until thickened. Set aside.

3. Boil onions according to package directions. Drain well and pour sauce over onions. Stir gently.

*Makes 2⅓ cups*

# Roasted Onions and Peppers

*6 to 7 medium-size onions, quartered (about 2½ pounds)*

*¾ cup olive oil*

*3 tablespoons honey*

*1½ teaspoons Ground Ginger*

*1½ teaspoons Bon Appétit*

*¾ teaspoon Hot Shot! Pepper Blend*

*½ teaspoon Italian Seasoning*

*2 green bell peppers, cut into 1½-inch strips*

*2 red bell peppers, cut into 1½-inch strips*

1. Preheat oven to 400°F.

2. Place onions in 13 x 9 x 2-inch baking pan.

3. Place oil, honey, ginger, Bon Appétit, Hot Shot!, and Italian seasoning in small bowl. Mix well and pour over onions. Stir and turn onions to coat.

4. Cover with aluminum foil and bake in preheated 400°F oven 30 minutes.

5. Remove foil and add green and red bell pepper strips. Stir gently to coat.

6. Bake, uncovered, 25 minutes, basting once with pan juices.

*Makes 12 servings, ½ cup each*

# Minted Peas

*1 package (10 ounces) frozen peas*

*¼ cup water*

*1 bottle (3½ ounces) tiny cocktail onions, drained and rinsed*

*1 tablespoon butter or margarine*

*1 teaspoon Chicken Flavor Base*

*½ teaspoon Mint Flakes*

1. Combine all ingredients in 2-quart saucepan. Cover and heat to boil. Reduce heat to low and cook 5 to 7 minutes.

*Makes 4 servings, ½ cup each*

# Tofu with Bell Peppers and Peanuts

⅓ cup vegetable oil

1 tablespoon Crushed Red Pepper

1 teaspoon Instant Minced Garlic

2 cups diced green bell peppers

1 cup diced red bell peppers

4 pounds tofu, cut into ½-inch cubes

1½ cups unsalted dry-roasted peanuts

1 tablespoon cornstarch

¾ cup water

¾ cup soy sauce

2 scallions, trimmed and cut into thin rounds

Hot cooked rice to serve, if desired

1. Heat oil in large skillet or wok over medium heat. Add crushed red pepper and minced garlic. Cook 1 minute.

2. Add green and red bell peppers, tofu, and peanuts. Cook, stirring, 5 minutes.

3. Place cornstarch in 2-cup glass measure. Gradually add 1 to 2 tablespoons water, stirring, to make smooth paste. Stir in remaining water and soy sauce. Pour over tofu mixture. Cook, stirring, until thickened and clear.

4. Sprinkle with sliced scallions and serve with hot cooked rice.

*Makes 12 servings, ¾ cup each*

# Candied Sweet Potatoes

2 pounds sweet potatoes

1 cup orange juice

½ cup firmly packed dark brown sugar

⅓ cup dry sherry

2 tablespoons butter or margarine

1 tablespoon Orange Peel

½ teaspoon Ground Cinnamon

¼ teaspoon Ground Ginger

⅛ teaspoon Ground Cloves

1. Scrub sweet potatoes and place in saucepan. Cover with cold water and heat to boil. Cook just until barely tender and still firm, about 25 to 35 minutes. Do not overcook. Drain and set aside to cool slightly.

2. When cool enough to handle, peel potatoes and cut into 2-inch pieces. Arrange in 8-inch square baking pan.

3. Preheat oven to 350°F.

4. Place remaining ingredients in saucepan and heat to boil, stirring. Boil 3 minutes and pour over potatoes.

5. Bake, uncovered, in preheated 350°F oven 1 hour, basting often to glaze.

*Makes 6 servings, ¾ cup each*

# Potatoes au Gratin

*1 cup hot water*

*1 teaspoon Chicken Flavor Base*

*6 large potatoes, peeled and quartered*

*4 tablespoons butter or margarine, divided*

*2 tablespoons all-purpose flour*

*1 teaspoon Season-All Seasoned Salt*

*¼ teaspoon salt*

*¼ teaspoon Ground White Pepper*

*¼ teaspoon Ground Mustard*

*⅛ teaspoon Ground Nutmeg*

*2 cups milk*

*1½ cups shredded Cheddar cheese, divided*

*1 cup soft bread crumbs*

*Paprika*

1. Place water in 4-quart saucepan, add flavor base, and stir to dissolve.

2. Add potatoes and heat to boil. Cook 20 minutes or until potatoes are fork tender. Drain well and cut into cubes. Arrange in 12 x 8 x 2-inch baking pan. Set aside.

3. Preheat oven to 350°F.

4. Melt 2 tablespoons butter in saucepan over medium heat. Stir in flour, seasoned salt, salt, white pepper, mustard, and nutmeg.

5. Gradually add milk, stirring constantly, until smooth and thickened.

6. Stir in 1 cup cheese and cook, stirring, until cheese has melted. Pour over potatoes.

7. Melt remaining 2 tablespoons butter, toss with bread crumbs, and spoon evenly over potatoes.

8. Top with remaining ½ cup cheese and sprinkle generously with paprika.

9. Bake, uncovered, in preheated 350°F oven 20 minutes.

*Makes 8 servings, 1 cup each*

# Bombay Potatoes

3 pounds potatoes, peeled and cut
   into 1-inch cubes

⅓ cup vegetable oil

3 tomatoes, chopped

¾ cup chopped fresh onion

3 tablespoons mango chutney

2 to 3 tablespoons Indian Curry Powder

½ cup water

¾ teaspoon salt

1. Place potatoes in 2-quart saucepan with small amount of water and boil until tender. Drain and set aside.

2. Heat oil in large skillet over medium heat.

3. Add tomatoes, onion, chutney, and curry powder. Cook over low heat 2 to 3 minutes. Add reserved potatoes, water, and salt. Cook 5 minutes to heat thoroughly.

*Makes 12 servings, ½ cup each*

# Potato Dumplings

3 medium-size potatoes, peeled
   and quartered

1 egg, beaten

½ cup dry bread crumbs

2 teaspoons salt, divided

¼ teaspoon Ground White Pepper

¼ teaspoon Onion Salt

3 to 4 tablespoons all-purpose flour

6 cups water

1. Boil potatoes in 2-quart saucepan in lightly salted water until tender. Drain well and set aside to cool slightly. Process through ricer or coarse sieve into medium-size bowl.

2. Add egg, bread crumbs, 1 teaspoon salt, white pepper, and onion salt. Mix well.

3. Stir in 3 tablespoons flour. Add up to 1 tablespoon additional flour, if needed, to make dough that is soft but not too sticky. Lightly flour hands and form mixture into 1½-inch balls.

4. Heat water and remaining 1 teaspoon salt to rapid boil in large saucepan. Add potato balls gently and cook 8 minutes or until dumplings change in appearance and begin to look fluffy.

5. Remove with slotted spoon and serve hot.

*Makes 16 to 18 dumplings*

# Sauerkraut Caraway

1 can (16 ounces) sauerkraut,
    undrained

½ cup port wine

1 tablespoon sugar

2 teaspoons Caraway Seed

1 teaspoon prepared horseradish

1 teaspoon Instant Minced Onion

½ teaspoon Ground Mustard

1. Preheat oven to 325°F.
2. Place all ingredients in 1-quart casserole and stir to combine.
3. Cover and bake in preheated 325°F oven 2 hours.

*Makes 5 servings, ½ cup each*

TIP:

Delicious with sausages, frankfurters, spareribs, roast pork, and pork chops.

# Country-Good Baked Squash

2 pounds small yellow squash

¼ cup water

3 tablespoons Instant Minced Onion

4 tablespoons butter or margarine,
    melted, divided

½ cup milk

2 eggs, beaten

1 teaspoon Bon Appétit

1 teaspoon Parsley Flakes

¼ teaspoon Ground Black Pepper

½ cup saltine cracker crumbs

1. Wash but don't peel squash. Slice ½ inch thick and place in 4-quart saucepan. Add water and minced onion. Heat to boil and cook about 10 minutes or just until tender.
2. Preheat oven to 350°F.
3. Drain squash and place in 11 x 7 x 2-inch baking pan. Pour 2 tablespoons melted butter over squash.
4. Place milk, eggs, Bon Appétit, parsley, and pepper in small bowl. Mix well and pour over squash. Place cracker crumbs in small bowl and stir in remaining 2 tablespoons melted butter. Sprinkle over squash.
5. Bake, uncovered, in preheated 350°F oven 20 minutes.

*Makes 10 servings, ½ cup each*

# Vegetable Korma

1 cup salted dry-roasted cashews

¼ cup light cream

1 tablespoon Poppy Seed

2 teaspoons Paprika

2 teaspoons Chicken Flavor Base

½ teaspoon Ground Cinnamon

½ teaspoon Ground Cardamom

½ teaspoon Ground Black Pepper

¼ teaspoon Ground Red Pepper

¼ teaspoon Ground Cloves

⅓ cup vegetable oil

3 medium-size onions, sliced

1 cup thinly sliced carrots

2 medium-size zucchini, cut into ½-inch slices

1½ cups small cauliflowerets

3 cups cold water

1 teaspoon Bon Appétit

3 cups peeled, cubed, cooked potatoes

1 cup frozen peas

1 cup frozen whole-kernel corn

1. Place cashews, cream, poppy seed, paprika, flavor base, cinnamon, cardamom, black and red pepper, and cloves in blender or food processor. Process until smooth and set aside.

2. Heat oil in 6-quart Dutch oven over medium heat. Add onions and carrots and cook until onions are transparent.

3. Add zucchini and cauliflower and cook, stirring occasionally, until vegetables have softened slightly. Stir in water and Bon Appétit and heat to boil.

4. Add reserved cashew mixture and stir to mix well.

5. Add potatoes, peas, and corn. Stir gently to mix, reduce heat, and simmer 5 minutes.

*Makes 12 servings, ¾ cup each*

# Thai Roasted Vegetables

½ cup olive oil

3 pounds yellow onions, halved or quartered if large

4 large red bell peppers, cut into 3 x 1-inch strips

4 large green bell peppers, cut into 3 x 1-inch strips

4 zucchini, each 6 inches long, cut in half lengthwise and crosswise

½ cup butter or margarine

4 teaspoons Thai Seasoning

1. Preheat oven to 350°F.

2. Pour ¼ cup oil into each of two 13 x 9 x 2-inch baking pans. Arrange half of onions in single layer in each pan and turn onions to coat well with oil.

3. Cover each pan with aluminum foil and bake in preheated 350°F oven 30 minutes.

4. Uncover pans and add half of red and green bell peppers and half of zucchini to each pan.

5. Melt butter in small saucepan over low heat and stir in Thai seasoning. Pour half of seasoned butter over vegetables in each pan. Stir to coat vegetables well.

6. Bake, uncovered, 30 minutes, basting 2 or 3 times with pan juices during cooking.

*Makes 12 servings, ½ cup each*

**POPPY**

## PASTA / RICE

# Cannelloni

PANCAKES

1 cup all-purpose flour

1 tablespoon cornmeal

½ teaspoon Bon Appétit

2 eggs

½ cup dairy sour cream

1 cup water

2 tablespoons vegetable oil

SAUCE

1 cup chili sauce

1 can (8 ounces) tomato sauce

2 tablespoons butter or
   margarine

2 tablespoons lemon juice

2 teaspoons Instant Minced
   Onion

⅛ teaspoon Garlic Powder

⅛ teaspoon Ground Oregano

Dash Ground Red Pepper

FILLING

2 tablespoons olive oil

1 pound ground turkey

½ pound ground veal

½ pound lean ground pork

4 slices prosciutto ham, chopped

2 tablespoons Instant Minced Onion

1½ teaspoons Season-All Seasoned Salt

¾ teaspoon Italian Seasoning

¼ teaspoon Rosemary Leaves

¼ teaspoon Ground Black Pepper

⅛ teaspoon Garlic Powder

½ cup dry sherry

½ pound ricotta cheese

½ cup milk

*  *  *

6 ounces Monterey Jack or
   Muenster cheese

Grated Parmesan cheese to serve

1. To make pancakes, place flour, cornmeal, and Bon Appétit in medium-size bowl and stir to combine.

2. Beat eggs in separate bowl. Stir in sour cream and water. Mix well.

3. Stir flour mixture and oil into egg mixture until smooth.

4. Grease griddle lightly and heat. Drop 3 tablespoons batter onto hot griddle for each pancake and cook until lightly browned on both sides. Set aside.

5. To make sauce, place all ingredients in 3-quart saucepan, cover, and simmer slowly about 20 minutes.

6. To make filling, heat oil in large skillet over high heat. Add turkey, veal, pork, and ham. Sauté 2 minutes, stirring frequently.

7. Reduce heat to low. Add minced onion, seasoned salt, Italian seasoning, rosemary, pepper, and garlic powder. Stir well, cover, and simmer slowly 45 minutes. Stir in sherry and cook 10 minutes.

8. Remove from heat and stir in ricotta cheese. Set aside to cool slightly. Stir in milk, mixing well.

9. Preheat oven to 350°F. Lightly grease baking pan and set aside.

10. To make Cannelloni, fill pancakes with meat mixture and fold sides of pancakes over filling to make long rolls. Place in prepared pan.

11. Bake, uncovered, in preheated 350°F oven 20 minutes. Top each roll with ½-ounce slice Monterey Jack or Muenster cheese. Bake until cheese has melted.

12. Serve with sauce and Parmesan cheese.

*Makes 12 Cannelloni and 2 cups sauce*

**ONION**

# Sausage and Wild Rice Casserole

¾ pound pork sausage meat

1½ cups hot water

1 can (10½ ounces) condensed
   cream of mushroom soup

1 cup wild rice

1 cup shredded American cheese

½ cup chopped celery

1 jar (4 ounces) chopped pimiento,
   drained

1 can (2 ounces) sliced mushrooms,
   drained

1 tablespoon Instant Minced Onion

1 teaspoon Chicken Flavor Base

½ teaspoon Marjoram Leaves

½ teaspoon Thyme Leaves

1. Preheat oven to 325°F.

2. Crumble sausage in large skillet and cook over medium heat until browned.
   Drain off excess fat.

3. Add remaining ingredients to skillet and stir to mix well.

4. Pour into 3-quart casserole, cover, and bake in preheated 325°F oven 2 hours.

*Makes 6 servings, ¾ cup each*

# Saffron Rice

¼ cup butter or margarine

1 cup long grain rice

½ cup slivered almonds

2½ cups water

1 cup chopped green bell peppers

1 can (4 ounces) mushrooms,
   stems and pieces, drained

1 tablespoon Instant Minced Onion

1 teaspoon salt

¼ teaspoon crushed Saffron threads

¼ teaspoon Ground Black Pepper

1. Melt butter in large skillet over low heat. Add rice and almonds. Cook,
   stirring, until rice is delicately browned.

2. Add remaining ingredients. Stir to combine.

3. Cover, heat to boil, reduce heat to very low, and simmer 25 minutes.

*Makes 8 servings, ½ cup each*

TIP:

Crush saffron with fingers to break into ⅛-inch-long pieces.

# Couscous with Variations

BASIC COUSCOUS

*1½ cups water*

*1 teaspoon Chicken Flavor Base*

*1¼ cups quick-cooking couscous*

*2 tablespoons butter or margarine*

*¼ teaspoon salt*

1. Place water and flavor base in medium-size saucepan and heat to boil.

2. Add couscous, butter, and salt.

3. Stir, remove from heat, and cover.

4. Let stand 5 minutes and fluff with fork.

*Makes 6 servings, ½ cup each*

VARIATIONS:

Mustard-Chive Couscous: Combine 1½ cups water, 1 teaspoon Chicken Flavor Base, ½ teaspoon Bon Appétit, ½ teaspoon Freeze-Dried Chives, ¼ teaspoon Ground Mustard, and ¼ teaspoon Ground Black Pepper in saucepan. Heat to boil. Follow steps 2, 3, and 4 but delete salt.

Curry Couscous: Combine 1½ cups water, 2 tablespoons raisins, 1 teaspoon Chicken Flavor Base, ½ teaspoon Madras Curry Powder, and ¼ teaspoon Basil Leaves in saucepan. Heat to boil. Follow steps 2, 3, and 4.

Thai Couscous: Combine 1½ cups water, 1 teaspoon Beef Flavor Base, ½ teaspoon Instant Minced Onion, ½ teaspoon Thai Seasoning, and ½ teaspoon Parsley Flakes in saucepan. Heat to boil. Follow steps 2, 3, and 4.

*Makes 6 servings, ½ cup each*

# Spaghetti with Meatballs

SAUCE

1 can (28 ounces) plum tomatoes

3 cups water

1 can (6 ounces) tomato paste

2 tablespoons olive or vegetable oil

2 tablespoons Instant Minced
    Onion

1 teaspoon Bon Appétit

1 teaspoon sugar

¾ teaspoon salt

½ teaspoon Oregano Leaves

½ teaspoon Garlic Powder

¼ teaspoon Ground Black Pepper

¼ teaspoon Crushed Red Pepper

1 Bay Leaf

1 tablespoon Arrowroot and
    1 tablespoon water to thicken
    (optional)

MEATBALLS

2 pounds lean ground beef

1 teaspoon Season-All Seasoned Salt

½ teaspoon Ground Black Pepper

½ teaspoon Onion Powder

¼ cup vegetable oil

1 teaspoon Beef Flavor Base

½ cup hot water

\* \* \*

16 ounces spaghetti, cooked according
    to package directions

Grated Parmesan cheese to serve

Sprigs of fresh basil to garnish

1. To make sauce, force tomatoes through coarse sieve to purée tomatoes and remove skin and seeds. Combine tomato purée with remaining sauce ingredients except arrowroot and 1 tablespoon water in 2-quart glass or stainless steel saucepan and stir to combine.

2. Heat to boil, reduce heat to very low, and simmer, uncovered, 1 hour. Remove and discard bay leaf.

3. For thicker sauce, simmer over very low heat an additional 20 minutes, or thicken by making thin, smooth paste of 1 tablespoon arrowroot and 1 tablespoon water. Stir into sauce and cook, stirring constantly, until thickened.

4. To make meatballs, place meat, seasoned salt, pepper, and onion powder in medium-size bowl. Mix thoroughly but lightly. Moisten hands and shape into 16 balls, 1½ inches each.

5. Heat oil in skillet over medium heat, add meatballs, and brown on all sides. Do not overcook.

6. Dissolve flavor base in hot water and pour over meatballs. Cover and simmer over very low heat 20 minutes.

7. Serve meatballs over hot cooked spaghetti. Top with sauce and Parmesan cheese. Garnish with sprigs of fresh basil.

*Makes 5 cups sauce and 16 meatballs (enough for 16 ounces spaghetti, cooked)*

TEN SPAGHETTI SAUCE VARIATIONS:

Recipe for Basic Sauce plus:

Meat Sauce: Crumble 1 pound lean ground beef. Place in skillet and cook over medium heat until meat is no longer pink. Drain off excess fat and stir meat into sauce.

Turkey Sauce: Crumble 1 pound ground turkey and add to sauce during last 30 minutes of cooking.

Mushroom Sauce: Add 1 can (4 ounces) mushrooms pieces and stems to sauce during last 30 minutes of cooking.

Vegetable Sauce: Add 1 cup chopped, cooked vegetables to sauce during last 30 minutes of cooking.

Shrimp Sauce: Add 1 cup small shrimp to sauce during last 10 minutes of cooking.

Bolognese Sauce: Add ½ cup minced ham and ½ cup chopped fresh onion to sauce during last 30 minutes of cooking.

Red Clam Sauce: Add 1 can (6½ ounces) minced clams with liquid and ½ teaspoon Instant Minced Garlic to sauce during last 30 minutes of cooking.

Creole Sauce: Add ½ cup chopped green bell pepper, ½ cup chopped celery, ½ cup sliced mushrooms, ¼ teaspoon Instant Minced Garlic, and ¼ teaspoon Thyme Leaves to sauce during last 30 minutes of cooking.

Sausage Sauce: Add ½ pound cooked, sliced or crumbled sausage to sauce during last 30 minutes of cooking.

Hot Dog Sauce: Add ½ pound sliced hot dogs to sauce during last 30 minutes of cooking.

*Spaghetti with Meatballs (see photo on page 264)*

# Superb Meat Sauce for Spaghetti

¼ cup all-purpose flour

3-pound round, chuck, or rump roast of beef

¼ cup olive oil

7 cups hot water, divided

4 cans (6 ounces each) tomato paste

1 cup dry red wine

2 cans (4 ounces each) sliced mushrooms, drained

4 anchovy fillets, mashed

½ cup sliced ripe olives

2 teaspoons sugar

2 teaspoons Season-All Seasoned Salt

1 teaspoon Onion Powder

1 teaspoon Celery Salt

1 teaspoon Italian Seasoning

1 teaspoon Ground Black Pepper

½ teaspoon Crushed Red Pepper

½ teaspoon Rosemary Leaves, crushed

¼ teaspoon Garlic Powder

⅛ teaspoon Ground Nutmeg

2 Bay Leaves

Hot cooked spaghetti and grated Parmesan cheese to serve

1. Rub flour over surface of meat.
2. Heat oil in Dutch oven or large saucepan over medium heat and brown meat on all sides. Add 3 cups hot water, cover, reduce heat, and cook slowly 2 to 3 hours or until meat almost falls apart. Tear meat into small pieces with fork.
3. Add remaining 4 cups hot water and remaining ingredients except spaghetti and Parmesan cheese. Mix well, cover tightly, and simmer 2 hours, stirring occasionally.
4. Remove cover and cook until sauce thickens to desired consistency.
5. Remove and discard bay leaves before serving.
6. Serve sauce over hot cooked spaghetti and sprinkle with grated Parmesan cheese.

*Makes 3½ quarts sauce (enough for 4 pounds spaghetti, cooked)*

TIP:

Freeze leftover sauce in covered freezer containers.

*Spaghetti with Meatballs (see recipe on page 262)*

# Seafood Lasagne

¾ cup butter or margarine, divided

½ cup all-purpose flour

1½ teaspoons Bon Appétit

1 teaspoon prepared horseradish

1 teaspoon Old Bay Seasoning, divided

½ teaspoon Ground Mustard

½ teaspoon Lemon & Pepper Seasoning

2 cups light cream

2 cups milk

2 tablespoons dry vermouth

8 ounces lasagne noodles, 9 strips

1 pound orange roughy, cooked and flaked

1 pound crab meat, picked over*

1 pound small shrimp, cooked, peeled, and deveined

1 pound ricotta cheese

½ pound mozzarella cheese, sliced

1 cup grated Parmesan cheese, divided

¼ cup dry bread crumbs

1. Melt ½ cup butter in 2-quart saucepan over low heat. Stir in flour, Bon Appétit, horseradish, ½ teaspoon Old Bay Seasoning, mustard, and Lemon & Pepper seasoning. Cook, stirring, until bubbly. Cook 1 minute more.

2. Stir in cream and milk gradually, stirring after each addition until sauce is smooth. Cook until thickened. Stir in vermouth and set aside.

3. Cook lasagne noodles according to package directions. Drain well and rinse under cold water. Separate carefully.

4. Place orange roughy, crab meat, and shrimp in bowl and mix lightly. Set aside.

5. Preheat oven to 350°F.

6. Arrange 3 cooked noodles in 13 x 9 x 2-inch baking pan so noodles cover bottom of pan.

7. Spoon ricotta cheese over noodles and spread evenly with back of spoon. Arrange half of mozzarella slices over ricotta cheese and sprinkle with ⅓ cup Parmesan cheese. Pour 1 cup reserved sauce over cheeses.

8. Add another layer of 3 noodles. Spread reserved seafood mixture over noodles and top with remaining slices of mozzarella. Sprinkle with ⅓ cup Parmesan cheese and pour 1 cup sauce over layer.

9. Top with remaining 3 noodles and pour remaining sauce over noodles.

10. Place remaining ⅓ cup Parmesan cheese, bread crumbs, and remaining ½ teaspoon Old Bay Seasoning in small bowl. Melt remaining ¼ cup butter and stir into mixture until well combined. Sprinkle evenly over lasagne.

11. Bake, uncovered, in preheated 350°F oven 35 minutes.

12. Let stand 10 minutes. Cut into 12 squares.

*Makes 12 squares, 3 x 3 inches each*

*(See page 47)

# Pasta Primavera

*6 ounces fettuccine, 3 cups cooked*

*¼ cup butter or margarine*

*1 tablespoon all-purpose flour*

*½ teaspoon Garlic Powder*

*¼ teaspoon Onion Powder*

*¼ teaspoon Parsley Flakes*

*¼ teaspoon Bon Appétit*

*⅛ teaspoon Ground White Pepper*

*Dash Ground Nutmeg*

*¾ cup heavy cream*

*½ cup shredded Havarti cheese*

*1 cup broccoli florets*

*⅓ pound Italian green beans, cut into 1-inch pieces (1 cup)*

*1 large carrot, cut into 1 x ¼ x ¼-inch sticks (½ cup)*

*½ cup peeled, coarsely chopped Italian plum tomatoes*

1. Cook fettuccine according to package directions while preparing sauce.

2. Melt butter in 2-quart saucepan over low heat. Stir in flour and add seasonings. Cook 1 minute, stirring.

3. Gradually add cream and shredded cheese, stirring constantly until cheese has melted. Remove from heat and set aside.

4. Drain fettuccine thoroughly and place in large bowl.

5. Add broccoli, green beans, carrot, and tomatoes. Stir reserved sauce and pour over pasta and vegetables. Toss gently and serve immediately.

*Makes 4½ cups*

TIP:

If desired, steam broccoli, green beans, and carrot 3 to 5 minutes until crisp-tender before adding to fettuccine.

# *Lasagne*

2 tablespoons olive oil

1 pound lean ground beef or
ground turkey

1 can (28 ounces) whole tomatoes,
undrained

2 cans (8 ounces each) tomato sauce

1 can (3 ounces) sliced mushrooms,
drained

2 tablespoons Instant Minced Onion

1½ teaspoons Oregano Leaves

1 teaspoon salt

1 teaspoon sugar

¼ teaspoon Basil Leaves

¼ teaspoon Rosemary Leaves

⅛ teaspoon Garlic Powder

8 ounces lasagne noodles, 9 strips

1 pound ricotta cheese

½ pound mozzarella cheese, sliced

½ cup grated Parmesan cheese

1. Heat oil in large skillet over medium heat. Add beef or turkey and cook, stirring, until beef is no longer pink or turkey is cooked. Drain off excess fat.

2. Add tomatoes, tomato sauce, mushrooms, minced onion, oregano, salt, sugar, basil, rosemary, and garlic powder to skillet. Mix well, cover, and cook over very low heat 2 hours or until sauce thickens.

3. Cook lasagne noodles according to package directions. Drain well and rinse under cold water. Separate carefully.

4. Preheat oven to 350°F.

5. Make first layer of lasagne in 12 x 8 x 2-inch baking pan by layering half of following ingredients in order given: noodles, meat sauce, ricotta cheese, sliced mozzarella, and Parmesan cheese. Repeat with remainder of same ingredients to make second layer, ending with Parmesan cheese.

6. Bake, uncovered, in preheated 350°F oven 30 minutes or until bubbly. Let stand 15 minutes before cutting.

*Makes 8 servings, 3 x 4 x 2 inches each*

VARIATION:

**Vegetable Lasagne:** Substitute 3 to 3½ cups cooked vegetables for meat in recipe.

## *SIDE DISHES / SAUCES*

# *Marinated Mushrooms*

*2 tablespoons vinegar*

*2 tablespoons olive oil*

*½ teaspoon Basil Leaves*

*½ teaspoon Marjoram Leaves*

*½ teaspoon Mustard Seed*

*¼ teaspoon Onion Salt*

*½ pound fresh mushrooms, sliced*

1. Place all ingredients except mushrooms in large bowl and stir to combine.
2. Add mushrooms, mix well, and cover.
3. Refrigerate at least 24 hours before serving.

*Makes 1 cup*

**MARJORAM**

# Cinnamon Baked Pineapple

1 large pineapple
¼ cup sugar

½ teaspoon Ground Cinnamon

1. Preheat oven to 400°F. Lightly grease shallow baking pan and set aside.
2. Cut off both ends of pineapple and remove skin and eyes with very sharp knife. Cut pineapple lengthwise into quarters. Cut each quarter in half lengthwise again. Remove core and cut each long wedge of pineapple into 1-inch-thick pieces about 1½ inches long.
3. Arrange pineapple pieces in single layer in prepared pan.
4. Mix sugar and cinnamon and sprinkle evenly over pineapple.
5. Bake in preheated 400°F oven 10 minutes.

*Makes 16 to 18 servings, 6 pieces each*
*(One large pineapple makes 100 to 110 bite-size wedges.)*

TIP:

Serve hot with ham, pork, chicken, or seafood.

# Vanilla Sauce

1 cup butter or margarine
½ teaspoon lemon juice

¼ teaspoon Pure Vanilla Extract

1. Melt butter in small saucepan over low heat.
2. Remove from heat and carefully pour off clear portion of butter into small bowl to make clarified butter.
3. Stir in lemon juice and vanilla.

*Makes ¾ cup*

TIP:

Serve hot with steamed lobster, Deviled Lobster Tails *(page 233)*, steamed vegetables, and/or other seafood.

*Lobster with Vanilla Sauce*

# Sauce Rémoulade

2 cups mayonnaise

1 can (6 ounces) tomato paste

2 anchovy fillets, rinsed and mashed

2 tablespoons India relish

1 tablespoon Instant Minced Onion

1 tablespoon chopped capers

1 tablespoon prepared mustard

1 teaspoon Parsley Flakes

¼ teaspoon Celery Salt

¼ teaspoon Tarragon Leaves

⅛ teaspoon Ground Red Pepper

1. Combine all ingredients in medium-size bowl and mix well.
2. Cover and refrigerate several hours to chill and allow flavors to blend.

*Makes 3½ cups*

TIP:

Serve with cold salmon, shrimp, lobster, or crab, picked over.* Excellent topping for lettuce, tossed salad, or avocados.

*(See page 47)

# Sauce Béarnaise

¼ cup white wine vinegar

1½ teaspoons Tarragon Leaves, divided

1 teaspoon Instant Minced Onion

1 teaspoon Parsley Flakes

¼ teaspoon salt

⅛ teaspoon Coarse Ground Black Pepper

Dash Ground Red Pepper

3 egg yolks

2 tablespoons cold butter, divided

½ cup butter, melted

1. Place vinegar, 1 teaspoon tarragon, minced onion, parsley, salt, and black and red pepper in small saucepan and stir to combine. Heat to boil and cook until mixture is reduced to 2 tablespoons. Strain through fine sieve into small bowl and set aside.
2. Beat egg yolks in top of double boiler until thick.
3. Add reserved vinegar mixture and 1 tablespoon cold butter. Cook over (not in) simmering water until mixture thickens, stirring constantly.

4. Remove from heat and add remaining 1 tablespoon cold butter. Stir to blend well.

5. Add melted butter very slowly, stirring constantly or beating with electric mixer at low speed.

6. Stir in remaining ½ teaspoon tarragon.

*Makes ¾ cup*

TIP:

Serve warm with chateaubriand, filet mignon, sirloin steak, roast leg of lamb, or broiled or poached fish.

# *Spicy Barbecue Sauce*

*3 cans (6 ounces each) tomato paste*

*2¼ cups (3 tomato paste cans) water*

*¼ cup vinegar*

*3 tablespoons Worcestershire sauce*

*3 tablespoons vegetable oil*

*2 tablespoons Instant Chopped Onions*

*2 teaspoons Season-All Seasoned Salt*

*1 teaspoon Ground Black Pepper*

*1 teaspoon Paprika*

*1 teaspoon Ground Mustard*

*½ teaspoon Ground Allspice*

*½ teaspoon Ground Cinnamon*

*½ teaspoon Chili Powder*

*½ teaspoon Ground Nutmeg*

*½ teaspoon Garlic Salt*

*¼ teaspoon Ground Red Pepper*

1. Place all ingredients in large saucepan and stir to combine.

2. Cover and slowly heat to boil. Reduce heat to very low and simmer 1 hour, stirring occasionally.

3. When cool, cover and refrigerate up to several weeks or keep in freezer.

*Makes 5 cups*

TIP:

Use to baste spareribs, pork chops, bologna roll, chicken, turkey, or beef during cooking.

# Molé Poblano

1 can (15 ounces) tomato purée

2 cans (4 ounces each) chopped green chilies

¼ cup lime juice

¼ cup unsweetened cocoa powder

2 tablespoons vegetable oil

1 tablespoon Instant Minced Onion

2 teaspoons Beef Flavor Base

1 teaspoon sugar

1 teaspoon Instant Minced Garlic

1 teaspoon Crushed Red Pepper

½ teaspoon Ground Cumin

¼ teaspoon Anise Seed

¼ teaspoon Coriander Seed

¼ teaspoon Ground Cinnamon

⅛ teaspoon Ground Cloves

1 cup water, divided

1. Combine all ingredients except water in food processor.
2. Add ½ cup water and process until well blended and smooth.
3. Pour into 1-quart saucepan and stir in remaining ½ cup water. Heat slowly to simmering and cook 2 to 3 minutes, stirring.

*Makes 3 cups*

TIP:

Serve over grilled or roasted chicken, pork, beef, lamb, or turkey.

# Spiced Cranberry Sauce

1 package (12 ounces) cranberries

1 cup sugar

1 cup water

1 Cinnamon Stick, 3 inches long

½ teaspoon Orange Peel

½ teaspoon Pure Vanilla Extract

1. Place all ingredients except vanilla in large saucepan. Stir to combine.
2. Heat to boil, reduce heat, and simmer 45 minutes or until very thick, stirring occasionally.
3. Remove from heat and set aside to cool to room temperature.
4. Remove and discard cinnamon stick and stir in vanilla. Cover and refrigerate until ready to serve.

*Makes 1¾ cups*

TIP:

Serve with poultry or ham.

# BREAD

## Quick Cinnamon Twists

*2 tablespoons sugar*

*½ teaspoon Ground Cinnamon*

*½ cup finely chopped nuts*

*1 can (10 ounces) refrigerator biscuits*

*2 tablespoons butter or margarine*

1. Preheat oven to 475°F.
2. Place sugar, cinnamon, and nuts in pie plate or other flat dish and stir to combine.
3. Remove refrigerator biscuits from package and pull each to about 6 inches in length.
4. Melt butter in small pan over low heat and leave butter in pan. Dip each biscuit in melted butter and roll in sugar-nut mixture.
5. Twist and place on ungreased cookie sheet.
6. Bake in preheated 475°F oven 8 minutes.
7. Remove from cookie sheet and place twists on wire rack to cool slightly. Serve warm.

*Makes 10 twists*

## Corn Sticks Rosemary

*1 package (12 ounces) corn bread mix*　　*1 teaspoon Rosemary Leaves*

1. Coat corn stick pans with no-stick cooking spray.
2. Pour corn bread mix into medium-size bowl. Add rosemary and prepare mix according to package directions.
3. Spoon batter into prepared pans, filling almost full.
4. Bake in preheated oven according to package directions.

*Makes 14 to 16 corn sticks or muffins*

TIP:

Instead of corn stick pans, muffin pans filled two-thirds full can be used.

# *Dilly Bread*

*1 package (16 ounces) hot roll mix*

*¼ cup butter or margarine*

*2 tablespoons Dill Weed*

*2 tablespoons Freeze-Dried Chives*

*2 tablespoons Parsley Flakes*

*½ teaspoon Onion Powder*

*¼ teaspoon salt*

*¼ teaspoon Ground Black Pepper*

1. Lightly grease 8½ x 4 x 2½-inch loaf pan and set aside.

2. Prepare hot roll mix according to package directions. Cover with damp towel and let rise in warm, draft-free place until dough doubles in size.

3. Punch dough down and turn out onto lightly floured surface. Roll out to 8 x 14-inch rectangle.

4. Melt butter in small saucepan over low heat and stir in remaining ingredients.

5. Spread butter-herb mixture over dough and roll tightly from 1 short side to make 3 x 8-inch roll. Pinch edge of dough to seal and place, seam side down, in prepared pan.

6. Lightly grease top of loaf. Cover with damp towel and let rise in warm, draft-free place until dough doubles in size.

7. Preheat oven to 375°F.

8. Bake in preheated 375°F oven 50 to 55 minutes. Serve warm.

*Makes 1 loaf, 8 x 4 inches*

**DILL**

# Rum Buns

1 package (16 ounces) hot roll mix

2 cups confectioners sugar

1 bottle (1 ounce) Rum Extract

4 teaspoons water

3 tablespoons butter or margarine, softened

Ground Cinnamon

1. Lightly grease 12-cup muffin pan and set aside.
2. Prepare hot roll mix according to package directions. Cover with damp towel and let rise in warm, draft-free place until dough doubles in size.
3. Punch dough down and turn out onto lightly floured surface. Roll out to 10 x 12-inch rectangle.
4. Place sugar in bowl and stir in rum extract and water. Mix until smooth.
5. Spread softened butter over surface of dough and spread half of sugar mixture over butter. Sprinkle with cinnamon.
6. Roll up dough from 1 long side and pinch edge of dough to seal. Cut into twelve 1-inch slices.
7. Place slices, cut side down, in prepared muffin pan.
8. Cover with damp towel and let rise in warm, draft-free place until dough doubles in size.
9. Preheat oven to 350°F.
10. Bake in preheated 350°F oven 25 minutes.
11. Remove from pan immediately and drizzle remaining half of sugar mixture over buns. Serve warm.

*Makes 12 buns*

TIP:

To make buns with milder rum flavor, reduce rum extract to ½ bottle and add 1 teaspoon additional water.

# Hot Cross Buns

1 package (16 ounces) hot roll mix

1 teaspoon Ground Cinnamon

¼ teaspoon Ground Allspice

¼ teaspoon Ground Cardamom

½ cup raisins

Yeast packet from hot roll mix

1 cup hot water (120°F to 130°F)

2 tablespoons butter or margarine, softened

1 egg

GLAZE

¾ cup confectioners sugar

¾ teaspoon Pure Lemon Extract

1 tablespoon water

1. Lightly grease cookie sheet and set aside.

2. Empty contents of flour mixture packet from hot roll mix into large bowl. Stir in cinnamon, allspice, cardamom, and raisins. Add contents of yeast packet and mix well.

3. Stir in 1 cup hot water, butter, and egg. Mix just until dough pulls away from sides of bowl.

4. Turn out onto lightly floured surface, flour hands, and knead 5 minutes. Cover dough with inverted bowl and let rest 5 minutes.

5. Shape dough into eighteen 2-inch balls and place on prepared cookie sheet. Cover with damp towel and let rise in warm, draft-free place until dough doubles in size.

6. Preheat oven to 400°F.

7. Bake in preheated 400°F oven 15 minutes. Remove from cookie sheet and cool on wire rack.

8. To make glaze, place sugar, lemon extract, and 1 tablespoon water in small bowl and stir until well combined. Drizzle cross on top of each bun.

*Makes 18 buns*

**CINNAMON**

# Belgian Waffles

4 eggs

1½ cups buttermilk

2 cups sifted all-purpose flour

2 tablespoons sugar

2 teaspoons baking powder

1 teaspoon baking soda

½ teaspoon salt

¼ teaspoon Ground Cinnamon

⅛ teaspoon Ground Nutmeg

6 tablespoons butter or margarine, melted

Honey Spice Butter (recipe below) or strawberries and whipped cream to serve, if desired

1. Beat eggs in large bowl until light. Stir in buttermilk.
2. Sift flour with sugar, baking powder, baking soda, salt, cinnamon, and nutmeg. Add to egg mixture gradually, beating with electric mixer until smooth.
3. Continue beating while slowly adding melted butter.
4. Cook in preheated electric or manual Belgian waffle iron.
5. Serve with Honey Spice Butter or strawberries and whipped cream.

*Makes 4 cups batter, 4 to 6 waffles*

TIP:

Batter can be made ahead of time, covered, and refrigerated up to 24 hours.

# Honey Spice Butter

½ cup butter or margarine, softened

2 teaspoons honey

½ teaspoon Ground Cinnamon

⅛ teaspoon Ground Nutmeg

1. Combine all ingredients, mixing well. Cover and refrigerate.
2. Use as spread on waffles, muffins, biscuits, toast, or pancakes.

*Makes ½ cup*

VARIATION:

Add 1 teaspoon Orange Peel and dash of Ground Cloves to butter-honey mixture instead of cinnamon and nutmeg.

# Cardamom Crescent

CARDAMOM FRUIT FILLING

1 cup chopped dates

⅓ cup orange juice

¼ cup granulated sugar

¼ teaspoon Ground Cardamom

⅛ teaspoon salt

¼ cup chopped walnuts or pecans

1 tablespoon butter or margarine

DOUGH

½ cup milk

1 package (¼ ounce) active dry yeast

1 egg, beaten

3 tablespoons granulated sugar

1 teaspoon salt

1 teaspoon Lemon Peel

½ teaspoon Ground Cardamom

2 to 2¼ cups all-purpose flour

6 tablespoons butter or margarine, softened, divided

GLAZE

1 cup confectioners sugar

4 teaspoons milk or water

1. To make filling, place dates, orange juice, ¼ cup granulated sugar, cardamom, and salt in small saucepan.

2. Cook, stirring, over medium heat until mixture thickens. Remove from heat and stir in nuts and butter. Set aside.

3. To prepare dough, scald milk and place in large bowl. Set aside to cool to lukewarm. Add yeast to warm milk and stir to dissolve.

4. Add egg, 3 tablespoons granulated sugar, salt, lemon peel, and cardamom to milk mixture. Stir to mix well.

5. Gradually beat in 2 cups flour, mixing to moderately stiff dough. If dough is soft, add up to ¼ cup additional flour.

6. Turn out onto lightly floured surface, flour hands, and knead just until smooth.

7. Place in lightly greased bowl and turn to coat entire surface of dough. Cover with damp towel and let rise in warm, draft-free place until dough doubles in size, about 1½ hours.

8. Turn out onto lightly floured surface and roll out to 15 x 12-inch rectangle. Spread 4 tablespoons softened butter over dough.

9. Fold 1 short end of dough in to middle of dough and fold other short end over to opposite edge of dough to make 3 even layers.

10. Roll out again to 15 x 12-inch rectangle. Spread remaining 2 tablespoons softened butter over dough.

11. Fold as before, cover with damp towel, and let stand 15 minutes.

12. Lightly grease cookie sheet and set aside.

13. Roll out dough to 16 x 10-inch rectangle and spread with reserved Cardamom Fruit Filling.

14. Roll up dough, from 1 long side and pinch seam and ends to seal.

15. Place, seam side down, on prepared cookie sheet and shape into crescent. Cut two-thirds of the way through top of crescent at about 1-inch intervals using scissors or razor blade.

16. Cover with damp towel and let rise in warm, draft-free place until dough doubles in size, about 1 hour.

17. Preheat oven to 350°F.

18. Bake in preheated 350°F oven 25 to 30 minutes. Remove from cookie sheet and cool on wire rack.

19. To make glaze, place confectioners sugar and milk in small bowl and stir to combine. Drizzle over top of cooled crescent.

*Makes 12 slices, 1 inch each*

**CARDAMOM**

# *Philadelphia Sticky Buns*

DOUGH

*1 cup milk*

*1 package (¼ ounce) active dry yeast*

*¼ cup warm water (110°F)*

*3 to 4½ cups sifted all-purpose flour, divided*

*¼ cup butter or margarine*

*⅓ cup granulated sugar*

*1 egg, well beaten*

*1 teaspoon salt*

*¼ teaspoon Ground Nutmeg*

SYRUP

*1 cup dark corn syrup*

*½ cup honey*

*½ cup firmly packed dark brown sugar*

*⅓ cup butter or margarine*

FILLING

*½ cup firmly packed dark brown sugar*

*1 tablespoon Ground Cinnamon*

*⅛ teaspoon Ground Ginger*

*¼ cup butter or margarine, softened*

*½ cup raisins*

1. Scald milk in small saucepan and cool to lukewarm. Pour into large bowl. Dissolve yeast in warm water and add to cooled milk.

2. Add 1½ cups flour to milk mixture and mix until smooth. Cover with damp towel and let rise in warm, draft-free place until top is bubbly, about 30 minutes.

3. Cream butter with ⅓ cup granulated sugar in small bowl. Add egg, salt, and nutmeg. Mix until smooth and add to dough.

4. Add additional flour, mixing well until mixing becomes difficult. Turn out onto floured work surface and knead in as much remaining flour as necessary to make soft dough that is easy to handle.

5. Place in lightly greased bowl and turn to coat entire surface of dough. Cover with damp towel and let rise in warm, draft-free place until dough doubles in size, 1 to 2 hours.

6. While dough is rising, prepare syrup by combining syrup ingredients in small saucepan. Heat over medium heat until butter has melted and sugar has dissolved. Set aside to cool slightly.

7. Roll out dough on lightly floured surface to 12 x 8-inch rectangle, ¾ inch thick.

8. To fill dough, combine ½ cup brown sugar with cinnamon and ginger in a small bowl. Spread ¼ cup softened butter over dough and sprinkle sugar-spice mixture over butter. Scatter raisins over all.

9. Roll up filled dough from 1 long side jelly-roll style. Pinch edge of dough to seal and cut into 12 slices.

10. Pour half of reserved syrup into 13 x 9 x 2-inch baking pan. Place buns, cut side down, on syrup and pour remaining syrup over.

11. Cover with damp towel and let rise in warm, draft-free place 30 minutes.

12. Preheat oven to 350°F.

13. Bake in preheated 350°F oven 45 minutes or until golden brown.

*Makes 12 sticky buns*

*Philadelphia Sticky Buns (see photo on page 284)*

# Apple-Nut Bread

2 eggs

1 cup sugar

½ teaspoon Pure Vanilla Extract

2 cups all-purpose flour

1 teaspoon baking soda

½ teaspoon salt

½ teaspoon Ground Nutmeg

½ teaspoon Ground Cinnamon

½ cup vegetable oil

2 tablespoons dairy sour cream

1 cup peeled, chopped apples

1 cup coarsely chopped walnuts

1. Preheat oven to 350°F. Lightly grease 9 x 5 x 3-inch loaf pan and set aside.

2. Beat eggs, sugar, and vanilla in large mixer bowl until light and fluffy.

3. Sift flour with baking soda, salt, nutmeg, and cinnamon. Add to egg mixture alternating with oil and sour cream and beating well after each addition.

4. Stir in apples and nuts and spoon into prepared pan.

5. Bake in preheated 350°F oven 1 hour.

6. Cool in pan on wire rack 10 minutes. Remove from pan and cool completely on rack.

*Makes 1 loaf, 9 x 5 x 3 inches*

# Maple-Walnut Bread

¼ cup butter or margarine, softened

1¼ cups sugar

1 egg

1 teaspoon Maple Flavor Extract

½ teaspoon Pure Vanilla Extract

¼ teaspoon Ground Cinnamon

1 cup mashed ripe bananas
   (2 to 3 medium-size bananas)

¼ cup dairy sour cream

2 cups all-purpose flour

1 teaspoon baking powder

½ teaspoon baking soda

½ teaspoon salt

½ cup chopped walnuts

1. Preheat oven to 350°F. Lightly grease and flour 9 x 5 x 3-inch loaf pan and set aside.

2. Cream butter with sugar in large mixer bowl until smooth.

3. Add egg, maple flavor extract, vanilla, and cinnamon. Beat with electric mixer at medium speed 2 minutes.

4. Add bananas and sour cream and mix well.

5. Sift flour with baking powder, baking soda, and salt. Add to banana mixture and mix well.

6. Stir in walnuts and spoon into prepared pan.

7. Bake in preheated 350°F oven 65 to 70 minutes or until toothpick inserted in center comes out clean.

8. Cool in pan on wire rack 10 minutes. Remove from pan and cool completely on rack.

*Makes 1 loaf, 9 x 5 x 3 inches*

VANILLA

*Philadelphia Sticky Buns (see recipe on page 282)*

## DESSERTS

# Pumpkin Cheesecake

CRUST

1¼ cups graham cracker or vanilla
    wafer crumbs

½ cup finely chopped walnuts

¼ cup granulated sugar

5 tablespoons butter or margarine,
    melted

½ teaspoon Ground Nutmeg

FILLING

3 packages (8 ounces each) Neufchâtel
    or cream cheese, softened

¾ cup granulated sugar

¾ cup firmly packed brown sugar

4 eggs

1 can (16 ounces) pumpkin

1 teaspoon Pure Vanilla Extract

1¼ teaspoons Ground Cinnamon

½ teaspoon Ground Nutmeg

¼ teaspoon Ground Cloves

Whipped cream to decorate,
    if desired

1. To make crust, place all crust ingredients in medium-size bowl and mix thoroughly.

2. Spoon into 10-inch springform pan and spread evenly on bottom of pan. Press firmly onto bottom and halfway up sides of pan with bottom of small, straight-sided glass.

3. Preheat oven to 350°F.

4. To make filling, place cheese, granulated sugar, and brown sugar in large mixer bowl and beat with electric mixer until fluffy. Add eggs, 1 at a time, beating well after each addition. Stir in pumpkin, vanilla, and spices. Mix thoroughly and pour into crust.

5. Bake in preheated 350°F oven 1 hour and 20 minutes.

6. Remove from oven and cool completely in pan on wire rack. Cover and refrigerate to chill overnight.

7. Run knife around inside edge of springform pan and release sides of pan. Place on serving plate and decorate with whipped cream.

*Makes 10-inch cheesecake, 16 wedges*

# Cheesecake *Élégante*

**CRUST**

*1½ cups graham cracker crumbs*

*¼ cup sugar*

*¼ cup butter or margarine, softened*

*½ teaspoon Ground Cinnamon*

**FILLING**

*4 packages (8 ounces each) cream cheese, room temperature*

*4 eggs, beaten*

*1⅓ cups sugar*

*1 tablespoon Pure Vanilla Extract*

**TOPPING**

*2 cups dairy sour cream*

*⅓ cup sugar*

*1 tablespoon Pure Vanilla Extract*

*¼ teaspoon Rum Extract*

1. To make crust, place all crust ingredients in medium-size bowl and mix thoroughly.

2. Spoon into 9-inch springform pan and spread evenly on bottom of pan. Press firmly onto bottom and 1 inch up sides of pan with bottom of small, straight-sided glass.

3. Preheat oven to 325°F.

4. To make filling, place cream cheese in mixer bowl and beat with electric mixer until soft and creamy. Add eggs, sugar, and vanilla and beat until very smooth. Pour into crust.

5. Bake in preheated 325°F oven 1 hour and 15 minutes.

6. Remove from oven and increase oven temperature to 450°F.

7. To make topping, place all topping ingredients in bowl and stir to mix well. Spoon over hot cheesecake and smooth top.

8. Return cake to oven and bake 7 minutes.

9. Remove from oven and cool to room temperature in pan on wire rack.

10. Cover and refrigerate 4 hours or overnight.

11. Run knife around inside edge of springform pan and release sides of pan. Place on serving plate.

*Makes 9-inch cheesecake, 12 wedges*

# Lady Baltimore Cake

CAKE

2½ cups sifted all-purpose flour

1 tablespoon baking powder

¼ teaspoon salt

1 cup butter or margarine, softened

2 cups sugar, divided

¾ cup milk

1 teaspoon Pure Almond Extract

6 egg whites, room temperature

FROSTING

1½ cups sugar

3 egg whites, room temperature

¼ cup water

3 tablespoons light corn syrup

¼ teaspoon Cream of Tartar

⅛ teaspoon salt

¼ teaspoon Pure Almond Extract

1 cup chopped pecans

1 cup chopped raisins

½ cup finely chopped dried figs

1. Preheat oven to 375°F. Lightly coat three 8-inch round cake pans with no-stick cooking spray and dust with flour. Set aside.

2. Sift flour with baking powder and salt.

3. Place butter and 1½ cups sugar in large mixer bowl and cream with electric mixer until light and fluffy. Add milk gradually, alternating with dry ingredients. Add almond extract, beat well, and scrape down bowl. Beat at medium speed 3 minutes.

4. Place egg whites in separate mixer bowl and beat until foamy. Gradually add remaining ½ cup sugar, beating at high speed until stiff peaks form when beaters are lifted. Gently fold beaten egg whites into batter. Divide batter evenly in prepared pans.

5. Bake in preheated 375°F oven 30 to 35 minutes or until toothpick inserted in center of cakes comes out clean.

6. Cool in pans on wire racks 5 minutes. Remove from pans and cool completely on racks.

7. To make frosting, place sugar, egg whites, water, corn syrup, cream of tartar, and salt in top of double boiler and beat with electric hand mixer at low speed over (not in) simmering water.

8. Adjust mixer to high speed and beat until soft peaks form, about 7 minutes. Remove from heat.

9. Add almond extract and continue beating at high speed until stiff peaks form when beaters are lifted. Scrape down sides occasionally. Add pecans, raisins, and figs. Stir with spoon to mix well.

10. Place cooled cake layer on serving plate bottom side up. Spread frosting over layer and top with second layer. Cover with frosting and add third layer top side up. Spread remaining frosting on top and sides of cake.

*Makes 3-layer, 8-inch cake*

# Gingerbread Chiffon Cake

*2 teaspoons baking soda*

*1 teaspoon salt*

*2 teaspoons Ground Ginger*

*2 teaspoons Ground Cinnamon*

*½ teaspoon Ground Cardamom*

*2¼ cups sifted all-purpose flour*

*1½ cups firmly packed
   dark brown sugar*

*¾ cup buttermilk*

*½ cup molasses*

*½ cup canola or other vegetable oil*

*4 egg yolks*

*8 egg whites (1 cup),
   room temperature*

*½ teaspoon Cream of Tartar*

1. Preheat oven to 325°F.

2. Add baking soda, salt, and spices to sifted flour and sift again.

3. Place sugar, buttermilk, molasses, oil, and egg yolks in large mixer bowl and beat with electric mixer until well combined. Add dry ingredients and mix until smooth.

4. Place egg whites in large mixer bowl with cream of tartar and beat with electric mixer until stiff peaks form when beaters are lifted. Fold into batter until blended.

5. Pour into ungreased 10-inch Bundt pan or tube pan.

6. Bake in preheated 325°F oven 1 hour and 10 minutes.

7. Cool in pan on wire rack 10 minutes. Remove from pan and cool completely on rack.

*Makes 10-inch cake*

# Golden Saffron Cake with Sour Cream Frosting

CAKE

½ cup butter or margarine, softened

⅛ teaspoon crushed Saffron threads

1 cup granulated sugar

2 eggs

1 teaspoon Pure Vanilla Extract

2½ cups sifted cake flour

1 tablespoon baking powder

¼ teaspoon salt

1 cup milk

SOUR CREAM FROSTING

2 boxes (16 ounces each) confectioners sugar (8 cups)

2 egg whites

¼ cup white vegetable shortening

¼ cup dairy sour cream

1 teaspoon Pure Vanilla Extract

1. Preheat oven to 375°F. Lightly grease and flour two 9-inch round cake pans and set aside.

2. Place butter and saffron in large mixer bowl and cream with electric mixer at medium speed 2 minutes. Add granulated sugar and beat until light and fluffy. Add eggs, 1 at a time, beating well after each addition. Stir in vanilla.

3. Sift flour with baking powder and salt. Add dry ingredients to batter alternating with milk, mixing at low speed. Divide batter evenly in prepared pans.

4. Bake in preheated 375°F oven 25 to 30 minutes.

5. Remove cake from oven and cool in pans on wire racks 5 to 10 minutes. Remove from pans and cool completely on racks.

6. To make frosting, sift all of the confectioners sugar into large bowl. Set 2 cups aside.

7. Place egg whites in small bowl and beat until stiff peaks form when beaters are lifted.

8. Place shortening in large mixer bowl and beat with electric mixer until fluffy. Add beaten egg whites, sour cream, vanilla and remaining 6 cups of confectioners sugar. Mix well. Beat in as much of the reserved 2 cups confectioners sugar as necessary to make frosting of desired spreading consistency.

9. Place 1 cake layer on serving plate bottom side up. Spread with frosting and add second layer top side up. Spread remaining frosting on top and sides of cake.

*Makes 2-layer, 9-inch cake*

TIP:

Crush saffron with fingers to break into ⅛-inch-long pieces.

# Cinnamon Chocolate Cake with Fudge Frosting

CAKE

2¼ cups sugar

¾ cup butter or margarine, softened

2 teaspoons Pure Vanilla Extract

1 teaspoon Ground Cinnamon

6 eggs

4 squares (4 ounces) unsweetened baking chocolate, melted

3 cups sifted cake flour

2 teaspoons baking soda

1 teaspoon salt

1½ cups ice water, divided

FUDGE FROSTING

2 packages (12 ounces each) semisweet chocolate morsels

1 can (14 ounces) sweetened condensed milk

1 teaspoon Pure Vanilla Extract

½ teaspoon Ground Cinnamon

½ cup coffee-flavored liqueur

1. Preheat oven to 350°F. Lightly grease three 9-inch round cake pans and line each pan with wax paper. Set aside.

2. Place sugar, butter, vanilla, and cinnamon in large mixer bowl. Cream with electric mixer until light and fluffy. Beat in eggs and melted chocolate.

3. Sift flour with baking soda and salt. Beat one-third of dry ingredients into chocolate mixture and stir in ¾ cup ice water.

4. Repeat, using one-third of dry ingredients and remaining ¾ cup ice water. Stir in remaining dry ingredients. Divide batter evenly in prepared pans.

5. Bake in preheated 350°F oven 35 to 40 minutes. Do not overbake.

6. To make frosting, place about 1 inch water in bottom of double boiler and heat to boil. Place chocolate morsels, condensed milk, vanilla, and cinnamon in top of double boiler. Cover and place over (not in) boiling water. Remove double boiler from heat. Let stand over water until chocolate has melted. Add liqueur and stir until smooth and glossy.

7. Remove cake from oven and cool in pans on wire racks 10 minutes. Remove from pans, peel off wax paper, and place 1 layer on serving plate bottom side up. Spread frosting over layer and top with second layer. Cover with frosting and add third layer top side up. Spread remaining frosting on top and sides of cake.

*Makes 3-layer, 9-inch cake*

# Rum Runner's Pound Cake

CAKE

1 teaspoon baking powder

½ teaspoon salt

¼ teaspoon Ground Mace

3½ cups sifted cake flour

1¾ cups butter or margarine, softened

2 cups superfine sugar

8 eggs

1 teaspoon Pure Vanilla Extract

½ teaspoon Pure Almond Extract

½ teaspoon Pure Lemon Extract

RUM SYRUP

1 cup confectioners sugar

½ cup butter or margarine, melted

¼ cup hot water

2 tablespoons Rum Extract

1. Preheat oven to 325°F. Lightly grease and flour 10-inch Bundt pan or two 9 x 5 x 3-inch loaf pans and set aside.

2. Add baking powder, salt, and mace to sifted flour and sift twice again. Set aside.

3. Place butter in large mixer bowl and cream with electric mixer until light and fluffy. Gradually add superfine sugar, beating at high speed. Continue beating until mixture resembles whipped cream. Add eggs, 1 at a time, beating well after each addition.

4. Stir in half of flour mixture, beating at lowest speed of mixer. Add extracts and remaining flour mixture. Mix well.

5. Pour batter into prepared pan(s). Cut through batter several times with knife to break air bubbles.

6. Bake in preheated 325°F oven 1 hour and 10 minutes.

7. Remove from pan(s) immediately and place on wire rack set on cookie sheet. Pierce cake(s) all over top with tines of fork.

8. To make syrup, place syrup ingredients in small bowl. Mix well to combine and pour slowly over hot cake(s). Allow cake(s) to cool and place on serving plate(s).

*Makes 10-inch Bundt cake or 2 loaf cakes*

# Old-Fashioned Spice Cake with Cinnamon Frosting

CAKE

2½ cups sifted cake flour

2 teaspoons baking powder

½ teaspoon baking soda

½ teaspoon salt

1 teaspoon Ground Cinnamon

½ teaspoon Ground Allspice

¼ teaspoon Ground Cloves

¼ teaspoon Ground Nutmeg

½ cup vegetable shortening

1¼ cups firmly packed brown sugar

3 eggs

1 cup buttermilk

CINNAMON FROSTING

1 box (16 ounces) confectioners sugar

1 tablespoon Ground Cinnamon

¼ cup butter or margarine, melted

1 egg white

Dash salt

3 tablespoons milk

1. Preheat oven to 350°F. Lightly grease and flour two 9-inch round cake pans and set aside.

2. Sift flour, baking powder, baking soda, salt, and spices into bowl.

3. Place shortening and brown sugar in large mixer bowl and cream with electric mixer until light and fluffy. Add eggs, 1 at a time, beating well after each addition. Stir in flour mixture alternating with buttermilk.

4. Divide batter evenly in prepared pans.

5. Bake in preheated 350°F oven 30 to 35 minutes.

6. Cool cakes in pans on wire racks 5 to 10 minutes. Remove from pans and cool completely on racks.

7. To make frosting, sift confectioners sugar and cinnamon into bowl.

8. Place melted butter and ½ cup sugar mixture in separate mixer bowl and cream with electric mixer or by hand. Beat in egg white and salt.

9. Add remaining sugar mixture and milk. Beat with mixer at high speed to spreading consistency.

10. Place 1 cake layer on serving plate bottom side up. Spread with frosting and add second layer top side up. Spread remaining frosting on top and sides of cake.

*Makes 2-layer, 9-inch cake*

# Chocolate Carrot Cake with Dark Chocolate Frosting

CAKE

2 cups cake flour

2 cups granulated sugar

3 tablespoons unsweetened cocoa powder

1 teaspoon baking powder

1 teaspoon Ground Cinnamon

¼ teaspoon Ground Mace

⅛ teaspoon Ground Nutmeg

1 cup butter or margarine, softened

4 eggs

1 tablespoon Pure Vanilla Extract

3 cups shredded carrots

4 squares (4 ounces) semisweet chocolate, cut into small pieces

1 cup finely chopped walnuts

DARK CHOCOLATE FROSTING

4 squares (4 ounces) semisweet chocolate

2 tablespoons light corn syrup

1 teaspoon Pure Vanilla Extract

⅛ teaspoon Pure Almond Extract

⅛ teaspoon Ground Cinnamon

1 cup confectioners sugar

2 tablespoons hot water

1. Preheat oven to 350°F. Lightly grease and flour 13 x 9 x 2-inch baking pan. Set aside.

2. Sift flour, granulated sugar, cocoa, baking powder, cinnamon, mace, and nutmeg into bowl.

3. Place butter in large mixer bowl and cream with electric mixer until fluffy. Add eggs and vanilla and beat until light and creamy.

4. Add dry ingredients and carrots. Beat at medium speed 2 minutes. Stir in chocolate and walnuts. Pour into prepared pan.

5. Bake in preheated 350°F oven 40 to 45 minutes.

6. To make frosting, melt chocolate in top of double boiler over (not in) simmering water. Add corn syrup, vanilla, almond extract, and cinnamon and mix well with spoon. Stir in confectioners sugar. Add hot water gradually, mixing until smooth.

7. Frost cake in pan while cake is still hot.

*Makes 1 cake, 13 x 9 x 2 inches*

# Poppy Seed Cake

4 eggs, room temperature

1½ cups sugar, divided

1 cup butter or margarine, softened

⅓ cup Poppy Seed

1 teaspoon baking soda

1 cup dairy sour cream, room temperature

2 cups sifted cake flour

1. Preheat oven to 350°F.

2. Separate eggs and set egg yolks aside.

3. Place egg whites in mixer bowl and beat with electric mixer until almost stiff. Gradually beat in ½ cup sugar and continue beating until stiff peaks form when beaters are lifted. Set aside.

4. Place butter and remaining 1 cup sugar in large mixer bowl. Cream with electric mixer until light and fluffy. Add reserved egg yolks, 1 at a time, beating well after each addition. Stir in poppy seed.

5. Combine baking soda and sour cream. Add to batter alternating with flour, and mixing after each addition just until smooth.

6. Gently fold in beaten egg whites.

7. Spoon into ungreased 9-inch tube pan.

8. Bake in preheated 350°F oven 1 hour.

9. Cool cake in pan on wire rack 5 to 10 minutes. Loosen around sides of pan and carefully turn out onto wire rack. Cool cake completely on rack.

*Makes 9-inch ring cake*

**POPPY**

# Applesauce Cake

½ cup butter or margarine, softened

1½ cups sugar

2 eggs, beaten

1 teaspoon baking powder

½ teaspoon baking soda

1 teaspoon Ground Cinnamon

½ teaspoon Ground Nutmeg

½ teaspoon Ground Cloves

¼ teaspoon salt

2 cups sifted all-purpose flour

1 cup applesauce

1 cup chopped golden seedless raisins

1 tablespoon all-purpose flour

1 cup chopped pecans

1. Preheat oven to 350°F. Lightly grease and flour 9 x 5 x 3-inch loaf pan and set aside.
2. Place butter and sugar in large mixer bowl and cream with electric mixer until light and fluffy. Add eggs and beat well.
3. Add baking powder, baking soda, spices, and salt to sifted flour and sift again. Add to butter mixture alternating with applesauce.
4. Coat raisins with remaining 1 tablespoon flour and stir into batter with pecans. Pour into prepared pan.
5. Bake in preheated 350°F oven 1 hour.
6. Cool cake in pan on wire rack 5 to 10 minutes. Remove from pan and cool completely on rack.

*Makes 1 loaf cake, 9 x 5 inches*

# Spiced Shortbread

1¼ cups butter or margarine, softened

¼ teaspoon Pure Almond Extract

⅛ teaspoon Ground Mace

⅛ teaspoon Ground Nutmeg

2½ cups sifted all-purpose flour

1 cup confectioners sugar

⅛ teaspoon salt

1. Preheat oven to 250°F.
2. Place butter in large mixer bowl and beat with electric mixer at low speed until fluffy. Add almond extract, mace, and nutmeg.

3. Add flour, sugar, and salt gradually. Mix thoroughly by hand. Do not use electric mixer.

4. Press firmly into 8 x 1-inch round shortbread mold, or place on ungreased cookie sheet and form into 8-inch circle.

5. Bake in preheated 250°F oven 2½ hours. Cool in pan on wire rack 30 minutes. Turn out onto serving plate.

*Makes 1 shortbread, 8 inches round*

# Tiramisu

*4 packages (8 ounces each) mascarpone or cream cheese, room temperature*

*1 cup plus 2 teaspoons sugar, divided*

*½ cup light cream*

*1 teaspoon Brandy Extract, divided*

*½ teaspoon Pure Orange Extract*

*½ teaspoon Pure Vanilla Extract*

*1½ cups cold strong black coffee*

*48 ladyfingers*

*8 ounces milk chocolate, grated*

1. Place mascarpone cheese in large mixer bowl and beat with electric mixer until light and fluffy.

2. Add 1 cup sugar, cream, ½ teaspoon brandy extract, orange extract, and vanilla, beating at high speed 1 minute. Set aside.

3. Place coffee, remaining 2 teaspoons sugar, and remaining ½ teaspoon brandy extract in 2-cup glass measure and stir until sugar has dissolved. Set aside.

4. Break ladyfingers into thirds and arrange half of pieces in bottom of 12 dessert dishes. Drizzle half of reserved coffee mixture evenly over ladyfingers and spoon half of cheese mixture on top. Sprinkle with half of grated chocolate.

5. Repeat with second layer of ladyfingers, coffee mixture, cheese mixture, and chocolate, ending with chocolate.

6. Cover and refrigerate at least 2 hours.

*Makes 12 servings, 1 cup each*

# Ginger Dessert Waffles

*½ cup butter or margarine*

*1 cup sugar*

*2 eggs*

*1 teaspoon Pure Vanilla Extract*

*1 teaspoon Orange Peel*

*2½ cups sifted all-purpose flour*

*1 tablespoon Ground Ginger*

*1 teaspoon Ground Cinnamon*

*1 teaspoon baking soda*

*¼ teaspoon salt*

*⅔ cup buttermilk*

*Ice cream, whipped cream, or maple syrup to serve, if desired*

1. Cream butter and sugar in large bowl until light and fluffy. Add eggs, 1 at a time, beating well after each addition. Stir in vanilla and orange peel.

2. Sift flour, ginger, cinnamon, baking soda, and salt into separate bowl.

3. Add dry ingredients and buttermilk alternately to butter mixture, beginning and ending with dry ingredients. Mix well after each addition.

4. Bake in preheated electric or manual waffle iron. Serve with ice cream, whipped cream, or maple syrup.

*Makes 10 waffles, 4 x 4 inches each*

# Strawberries with Brie Sauce

*1 quart strawberries, washed and hulled*

*8 ounces Brie*

*1 cup heavy cream*

*4 teaspoons sugar*

*⅛ teaspoon Ground Cardamom*

*½ teaspoon Pure Vanilla Extract*

*¼ teaspoon Pure Orange Extract*

1. Place strawberries in serving dish, cover, and refrigerate until chilled.

2. Trim rind from Brie and allow cheese to soften at room temperature. Cut into small pieces and set aside.

3. Place cream, sugar, and cardamom in top of double boiler over (not in) simmering water. Heat, stirring, just until sugar has dissolved.

4. Add reserved Brie and melt very slowly, stirring gently. Remove from heat when smooth and creamy. Gently stir vanilla and orange extracts into Brie mixture.

5. Pour sauce into small pitcher and serve hot over chilled whole strawberries.

*Makes 4 to 6 servings*

*Strawberries with Brie Sauce*

# Strawberries Romanoff

1 quart strawberries, washed
   and hulled

¼ cup orange juice

¼ cup Cognac

¼ cup Cointreau

½ teaspoon plus ⅛ teaspoon
   Ground Mace, divided

1 cup heavy cream

¼ cup sugar

1 quart vanilla ice cream

1. Place strawberries in 2-quart glass or stainless steel bowl. Add orange juice, Cognac, Cointreau, and ½ teaspoon mace. Mix well, cover, and refrigerate to marinate overnight.

2. Place cream, sugar, and remaining ⅛ teaspoon mace in chilled bowl and beat with electric mixer until stiff.

3. Allow ice cream to soften slightly at room temperature, but do not allow it to melt. Place in mixer bowl and beat with electric mixer. Fold in whipped cream.

4. Use slotted spoon to remove berries from marinade, reserving marinade. Add berries to cream mixture and stir gently.

5. Spoon into serving bowls and serve immediately. Spoon reserved marinade over each serving.

*Makes 8 servings, 1 cup each*

# Homemade Peppercorn Ice Cream

3 cups half and half

2 cups heavy cream

1 can (15 ounces) sweetened
   coconut milk

1⅓ cups sugar, divided

12 Whole Allspice

1 Vanilla Bean, 2 inches long,
   split lengthwise

½ teaspoon salt

5 egg yolks

2 tablespoons crushed Green Peppercorns

1 tablespoon Coarse Ground Black Pepper

Sliced strawberries to serve, if desired

1. Place half and half, heavy cream, coconut milk, ⅔ cup sugar, allspice, vanilla bean, and salt in saucepan. Stir to mix well and heat to simmer.

2. Place egg yolks and remaining ⅔ cup sugar in medium-size bowl and beat until fluffy. Add 1 cup cream mixture in slow steady stream, beating constantly. Pour back into saucepan and cook, stirring, over medium heat until slightly thickened.

3. Remove from heat and set aside 45 minutes.

4. Strain through fine sieve into bowl or remove whole spices with spoon. Discard spices.

5. Stir in green peppercorns and black pepper. Cover and refrigerate to chill.

6. Freeze in crank-type, electric, or hand-operated ice cream freezer. Store in freezer in covered freezer containers.

*Makes 2½ quarts*

TIP:

Crush green peppercorns with mortar and pestle or in small electric spice grinder.

# Cardinal Punch

1 bottle (48 ounces) cranberry juice cocktail
2 cups light corn syrup
2 tablespoons lemon juice
1 Cinnamon Stick, 3 inches long
1 piece Whole Ginger, 1 inch long
2 Cardamom Seeds
1 Bay Leaf
Fresh mint sprigs to decorate, if desired

1. Combine all ingredients except mint in glass or stainless steel saucepan. Heat slowly and keep over low heat 10 minutes.

2. Remove and discard whole spices.

3. Pour mixture into 11 x 8 x 2-inch pan. Place in freezer until solid.

4. Remove from freezer and scratch with tines of fork to break all of mixture into small flakes. Work quickly and return pan to freezer.

5. To serve, spoon frozen slush into sherbet glasses and decorate with fresh mint sprigs.

6. Serve between courses to refresh the palate or serve as light dessert.

*Makes 16 servings, ½ cup each*

*Cardinal Punch (see photo on page 302)*

# Pecan Pie

*Pastry for 9-inch 1-crust pie*

*4 eggs*

*1 cup sugar*

*1 cup dark corn syrup*

*¼ cup butter or margarine, melted*

*1 tablespoon cornstarch*

*1 teaspoon Pure Vanilla Extract*

*½ teaspoon Brandy Extract*

*⅛ teaspoon salt*

*2 cups pecan halves*

1. Preheat oven to 425°F. Line pie plate with pastry and set aside.

2. Place eggs in bowl and beat until lemon colored. Beat in sugar, corn syrup, melted butter, cornstarch, vanilla, brandy extract, and salt.

3. Arrange pecan halves in single layer in bottom of pastry-lined pie plate and pour egg mixture over pecans.

4. Bake in preheated 425°F oven 10 minutes.

5. Reduce oven temperature to 325°F and bake 50 to 55 minutes. Cool on wire rack.

*Makes 9-inch pie*

# Wonderful Apple Pie

*Pastry for 9 or 10-inch 1-crust pie*

*1 cup firmly packed light brown sugar*

*½ cup all-purpose flour*

*½ cup butter or margarine, softened*

*1 teaspoon Ground Cinnamon*

*½ teaspoon Lemon Peel*

*⅛ teaspoon Ground Allspice*

*⅛ teaspoon Ground Cloves*

*⅛ teaspoon Ground Nutmeg*

*6 medium-size apples, peeled, cored, and sliced*

1. Preheat oven to 400°F. Line pie plate with pastry and set aside.

2. Place sugar, flour, butter, and spices in medium-size bowl and mix until crumbly.

3. Spread one-third of mixture over bottom of pastry-lined pie plate and arrange apples on top.

4. Spoon remaining two-thirds of flour-sugar mixture evenly over apples.

5. Bake in preheated 400°F oven 50 to 55 minutes.

*Makes 9 or 10-inch pie*

*Cardinal Punch (see recipe on page 301)*

# Spiced Coconut Chiffon Pie

FILLING

1½ cups flaked coconut, divided

1 teaspoon Ground Cinnamon

¼ teaspoon Ground Ginger

⅛ teaspoon Ground Cardamom

1 envelope unflavored gelatin

¼ cup cold water

4 eggs, room temperature

½ cup granulated sugar

¼ teaspoon salt

1 cup milk, scalded

1 cup heavy cream

¼ teaspoon Cream of Tartar

1 teaspoon Pure Vanilla Extract

\* \* \*

Baked 10-inch pie crust

TOPPING

1 cup heavy cream

¼ cup confectioners sugar

¼ teaspoon Coconut Extract

1. Preheat oven to 350°F. Put small bowl in refrigerator.
2. Combine 1 cup coconut with spices and spread in shallow baking pan. Toast in preheated 350°F oven 8 minutes or until light brown, stirring occasionally. Set aside.
3. Soften gelatin in cold water and set aside.
4. Separate eggs and set egg whites aside.
5. Place egg yolks in large saucepan, add granulated sugar and salt, and beat until light in color. Add scalded milk to egg yolk mixture in thin, slow trickle, beating constantly. Cook over low heat, stirring, until mixture thickens.
6. Add reserved gelatin and stir to dissolve. Spoon into large bowl and set aside to cool.
7. Place egg whites and cream of tartar in mixer bowl and beat with electric mixer until stiff but not dry.
8. Place cream in chilled bowl and beat with electric mixer until stiff.
9. Stir vanilla and remaining ½ cup untoasted coconut into reserved egg yolk mixture. Fold in whipped cream and beaten egg whites.
10. Cover and refrigerate until mixture holds its shape when dropped from spoon.
11. Spread half reserved toasted coconut over bottom of baked pie shell. Spoon filling over coconut, mounding high in center. Refrigerate at least 1 hour.

12. To make topping, combine all topping ingredients in 2-quart mixer bowl and beat with electric mixer at high speed until stiff. Spread over chilled pie.

13. Sprinkle top of pie with remaining half of toasted coconut and refrigerate at least 1 hour.

*Makes 10-inch pie*

# Chiffon Pumpkin Pie

FILLING

3 eggs, room temperature

1½ cups canned pumpkin

¾ cup firmly packed brown sugar

½ cup milk

½ teaspoon salt

1 teaspoon Ground Cinnamon

½ teaspoon Ground Ginger

½ teaspoon Ground Nutmeg

1 envelope unflavored gelatin

¼ cup cold water

¼ cup granulated sugar

* * *

Baked 9-inch graham cracker crumb crust

Whipped cream to decorate

1. Separate eggs and set egg whites aside.

2. Place egg yolks in top of double boiler and beat until thick and light. Add pumpkin, brown sugar, milk, salt, and spices. Cook over (not in) simmering water, stirring constantly until thickened.

3. Soften gelatin in cold water and stir into pumpkin mixture. Pour into large bowl, cover, and refrigerate until partially set.

4. Place reserved egg whites in large mixer bowl and beat with electric mixer until foamy. Gradually beat in granulated sugar and beat until stiff but not dry. Fold into pumpkin mixture.

5. Pour into graham cracker crust and refrigerate 4 hours or overnight. Decorate with whipped cream.

*Makes 9-inch pie*

# Chocolate Sin

CRUST

1 package (9 ounces) round chocolate
    wafer cookies, crushed

¼ cup butter or margarine, softened

FILLING

2 packages (12 ounces each)
    semisweet chocolate morsels

4 eggs, room temperature

¼ cup granulated sugar

1 cup heavy cream

6 tablespoons confectioners sugar

1 teaspoon Pure Vanilla Extract

½ teaspoon Rum Extract

TOPPING

1 cup heavy cream

6 tablespoons confectioners sugar

1 teaspoon Pure Vanilla Extract

½ teaspoon Rum Extract

Chocolate curls to decorate,
    if desired (see below)

1. Preheat oven to 350°F. Chill small mixer bowl.

2. Place crushed cookies in bowl, add butter, and mix thoroughly. Press crumb mixture firmly onto bottom and up sides of 10-inch quiche pan or pie plate.

3. Bake in preheated 350°F oven 5 minutes. Set aside to cool.

4. Melt chocolate morsels in double boiler over (not in) hot water. (Do not allow water to boil.) Remove from heat.

5. Separate eggs and place egg yolks in 2-cup glass measure or small bowl. Set egg whites aside in large mixer bowl. Beat egg yolks with fork. Add about 1 tablespoon hot melted chocolate to beaten yolks in slow, steady stream, beating constantly. Pour egg mixture back into melted chocolate slowly. Mix throughly with fork. Set aside.

6. Beat reserved egg whites with electric mixer until foamy. Continue beating while gradually adding granulated sugar. Beat until stiff but not dry.

7. Place cream, confectioners sugar, vanilla, and rum extract in chilled bowl and beat with electric mixer until stiff.

8. Add beaten egg whites and whipped cream to chocolate mixture and beat with electric mixer at low speed until blended. Pour into reserved chocolate crust and refrigerate 4 hours or overnight.

9. To make topping, place cream, confectioners sugar, vanilla, and rum extract in chilled bowl and beat with electric mixer until stiff. Spoon into pastry bag

fitted with large star tip. Pipe in decorative design on top of chilled tart and decorate with chocolate curls.

*Makes 16 wedge-shaped servings*

TIP:

To make chocolate curls, soften large bar of semisweet or milk chocolate by placing chocolate in warm place (75°F to 80°F). Do not allow surface of chocolate to melt. Place on flat surface and use potato peeler to shave curls from top surface of bar.

# Cream Cheese Pie

FILLING

*2 packages (8 ounces each) cream cheese, softened*

*2 eggs, beaten*

*¾ cup sugar*

*1 tablespoon lemon juice*

*1 teaspoon Pure Vanilla Extract*

⋆  ⋆  ⋆

*Baked 9-inch graham cracker crumb crust*

TOPPING

*1 cup dairy sour cream*

*¼ cup sugar*

*1 teaspoon Pure Vanilla Extract*

1. Preheat oven to 350°F.
2. Place cream cheese, eggs, ¾ cup sugar, lemon juice, and 1 teaspoon vanilla in large bowl and beat until light and smooth. Pour into graham cracker crust.
3. Bake in preheated 350°F oven 35 minutes.
4. Remove from oven and set aside to cool 5 minutes. (Do not turn oven off.)
5. Place sour cream, ¼ cup sugar, and 1 teaspoon vanilla in bowl and mix well. Spread carefully over top of pie.
6. Return pie to oven and bake 10 minutes. Cool to room temperature and place in refrigerator to chill 4 hours or overnight.

*Makes 9-inch pie*

# Sweet Potato and Pecan Pie

Pastry for 9-inch 1-crust pie

FILLING

1 cup firmly packed brown sugar

½ teaspoon salt

1 teaspoon Ground Cinnamon

½ teaspoon Ground Ginger

¼ teaspoon Ground Nutmeg

⅛ teaspoon Ground Cloves

3 eggs, beaten

1½ cups milk

1½ cups cooked, mashed sweet
    potatoes

PECAN TOPPING

¼ cup firmly packed dark brown sugar

2 tablespoons butter, melted

1 cup chopped pecans

½ teaspoon Ground Cinnamon

⅛ teaspoon Ground Ginger

⅛ teaspoon Ground Nutmeg

1. Preheat oven to 425°F. Line pie plate with pastry and set aside.
2. Place 1 cup sugar, salt, and spices in large bowl and stir to combine. Stir in beaten eggs and mix well. Add milk and sweet potatoes. Mix thoroughly and pour into pie shell.
3. Bake in preheated 425°F oven 10 minutes.
4. Reduce oven temperature to 300°F and bake 30 minutes.
5. To make topping, place ¼ cup sugar in bowl and stir in melted butter. Add remaining ingredients and mix well. Spoon over pie and bake 30 minutes.

*Makes 9-inch pie*

# Macaroon Pie

3 eggs, room temperature

1 cup sugar, divided

¾ teaspoon Pure Almond Extract

1 cup graham cracker crumbs

½ cup chopped walnuts

½ teaspoon Pure Vanilla Extract

Whipped cream or ice cream to serve,
    if desired

1. Preheat oven to 350°F. Grease 9-inch pie plate and set aside.
2. Separate eggs and set egg whites aside.

3. Place egg yolks in large mixer bowl and beat with electric mixer until thick and light. Beat in ½ cup sugar and almond extract. Stir in graham cracker crumbs and walnuts.

4. Place reserved egg whites in separate mixer bowl and beat with electric mixer until foamy. Gradually beat in remaining ½ cup sugar and vanilla. Fold into egg yolk mixture and pour into prepared pie plate.

5. Bake in preheated 350°F oven 30 minutes.

6. Serve with whipped cream or ice cream.

*Makes 8 wedges, 3 inches each*

# *Cherry Clafouti*

*2 cans (16 ounces each) sour pitted cherries*

*1 cup sugar, divided*

*4 teaspoons quick-cooking tapioca*

*1 tablespoon plus ½ teaspoon Pure Vanilla Extract, divided*

*1 teaspoon lemon juice*

*¼ teaspoon Pure Almond Extract*

*⅛ teaspoon Ground Cinnamon*

*1¼ cups milk*

*⅔ cup all-purpose flour*

*3 eggs*

*Dash salt*

*2 tablespoons butter or margarine*

*Cream, whipped cream, or vanilla ice cream to serve, if desired*

1. Drain cherries, reserving ⅓ cup juice. Place cherries in large bowl. Add reserved ⅓ cup cherry juice, ⅔ cup sugar, tapioca, ½ teaspoon vanilla, lemon juice, almond extract, and cinnamon. Mix well and set aside at room temperature.

2. Preheat oven to 350°F. Grease bottom and sides of 2-quart oval, round, or rectangular 2-inch-deep baking pan and set aside.

3. Place milk, flour, remaining ⅓ cup sugar, eggs, remaining 1 tablespoon vanilla, and salt in blender and blend 1 minute at highest speed. Pour 1½ cups batter into prepared pan. Set aside remaining batter.

4. Bake in preheated 350°F oven 10 minutes.

5. Remove from oven and pour reserved cherry mixture over baked crust. Dot with butter and pour remaining batter evenly over cherries. Return to oven and bake 35 minutes. Serve immediately with cream, whipped cream, or vanilla ice cream.

*Makes 12 servings, ½ cup each*

# *Pavlova*

*Cornstarch for dusting cookie sheet*

*4 egg whites, room temperature*

*Dash salt*

*1 cup superfine sugar*

*1 teaspoon vinegar*

*1 teaspoon cornstarch*

*1½ teaspoons Pure Vanilla Extract, divided*

*2 cups heavy cream*

*¾ cup confectioners sugar*

*1 pint strawberries, washed and hulled*

*3 kiwi, peeled and sliced*

1. Preheat oven to 250°F. Grease cookie sheet and dust heavily with cornstarch. Set aside.

2. Place egg whites in large mixer bowl, add salt, and beat with electric mixer until foamy. Gradually beat in superfine sugar until mixture is very thick. Add vinegar, cornstarch, and ½ teaspoon vanilla.

3. Beat egg white mixture with electric mixer at high speed 8 to 10 minutes. Scrape down sides of bowl 2 or 3 times during beating.

4. Spoon meringue onto center of prepared cookie sheet. Use back of large spoon to spread meringue into 8-inch round or oval shape.

5. Bake in preheated 250°F oven 1 hour. Do not allow to brown. Turn off oven and let cool in oven with door ajar.

6. Carefully transfer cooled meringue to large serving plate and set aside.

7. Place cream, confectioners sugar, and remaining 1 teaspoon vanilla in chilled bowl and beat with electric mixer until stiff. Refrigerate to chill.

8. Set aside 8 whole strawberries for decoration and slice remaining berries. Set aside 8 kiwi slices for decoration.

9. Arrange sliced strawberries and remaining slices of kiwi on top of cooled meringue. Spread one-third of chilled whipped cream over fruit.

10. Place remaining whipped cream in pastry bag fitted with large star tip. Pipe cream to cover sides of meringue and fruit layer, and pipe large rosettes around base and top edge of meringue.

11. Decorate with reserved whole strawberries and reserved slices of kiwi. Cut into wedges to serve.

*Makes 12 wedges, 2 inches each*

# *Trifle*

4 eggs

1 cup granulated sugar

3 tablespoons cornstarch

⅛ teaspoon salt

4 cups milk

1 Bay Leaf

1 Whole Nutmeg

1 teaspoon Pure Vanilla Extract

¼ teaspoon Pure Orange Extract

¼ teaspoon Coconut Extract

1 frozen pound cake, 10¾ ounces

¾ cup strawberry preserves

1 can (29 ounces) sliced peaches, drained

TOPPING

1 cup heavy cream

¼ cup confectioners sugar

½ teaspoon Pure Vanilla Extract

⅛ teaspoon Pure Orange Extract

⅛ teaspoon Coconut Extract

1. Place eggs in large mixer bowl and beat with electric mixer at high speed.

2. Place granulated sugar, cornstarch, and salt in small bowl and mix well. Add to eggs and beat at high speed 2 minutes. Reduce speed to low and slowly add milk. Add bay leaf and nutmeg.

3. Pour mixture into 4-quart stainless steel bowl and place bowl over (not in) saucepan containing 1 inch simmering water.

4. Cook over medium heat, stirring, until mixture thickens and coats a spoon.* Cool to room temperature. Remove and discard nutmeg and bay leaf. Stir in 1 teaspoon vanilla, ¼ teaspoon orange extract, and ¼ teaspoon coconut extract.

5. Cut pound cake into fifteen ⅜-inch-thick slices.

6. Line bottom of 3-quart glass bowl with 5 slices pound cake. Dot with one-third of strawberry preserves, add one-third of peaches, and cover with one-third of custard.

7. Continue layering pound cake, preserves, peaches, and custard to make 2 additional layers, ending with custard. Smooth top.

8. Cover and refrigerate at least 2 hours.

9. To make topping, place cream and remaining ingredients in chilled bowl and beat with electric mixer until stiff. Spread over Trifle.

*Makes 10 servings, ½ cup each*

*(See page 53)

# Coffee Torte

MERINGUE

6 egg whites, room temperature

¼ teaspoon Cream of Tartar

1½ cups sifted confectioners sugar

1 cup granulated sugar

1 teaspoon Pure Almond Extract

Dash Ground Allspice

Dash Ground Mace

FILLING

6 egg yolks, beaten

½ cup granulated sugar

½ cup cold strong black coffee

1 tablespoon all-purpose flour

½ cup butter or margarine, softened

*   *   *

1 cup heavy cream

⅓ cup confectioners sugar

1 teaspoon Pure Vanilla Extract

1. Preheat oven to 250°F. Chill small mixer bowl.

2. Place egg whites in large mixer bowl and beat with electric mixer until foamy. Add cream of tartar and beat until stiff peaks form when beaters are lifted. Add confectioners and granulated sugars, 1 tablespoon at a time, beating well after each addition. Add almond extract, allspice, and mace. Beat 2 minutes.

3. Cut four 8-inch circles out of heavy brown paper and place circles on cookie sheets. Divide meringue into 4 equal parts and spread evenly over each circle of paper with back of large spoon.

4. Bake in preheated 250°F oven 1 hour and 15 minutes. Remove from oven and set aside to cool.

5. When cool, carefully peel paper off bottoms of meringue layers.

6. To make filling, place egg yolks, granulated sugar, coffee, and flour in top of double boiler over (not in) simmering water. Cook, stirring constantly, until mixture thickens. Set aside to cool to lukewarm. Add butter and stir until well blended.

7. Place l meringue layer on flat cake plate. Spread one-quarter of filling over layer. Top with second layer and spread with one-quarter of filling. Continue until all layers are stacked, ending with filling.

8. Place cream, confectioners sugar, and vanilla in chilled bowl and beat with electric mixer until stiff. Decorate top of torte with whipped cream.

*Makes 4-layer, 8-inch torte*

# Baked Alaska

ICE CREAM

1 quart vanilla ice cream

1 pint orange sherbet

1 pint strawberry ice cream

CAKE

9-inch round cake layer of any flavor
    desired

MERINGUE

6 egg whites, room temperature

1½ cups sugar

1 teaspoon Pure Vanilla Extract

¼ teaspoon Pure Orange Extract

1. Chill 2-quart mixing bowl in which to mold ice cream.

2. Cut vanilla ice cream crosswise into 1-inch-thick slices and line bottom and sides of chilled bowl with ice cream slices, leaving center empty. Smooth surface to even thickness.

3. Slice orange sherbet and make even, smooth layer of sherbet inside ice cream lining. Fill center with strawberry ice cream and smooth top.

4. Cover bowl with plastic wrap and place in freezer until ice cream and sherbet are firmly frozen.

5. Place cake on freezerproof and ovenproof serving dish. Unmold ice cream onto cake and return to freezer.

6. Place egg whites in large mixer bowl and beat with electric mixer until foamy. Gradually add sugar to egg whites, beating at high speed. Add vanilla and orange extracts and beat until stiff peaks form when beaters are lifted.

7. Remove cake and ice cream from freezer. Working quickly, spread meringue over ice cream and cake, covering surface evenly and completely. Be sure meringue completely covers cake all around edge to seal in ice cream. Cake can be frozen up to 4 hours before serving.

8. When ready to serve, preheat oven to 450°F.

9. Bake in preheated 450°F oven 3 to 5 minutes or just until meringue starts to brown. Serve immediately.

*Makes 10 to 12 wedge-shaped servings*

*Baked Alaska*

# Cinnamon Sandies

1 cup butter or margarine, softened

1½ cups confectioners sugar, divided

2 teaspoons Pure Vanilla Extract

1 tablespoon water

2 cups sifted all-purpose flour

1 cup finely chopped nuts

2 teaspoons Ground Cinnamon

1. Preheat oven to 300°F.
2. Place butter and ½ cup sugar in large mixer bowl and cream until light and fluffy. Stir in vanilla and water. Gradually add flour and mix well. Stir in nuts.
3. Shape teaspoonfuls of dough into crescents and place 1 inch apart on ungreased cookie sheets.
4. Bake in preheated 300°F oven 20 minutes or until very lightly browned.
5. Sift remaining 1 cup sugar with cinnamon and roll hot cookies in mixture.
6. Place on wire racks to cool. When cool, roll again in sugar mixture.

*Makes 5 dozen*

# Cinnamon Sledges

1 cup butter or margarine, softened

1 cup sugar

1 egg, separated

2 cups sifted all-purpose flour

1 tablespoon Ground Cinnamon

½ cup chopped pecans

1. Preheat oven to 300°F.
2. Place butter and sugar in large mixer bowl and cream with electric mixer at high speed until light and fluffy. Add egg yolk and beat well. Add flour and cinnamon and mix at low speed until well blended.
3. Spread dough on ungreased 15 x 12-inch cookie sheet, leaving 1½-inch border to allow for spreading.
4. Beat egg white in small bowl with fork until foamy. Brush over top of dough. Sprinkle with nuts and lightly press nuts into dough.
5. Bake in preheated 300°F oven 45 to 50 minutes.
6. Cut into 2-inch squares while still hot. Remove from cookie sheet and place on wire racks to cool.

*Makes 3 dozen squares*

# Date Sticks

*½ cup butter or margarine, softened*

*1 cup sugar*

*1 egg*

*1 teaspoon Pure Vanilla Extract*

*1 teaspoon Lemon Peel*

*2 cups all-purpose flour*

*1 teaspoon Ground Cinnamon*

*½ teaspoon baking powder*

*¼ teaspoon baking soda*

*¼ teaspoon salt*

*⅛ teaspoon Ground Nutmeg*

*1 cup chopped dates*

1. Preheat oven to 350°F. Lightly grease cookie sheets and set aside.

2. Place butter in large mixer bowl and cream with electric mixer until fluffy. Gradually add sugar and beat until light and fluffy. Beat in egg, vanilla, and lemon peel.

3. Sift flour with cinnamon, baking powder, baking soda, salt, and nutmeg. Gradually add to creamed mixture, mixing at low speed until well blended. Stir in dates.

4. Shape dough into thin sticks about 1½ inches long. Place 1 inch apart on prepared cookie sheets.

5. Bake in preheated 350°F oven 15 to 20 minutes.

6. Remove from cookie sheets and place on wire racks to cool.

*Makes 6 dozen sticks*

**CINNAMON**

# Pecan Cookie Balls

1 cup butter or margarine

2½ cups sifted confectioners sugar, divided

2 teaspoons Pure Vanilla Extract

½ teaspoon Ground Nutmeg

⅛ teaspoon salt

2 cups sifted all-purpose flour

2 cups finely chopped pecans

1. Preheat oven to 350°F.
2. Place butter in large mixer bowl and cream until soft. Add ½ cup sugar, vanilla, nutmeg, and salt. Cream until thoroughly mixed. Stir in flour and pecans.
3. Shape dough into 1-inch balls and place 1 inch apart on ungreased cookie sheets.
4. Bake in preheated 350°F oven 15 minutes.
5. Remove from cookie sheets and immediately roll hot cookies in remaining 2 cups sugar.
6. Place sugared cookies on wire racks and set aside to cool. When cool, roll again in sugar.

*Makes 4 to 5 dozen cookies*

# Anise Cookies

½ cup butter or margarine, softened

1 cup sugar

1 egg

½ teaspoon Pure Vanilla Extract

1½ teaspoons baking powder

½ teaspoon salt

1¾ cups sifted all-purpose flour

1½ teaspoons Anise Seed

1. Place butter and sugar in large mixer bowl and cream until light and fluffy. Add egg and vanilla and mix well.
2. Add baking powder and salt to sifted flour and sift again.
3. Gradually add dry ingredients and anise seed to butter mixture, mixing thoroughly after each addition.
4. Shape dough into roll and wrap in wax paper. Refrigerate at least 2 hours.

5. Preheat oven to 400°F. Lightly grease cookie sheets.

6. Cut chilled dough into thin slices and place 1 inch apart on prepared cookie sheets.

7. Bake in preheated 400°F oven 8 minutes or until golden brown.

8. Remove from cookie sheets and place on wire racks to cool.

*Makes 5 dozen*

# Pfeffernüsse

| | |
|---|---|
| *1 cup firmly packed light brown sugar* | *1 teaspoon Ground Cinnamon* |
| *½ cup butter or margarine, softened* | *½ teaspoon salt* |
| *2 eggs* | *½ teaspoon Ground Black Pepper* |
| *1 teaspoon Pure Vanilla Extract* | *⅛ teaspoon Ground Nutmeg* |
| *½ teaspoon Pure Lemon Extract* | *⅛ teaspoon Ground Cloves* |
| *½ teaspoon Pure Anise Extract* | *2¾ cups sifted all-purpose flour* |
| *1 teaspoon baking powder* | *Confectioners sugar* |

1. Place brown sugar and butter in large mixer bowl. Cream with electric mixer until smooth and fluffy. Beat in eggs and extracts.

2. Add remaining ingredients except confectioners sugar to sifted flour and sift again. Gradually add to butter mixture, mixing well.

3. Cover and refrigerate 2 hours.

4. Preheat oven to 375°F.

5. Shape teaspoonfuls of dough into ovals and place 1 inch apart on ungreased cookie sheets.

6. Bake in preheated 375°F oven 10 minutes.

7. Remove from cookie sheets and place on wire racks.

8. Sprinkle with confectioners sugar while cookies are still warm.

9. When cookies are cool, store in airtight containers.

*Makes 55 to 60 cookies*

# Gingersnaps

¾ cup butter or margarine, softened

1 cup sugar

¼ cup molasses

1 egg

2 cups all-purpose flour

2 teaspoons baking soda

¼ teaspoon salt

1 teaspoon Ground Cinnamon

1 teaspoon Ground Cloves

1 teaspoon Ground Ginger

Sugar for rolling, if desired

1. Place butter and sugar in large mixer bowl and cream until light and fluffy. Add molasses and egg and beat well.

2. Sift flour with baking soda, salt, and spices. Gradually add to butter mixture and mix well.

3. Cover and refrigerate at least 2 hours.

4. Preheat oven to 375°F. Lightly grease cookie sheets and set aside.

5. Shape dough into 1-inch balls and roll in sugar. Place 2 inches apart on prepared cookie sheets.

6. Bake in preheated 375°F oven 10 minutes.

7. Remove from cookie sheets and place on wire racks to cool.

*Makes 4 to 5 dozen*

# Orange Butter Gems

1 cup butter or margarine, softened

1 cup confectioners sugar

¼ teaspoon Ground Mace

¼ teaspoon salt

2½ cups sifted all-purpose flour

1 egg

2 teaspoons Orange Peel

2 teaspoons Pure Orange Extract

1. Preheat oven to 375°F.

2. Place butter and sugar in large mixer bowl and cream until light and fluffy.

3. Add mace and salt to sifted flour and sift again. Add 1 cup flour mixture to butter mixture and mix well. Beat in egg, orange peel, and orange extract.

4. Gradually add remaining 1½ cups flour mixture and mix well.

5. Spoon dough into cookie press and press out 1 inch apart onto ungreased cookie sheets.

6. Bake in preheated 375°F oven 10 minutes or until edges are lightly browned. Remove from cookie sheets and place on wire racks to cool.

*Makes 3½ to 4 dozen*

VARIATION:

Substitute 2 teaspoons Lemon Peel and 2 teaspoons Pure Lemon Extract for Orange Peel and Orange Extract in recipe.

# Sugared Vanilla Wafers

*1½ cups sugar*

*1 cup butter or margarine, softened*

*2 eggs*

*1 tablespoon Pure Vanilla Extract*

*2 teaspoons baking powder*

*3 cups sifted all-purpose flour*

*2 tablespoons milk*

*Sugar for rolling and sprinkling*

*Cinnamon Sugar, if desired*

1. Place 1½ cups sugar and butter in large mixer bowl and cream with electric mixer until light and fluffy. Beat in eggs and vanilla.

2. Gradually add baking powder to sifted flour and sift again. Gradually add to butter mixture, mixing well. Stir in milk and mix until well combined.

3. Cover and refrigerate at least 2 hours.

4. Preheat oven to 400°F. Lightly grease cookie sheets and set aside.

5. Lightly flour work surface and sprinkle with 1 tablespoon sugar.

6. Roll out chilled dough to ⅛-inch thickness and cut with 2-inch cookie cutters.

7. Place cookies 1 inch apart on prepared cookie sheets and sprinkle with sugar or cinnamon sugar.

8. Bake in preheated 400°F oven 6 to 8 minutes.

9. Remove from cookie sheets and place on wire racks to cool.

*Makes 5 dozen cookies, 2 inches each*

# *BEVERAGES*

# *Spiced Fruit Ring*

*About 1 quart ginger ale*

*Lemon slices, cut ¼ inch thick*

*Orange slices, cut ¼ inch thick*

*Whole Cloves*

*Cardamom Seed*

*Pineapple spears, drained if canned*

*Pineapple slices, drained if canned*

*Red maraschino cherries with stems, drained and rinsed*

*Green maraschino cherries, drained and rinsed*

*Whole Ginger*

*Cinnamon Sticks*

*Whole Allspice*

1. Pour enough ginger ale into ring or other attractive mold to cover bottom of ring or mold. Set remaining ginger ale aside. Place ring in freezer until well frozen.

2. Stud outer edges of lemon and orange slices with cloves and place cardamom seed in center of each slice.

3. Arrange prepared lemon and orange slices, remaining fruit, and remaining spices in attractive pattern on top of frozen ginger ale.

4. Pour enough reserved ginger ale over fruit and spices to barely cover and return to freezer until well frozen.

5. When ready to serve, remove ring from mold and place in punch bowl. Add punch and serve.

*Makes 1 ice ring*

TIP:

Any leftover ginger ale can be used in punch or can be frozen to make an additional plain ice ring. Ice rings can be made ahead of time, unmolded, and stored in plastic bag in freezer.

# Party Punch

1 can (46 ounces) pineapple-grape
    fruit juice

1 quart apple juice

3 cans (6 ounces each) frozen orange
    juice concentrate

1 can (5¾ ounces) frozen lemon juice

½ cup sugar

24 Whole Cloves

6 Cardamom Seeds

4 Cinnamon Sticks,
    each 3 inches long

½ teaspoon Ground Ginger

½ teaspoon Ground Allspice

½ teaspoon Ground Mace

Spiced Fruit Ring (page 322)
    to serve, if desired

4 quarts ginger ale

1. Combine fruit juices in 4-quart bowl.

2. Add sugar and spices to fruit juice and stir until sugar has dissolved.

3. Refrigerate several hours, remove and discard whole spices, and stir punch.

4. When ready to serve, place ice or Spiced Fruit Ring in punch bowl and pour
   punch over. Add ginger ale.

*Makes 2 gallons, 64 servings, 4 ounces each*

TIP:

For punch with more sparkle, substitute champagne for ginger ale. To make
punch in small batches, use 1 cup spiced fruit juice mixture to 1 cup ginger ale.

**CLOVES**

# Easy Eggnog

1 gallon prepared eggnog
½ cup light rum
½ cup brandy

½ cup bourbon
1 quart eggnog-flavored ice cream
Ground Nutmeg to garnish

1. Pour eggnog into large punch bowl. Add rum, brandy, and bourbon. Stir gently.
2. Add ice cream to eggnog by spoonfuls. Sprinkle nutmeg on top.

*Makes about 25 servings*

# Party Eggnog

6 eggs
2 cups granulated sugar, divided
1 quart milk
1 teaspoon Pure Vanilla Extract
1 cup brandy

1 cup light rum
½ cup apricot or peach brandy
1 cup heavy cream
¼ cup confectioners sugar
Nutmeg to garnish

1. Separate eggs and refrigerate egg whites. Place egg yolks in top of double boiler, add 1½ cups granulated sugar, and beat until light colored and fluffy. Stir in milk.
2. Place top of double boiler over (not in) simmering water and cook, stirring, until mixture thickens slightly. Remove from heat and cool slightly.
3. Stir in vanilla, cover, and refrigerate several hours or overnight.
4. When ready to serve, pour chilled egg yolk mixture into punch bowl. Stir in brandy, rum, and apricot brandy.
5. Allow egg whites to come to room temperature (30 minutes), then beat egg whites until foamy. Add remaining ½ cup granulated sugar, and beat until soft peaks form when beaters are lifted.
6. Place cream in chilled bowl and beat just until it begins to thicken. Add confectioners sugar and beat until soft peaks form. Do not overbeat.
7. Fold beaten egg whites and whipped cream into chilled egg yolk mixture until well combined. Sprinkle with nutmeg.

*Makes 20 servings, ½ cup each*

# Traditional Wassail Bowl

*3 apples*

*1 cup water*

*1 cup sugar*

*4 Coriander Seeds*

*3 Whole Cloves*

*3 Whole Allspice*

*1 piece Whole Ginger, bruised
(slightly crushed)*

*1 Cinnamon Stick, 3 inches long*

*1 teaspoon Lemon Peel*

*½ teaspoon Ground Nutmeg*

*½ teaspoon Ground Mace*

*1 bottle (750 ml) sherry*

*3 bottles (12 ounces each) ale*

*3 eggs, separated*

1. Preheat oven to 350°F.

2. Wash apples and place in 8-inch square baking pan. Bake in preheated 350°F oven 45 minutes. Remove from oven and set aside.

3. Place water, sugar, and seasonings in large saucepan. Heat to boil, reduce heat, and simmer 10 minutes.

4. Add sherry and ale. Heat but do not boil. Remove and discard whole spices. Keep warm.

5. Place egg yolks in large bowl and beat until thickened. Beat egg whites in separate bowl until stiff. Fold beaten whites into yolks.

6. Add hot liquid to eggs in very slow, steady stream, beating constantly. Pour into heatproof punch bowl.

7. Float baked apples on top of punch and serve hot.

*Makes 2 quarts*

**ALLSPICE**

# Glögg

6 Cardamom Seeds, split

5 Whole Cloves

1 Cinnamon Stick, 3 inches long, broken

1 piece Whole Ginger, broken

1 tablespoon Orange Peel

2 cups port wine

2 cups dry red wine

1 cup water

½ cup seedless raisins

½ cup blanched almonds

½ cup sugar

1 cup brandy

1. Cut 6-inch square piece of cheesecloth. Place split cardamom seeds, cloves, cinnamon stick, ginger, and orange peel in center of cheesecloth. Bring corners of cheesecloth together and tie tightly to enclose spices. Place in 2-quart saucepan.

2. Add remaining ingredients except brandy. Heat to just under boiling point and cook 15 minutes. (Do not boil.)

3. Remove and discard spice bag. Add brandy and serve hot.

*Makes 6 servings, 8 ounces each*

# Tropical Delight

1 can (46 ounces) unsweetened grapefruit juice

1 can (12 ounces) apricot juice

1 can (12 ounces) papaya juice

1 can (12 ounces) guava nectar

1 can (12 ounces) pear nectar

1 cup water

¾ cup sugar

4 Cardamom Seeds

1 Cinnamon Stick, 3 inches long

⅛ teaspoon Ground Mace

1 quart ginger ale

1 teaspoon Pure Vanilla Extract

1. Combine fruit juices in punch bowl and set aside.

2. Place water, sugar, cardamom seeds, cinnamon stick, and mace in small saucepan. Simmer 10 minutes and set aside to cool.

3. When cool, strain into juice mixture and add ginger ale and vanilla. Serve over ice.

*Makes 32 servings, 4 ounces each*

# Spiced Sangria

| | |
|---|---|
| 1 orange | 8 Whole Allspice |
| 1 lemon | 1 Cinnamon Stick, 3 inches long |
| 1 lime | 1 Vanilla Bean, 2 inches long |
| 1 apple, cored | 2 bottles (750 ml) red wine |
| 1 cup sugar | 2 bottles (10 ounces each) lemon-flavored |
| ½ cup brandy | carbonated soft drink |

1. Cut orange, lemon, lime, and apple into ½-inch pieces and place in glass bowl.
2. Add sugar, brandy, allspice, cinnamon stick, and vanilla bean. Mix well and refrigerate at least 2 hours. Remove and discard whole spices.
3. Divide fruit in half and place each half in large pitcher.
4. Add 1 quart wine and 1 bottle soft drink to each pitcher. Stir gently and serve over ice, if desired.

*Makes 10 servings, 8 ounces each*

**CINNAMON**

# ENTERTAINING

～

MOST OF US have taken off the white gloves and dropped the engraved calling cards and other trademarks of earlier eras of formal entertaining in favor of more casual parties, where even the host and hostess can have fun, too.

But even with this more informal style, it is often difficult to find recipes that serve more than six or eight guests. We have solved that problem for you by suggesting these recipes for large groups. Most of the recipes in this section can be doubled or halved with confidence. But be aware that other changes may not work.

We have also suggested a number of creative party themes along with several menu variations for you to choose from. Treat your guests to the intrigue of Casablanca, or the exotic spell of India, or "go native" with an Island party.

We have even included ideas for children's parties that will be almost as much fun for you as for the youngsters.

Make life a Fiesta!

## CHESAPEAKE BRUNCH

Early explorers of the vast Chesapeake Bay area called it "a fair and pleasant land," which James Michener confirmed when he captured the history, folklore, and scenic splendor of the region in his book *Chesapeake.*

Bay food is essentially simple food. But in contrast, seafood from the area is elegant — backfin crab meat, oysters, and striped bass, which the natives call "rockfish."

The recipes that follow capture a skipjack captain's mood for your guests — everything but the sea breeze and chirping gulls.

MENU

# CHESAPEAKE BRUNCH

*Cream of Crab Soup*

*Old Bay Crab Cakes or Oyster Fritters*

*Maryland Fried Chicken*

*Broiled Tomatoes*　　　*Tossed Green Salad\**

*Spoonbread*

*Spiced Fruit*

*Elegant Peach Pie*

OTHER MENU IDEAS:

Crab Meat Dunk *(page 160)* — (Double recipe to serve 12)

Maryland Crab Soup *(page 170)* — (Make recipe 1½ times to serve 12)

Golden Clove-Glazed Ham *(page 208)*

Country-Good Baked Squash *(page 255)* — (Make recipe 1½ times to serve 12)

Lady Baltimore Cake *(page 288)*

*\*(No recipe provided)*

# Cream of Crab Soup

¼ cup butter or margarine

2 tablespoons Instant Minced Onion

2 teaspoons Chicken Flavor Base

2 teaspoons Season-All Seasoned Salt

¼ teaspoon Ground Mace

¼ teaspoon Ground White Pepper

⅛ teaspoon Ground Red Pepper

1 quart milk

1 quart half and half

1½ pounds lump crab meat, picked over*

1 tablespoon Parsley Flakes

Paprika to garnish, if desired

1. Melt butter in 6-quart stockpot over low heat. Stir in minced onion, flavor base, seasoned salt, mace, and white and red pepper. Simmer 1 minute.

2. Stir in milk and half and half. Heat slowly.

3. Add crab meat and parsley. Simmer gently just until heated through. (Do not boil.)

4. Spoon into soup bowls and sprinkle with paprika.

*Makes 12 servings, 1 cup each*

*(See page 47)

**PAPRIKA**

# Old Bay Crab Cakes

6 slices stale white bread, crusts removed

Small amount milk

3 tablespoons mayonnaise

3 tablespoons Worcestershire sauce

3 tablespoons Parsley Flakes

3 tablespoons baking powder

1 tablespoon Old Bay Seasoning

¾ teaspoon salt

3 eggs, beaten

3 pounds lump crab meat, picked over*

Tomato slices and lettuce to serve

Lemon slices and sprigs of parsley to garnish

1. Break bread into small pieces and place in medium-size bowl. Add just enough milk to moisten.

2. Add remaining ingredients and mix well. Shape into 12 patties.

3. Preheat broiler or skillet.

4. Broil or panfry patties until golden brown on both sides.

5. Serve with tomato slices and lettuce and garnish with lemon slices and sprigs of parsley.

*Makes 12 servings, 3 ounces each*

*(See page 47)*

**RED PEPPER**

# Oyster Fritters

*2 cups all-purpose flour*

*1 tablespoon baking powder*

*1 tablespoon sugar*

*2 teaspoons Bon Appétit*

*1 teaspoon Onion Powder*

*½ teaspoon Ground Black Pepper*

*⅛ teaspoon Ground Red Pepper*

*4 eggs*

*⅔ cup milk*

*2 tablespoons butter or margarine, melted*

*2 cups drained, coarsely chopped oysters*

*Vegetable oil for frying*

1. Sift flour and baking powder into large bowl.

2. Combine sugar, Bon Appétit, onion powder, and black and red pepper. Stir into flour mixture.

3. Separate eggs and set egg whites aside. Beat egg yolks in medium-size bowl. Beat in milk and melted butter and stir into flour mixture.

4. Place egg whites in mixer bowl and beat with electric mixer until soft peaks form when beaters are lifted. Fold into batter lightly but thoroughly. Stir in oysters quickly.

5. Pour 3 inches oil into 5-inch-deep heavy saucepan. Heat oil to 350°F on deep-fry thermometer.

6. Carefully drop batter by teaspoonfuls into hot oil and fry until browned on both sides.

7. Remove with slotted spoon and drain on paper towels. Serve hot.

*Makes 12 servings, 4 fritters each*

**ONION**

# Maryland Fried Chicken

Vegetable oil for frying
1½ cups all-purpose flour
1 tablespoon Paprika
2 teaspoons Bon Appétit
1½ teaspoons Season-All Seasoned Salt
1 teaspoon Ground Black Pepper
1 cup milk
3 frying chickens, cut into 24 pieces

1. Preheat oven to 350°F.
2. Pour ½ inch oil into 15 x 3-inch-deep skillet or chicken frying pan. Heat oil slowly to 350°F on deep-fry thermometer.
3. Mix flour, paprika, Bon Appétit, seasoned salt, and pepper in shallow pan or pie plate. Place milk in bowl.
4. Dip chicken pieces in milk and roll in flour mixture.
5. Carefully place chicken, a few pieces at a time, in hot oil and cook 10 minutes, turning once to brown on both sides. (Do not overcrowd pan.) Transfer browned chicken to two 13 x 9 x 2-inch baking pans.
6. Bake, uncovered, in preheated 350°F oven 40 to 50 minutes.

*Makes 12 servings, 2 pieces chicken each*

# Broiled Tomatoes

6 ripe tomatoes
½ cup butter or margarine
½ cup dry bread crumbs
½ teaspoon Dill Weed
½ teaspoon Bon Appétit

1. Preheat broiler or preheat oven to 375°F.
2. Cut tomatoes in half crosswise and place, cut side up, on cookie sheet.
3. Melt butter in saucepan over low heat and stir in remaining ingredients.
4. Spread buttered crumb mixture evenly on cut side of tomatoes.
5. Broil, 8 inches from source of heat, 5 to 7 minutes, or bake in preheated 375°F oven 10 minutes.

*Makes 12 servings, ½ tomato each*

# Spoonbread

*1 cup yellow cornmeal*

*3¼ cups milk*

*1 can (16 ounces) whole-kernel corn, drained*

*¾ cup butter or margarine, melted*

*1¼ cups all-purpose flour*

*3 tablespoons sugar*

*1 tablespoon baking powder*

*1½ teaspoons Bon Appétit*

*¼ teaspoon Ground Nutmeg*

*¼ teaspoon Ground Red Pepper*

*5 eggs, beaten*

1. Preheat oven to 350°F. Lightly grease 13 x 9 x 2-inch baking pan and set aside.

2. Place cornmeal and milk in large stainless steel bowl set over (not in) saucepan containing 2 inches of boiling water. Stir until smooth and cook, stirring, 10 minutes. Stir in corn and butter. Remove from heat.

3. Place flour, sugar, baking powder, Bon Appétit, nutmeg, and red pepper in bowl and mix well. Stir into corn meal mixture. Add beaten eggs and stir until well combined. Pour into prepared pan.

4. Bake in preheated 350°F oven 40 to 45 minutes. Serve immediately, scooping out servings with large spoon.

*Makes 12 servings, ½ cup each*

# Spiced Fruit

*1 can (29 ounces) peach halves in syrup*

*1 can (29 ounces) pear halves in syrup*

*2 cans (17 ounces each) apricot halves in syrup*

*3 bananas, sliced*

*3 large apples, peeled, cored, and cut into bite-size pieces*

*12 Whole Cloves*

*4 Whole Allspice*

*1 Cinnamon Stick, 3 inches long*

*1 Cardamom Seed*

*1 Whole Nutmeg*

*1 piece Whole Ginger, 1 inch long*

*Maraschino cherries to garnish, if desired*

1. Drain syrup from canned fruit into large saucepan and place fruit in large heatproof bowl. Add bananas and apples to bowl and set fruit aside.

2. Add spices to syrup in saucepan and heat to boil. Reduce heat and simmer 5 minutes. Pour over fruit.

3. Cover and refrigerate overnight.

4. Remove whole spices. Spoon fruit into large glass serving bowl and garnish with cherries.

*Makes 12 servings, 1 cup each*

# Elegant Peach Pie

CRUST

¼ cup Sesame Seed

2 cups all-purpose flour

½ teaspoon salt

⅔ cup vegetable shortening

¼ cup cold water

FILLING

¾ cup firmly packed brown sugar

3 tablespoons quick-cooking tapioca

¾ teaspoon Ground Ginger

½ teaspoon Lemon Peel

4 cups peeled, sliced peaches

2 tablespoons butter or margarine

¼ teaspoon Pure Almond Extract

1. Preheat oven to 350°F.

2. Place sesame seed in shallow baking pan and toast in preheated 350°F oven 15 minutes or until golden brown. Set aside to cool.

3. Sift flour and salt into medium-size bowl. Measure ¼ cup flour mixture and set aside in small bowl.

4. Cut shortening into remaining flour mixture with pastry blender or 2 knives until particles are about size of peas.

5. Add cold water to ¼ cup reserved flour mixture and stir to make smooth paste. Sprinkle paste over flour-shortening mixture. Add toasted sesame seed and blend quickly until dough is moist and can be shaped into 2 equal-size balls.

6. Set 1 ball of dough aside and roll out other ball on lightly floured surface to ⅛-inch thickness. Line 9-inch pie plate.

7. Roll out remaining ball of dough on floured surface to ⅛-inch thickness and cut into ¾-inch strips. Set strips aside to use for lattice top.

8. Increase oven temperature to 425°F.

9. To make filling, place sugar, tapioca, ginger, and lemon peel in small bowl and mix well. Sprinkle half of mixture over bottom of pie shell.

10. Arrange peach slices over sugar-spice mixture and sprinkle remaining sugar mixture over peaches. Dot with butter and drizzle almond extract over all. Use pastry strips to form lattice top over fruit. Press ends of strips to bottom crust to seal.

11. Bake in preheated 425°F oven 10 minutes. Reduce oven temperature to 350°F and bake 30 minutes.

*Makes 9-inch pie*

TIP:

To serve 12, make 2 pies.

# HIGH TEA

During the period of time the British were establishing colonies around the world, they invariably took one indispensable item with them — tea. Although tea drinking had been a ceremonial ritual in Oriental cultures for many centuries, it was the British who turned the drinking of tea into a social event as well as a mini-meal.

Almost any place in the world you find people from Britain, it's likely you'll also find tea served between three and five in the afternoon. But High Tea involves more than just the drinking of tea. A wide variety of traditional foods are served with tea, along with many delicious local specialties.

The following teatime suggestions are for food appropriate to serve at High Tea in either a formal or casual manner.

GINGER

MENU

# HIGH TEA

Tea Punch        Hot Tea*

Cinnamon-Raisin Scones

Tea Sandwiches

Phyllo Turnovers        Herb Omelets

Filled Benne Lace Cookies

Coconut Tea Cakes        Madeleines

Spiced Almonds

Crackling Fruit

*(No recipe provided)

# Tea Punch

6 tea bags

1 piece Whole Ginger, 1 inch long

1 quart boiling water

2 quarts pineapple juice

1 quart apricot nectar

1 quart cranberry juice cocktail

¼ teaspoon Pure Almond Extract

¼ teaspoon Pure Orange Extract

6 drops Red Food Color

1 quart ginger ale

1. Place tea bags and ginger in 1½-quart heatproof glass bowl. Pour boiling water over and let stand 5 minutes. Remove and discard tea bags, but leave ginger in tea.

2. Pour tea into 8-quart container and add remaining ingredients except ginger ale. Cover and refrigerate to chill several hours or overnight.

3. Just before serving, remove ginger and pour tea into punch bowl. Add ginger ale.

*Makes 6 quarts*

TIP:

Freeze some tea in ring mold, unmold, and float frozen ring in punch.

# Cinnamon-Raisin Scones

4 cups all-purpose flour

2 tablespoons sugar

4 teaspoons baking powder

1½ teaspoons baking soda

1 teaspoon salt

1 teaspoon Ground Cinnamon

1 cup vegetable shortening

¼ cup butter or margarine, softened

2 cups buttermilk

⅓ cup raisins, soaked 30 minutes in ⅓ cup hot water

1. Preheat oven to 425°F. Lightly grease cookie sheets.

2. Place flour, sugar, baking powder, baking soda, salt, and cinnamon in large bowl and mix well. Cut in shortening and butter with pastry blender or 2 knives until mixture resembles coarse meal. Stir in buttermilk.

3. Turn dough out onto lightly floured work surface.

4. Drain raisins and knead into dough just until raisins are distributed throughout dough.

5. Divide dough into 3 equal-size portions and shape each portion into 1½ inch-thick round. Place on prepared cookie sheets.

6. Cut each round into 6 equal-size wedges with floured knife, but don't separate wedges.

7. Bake in preheated 425°F oven 25 minutes.

8. Serve warm, or cool on wire racks.

*Makes 18 scones*

# Tea Sandwiches

*½ cup butter or margarine, softened*
*¼ teaspoon Bon Appétit*
*⅛ teaspoon Caraway Seed*
*⅛ teaspoon Ground White Pepper*

*16 to 20 slices party-size rye or pumpernickle bread or small rounds white bread to serve*

*Toppings to serve (see below)*

1. Place butter, Bon Appétit, caraway seed, and white pepper in small bowl and mix well.

2. Spread on slices or rounds of bread.

3. Arrange choice of toppings on sandwiches to form delicate, appetizing and colorful combinations.

| | |
|---|---|
| Thinly sliced cucumbers | Herring |
| Thinly sliced tomatoes | Small cooked shrimp |
| Thinly sliced red or white onions | Anchovies |
| Thinly sliced radishes | Caviar |
| Shredded red or green bell peppers | Sliced smoked salmon |
| Lettuce, watercress, parsley | Rolled sliced roast beef |
| Thinly sliced pickles | Crumbled cooked bacon |
| Sliced hard-cooked eggs* | Variety of cheeses |

*Makes enough spread for 16 to 20 party sandwiches*

*(To hard-cook eggs, see page 48)

# Phyllo Turnovers

*1 pound lean ground beef*

*1 package (9 ounces) frozen creamed spinach, cooked*

*2 teaspoons Instant Minced Onion*

*½ teaspoon Bon Appétit*

*¼ teaspoon Ground Black Pepper*

*1 package (16 ounces) frozen phyllo leaves, thawed*

*½ cup butter or margarine, melted*

1. Place ground beef in skillet and cook over medium heat, stirring, until no longer pink. Drain off excess fat. Add cooked spinach, minced onion, Bon Appétit, and pepper. Mix well and set aside.

2. Preheat oven to 375°F. Set aside 2 cookie sheets.

3. Unfold phyllo leaves and place between damp towels. Remove 2 leaves together and place on flat, dry work surface. Cut into 2½ x 20-inch strips.

4. Brush both sides with melted butter. Place 2 teaspoons meat filling on corner at 1 end of double phyllo strip.

5. Pick up corner and fold over to opposite edge of strip to make filled triangle. Continue to fold filled triangle to end of leaf, alternating from left to right in triangle shape, folding as you would fold a flag.

6. Press end seam gently to seal. Place, seam side down, on cookie sheet and brush top with melted butter.

7. Repeat with remaining phyllo leaves and filling.

8. Bake in preheated 375°F oven 15 minutes or until lightly browned. Serve warm.

*Makes 32 to 40 turnovers*

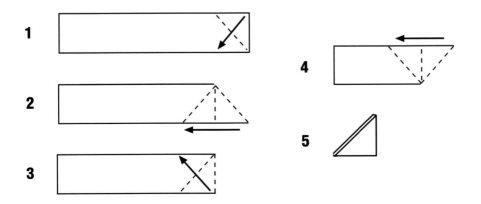

# Herb Omelets

12 large eggs

1 tablespoon water

1 teaspoon salt

¼ teaspoon Ground White Pepper

Butter or margarine

Choice of herbs (see below)

1. Place eggs in medium-size bowl, add water, salt, and white pepper, and beat until well combined.

2. Melt ½ teaspoon butter in nonstick 7-inch skillet or omelet pan.

3. Pour ¼ cup egg mixture into pan and sprinkle lightly with one of following:

   | | |
   |---|---|
   | Tarragon Leaves | Thyme Leaves |
   | Basil Leaves | Dill Weed |
   | Curry Powder | Oregano Leaves |

4. Cook just until omelet is set but still soft on top.

5. Fold 1 side of omelet to center and roll omelet over onto serving plate so both edges are folded under omelet.

6. Repeat with remaining egg mixture, adding butter as needed.

*Makes 16 omelets*

**TARRAGON**

# Filled Benne Lace Cookies

⅓ cup Sesame Seed

¼ cup butter

¼ cup light corn syrup

¼ cup firmly packed light
   brown sugar

½ cup plus 2 tablespoons sifted
   all-purpose flour

¼ teaspoon baking powder

¼ teaspoon Ground Cinnamon

3 ounces sweet baking chocolate

1. Preheat oven to 350°F. Lightly grease cookie sheets and set aside.

2. Place sesame seed in shallow baking pan and toast in preheated 350°F oven 15 minutes or until golden brown. Set aside to cool.

3. Reduce oven temperature to 325°F.

4. Place butter, corn syrup, and sugar in top of double boiler over (not in) boiling water. Cook until butter has melted. Stir to combine and remove from heat.

5. Sift flour, baking powder, and cinnamon and stir into butter mixture. Stir in reserved sesame seed and mix well.

6. Drop by ½ teaspoonfuls 3 inches apart onto prepared cookie sheets.

7. Bake in preheated 325°F oven 8 minutes.

8. Remove from oven and cool on cookie sheets 2 minutes.

9. Remove from cookie sheets with thin flexible spatula and place on flat work surface. Let cool on flat surface.

10. Melt chocolate over low heat.

11. Spread bottom of 1 cookie with thin coating of chocolate. Place second cookie on top of chocolate to make "sandwich." Repeat with remaining cookies and chocolate, making only 1 cookie "sandwich" at a time. Work quickly before chocolate cools.

*Makes about 3 dozen filled cookies*

TIP:

For best results, and nice crisp cookies, choose a dry, sunny day to make them.

# Coconut Tea Cakes

CAKE

1 package (17 ounces) pound
    cake mix

⅛ teaspoon Ground Mace

ICING

¼ cup butter or margarine,
    softened

¼ cup dairy sour cream

½ teaspoon Pure Vanilla Extract

¼ teaspoon Ground Cinnamon

¼ teaspoon Coconut Extract

2½ cups confectioners sugar

1 can (3½ ounces) flaked coconut

1. Prepare pound cake according to package directions, adding mace with
   dry ingredients. Bake as directed and cool on wire rack. Cut cake into
   3 x 1 x 1-inch rectangles.

2. Preheat broiler.

3. Place all icing ingredients except coconut in small mixing bowl and mix well.

4. Spread thin layer of icing on tops, sides, and ends of cake pieces. (Do not
   spread icing on bottom of pieces.)

5. Pour coconut into shallow dish and roll iced sides of cake pieces in coconut.
   Arrange on cookie sheet, iced sides up.

6. Broil 6 to 8 inches from source of heat, just until coconut is lightly browned.

7. Cool on cookie sheet.

*Makes 24 tea cakes*

**SESAME**

# Madeleines

*4 eggs*

*1¼ cups superfine sugar*

*2 cups sifted cake flour*

*1 teaspoon Pure Vanilla Extract*

*Dash Ground Mace*

*1 cup butter or margarine, melted and cooled to room temperature*

*Confectioners sugar for sprinkling, if desired*

1. Separate eggs and set egg whites aside.

2. Place egg yolks and superfine sugar in 2-quart bowl and beat until light colored and creamy. Stir in flour, vanilla, and mace, mixing well. Gradually beat melted butter into flour mixture.

3. Preheat oven to 350°F. Lightly grease twenty-four 2½-inch madeleine molds and set aside.

4. Place egg whites in mixer bowl and beat with electric mixer until soft peaks form when beaters are lifted. Fold egg whites into batter, folding gently until no streaks are visible.

5. Spoon batter into prepared madeleine molds, filling molds two-thirds full.

6. Bake in preheated 350°F oven 15 minutes.

7. Remove from molds and cool on wire rack. Sprinkle with confectioners sugar before serving.

*Makes 24 Madeleines*

**CUMIN**

# Spiced Almonds

*1 egg white*

*4 teaspoons sugar*

*4 teaspoons California Style
  Garlic Salt*

*2 teaspoons Hot Shot! Pepper Blend*

*2 teaspoons Ground Cumin*

*1 teaspoon Chili Powder*

*1 pound whole almonds with skins*

1. Preheat oven to 275°F. Line 15 x 10½ x 1-inch jelly-roll pan with aluminum foil. Lightly coat with no-stick cooking spray.

2. Beat egg white in small bowl until frothy. Add sugar, spices, and almonds. Stir to coat almonds evenly and place almonds in single layer in prepared pan.

3. Bake in preheated 275°F oven 40 minutes, stirring every 10 minutes.

4. Remove from oven and set aside to cool.

5. Store in airtight container up to 3 weeks.

*Makes 3½ cups (1 pound)*

VARIATIONS:

Follow recipe above, but in place of spices, substitute either of the following spice mixtures and add to beaten egg white with sugar and almonds.

*2 teaspoons Hot Shot! Pepper Blend*

*2 teaspoons California Style Garlic Powder*

*1 teaspoon Onion Salt*

OR

*2 teaspoons Curry Powder*

*2 teaspoons Onion Salt*

*2 teaspoons Hot Shot! Pepper Blend*

# Crackling Fruit

30 bite-size pieces fresh fruit such
  as strawberries, pineapple
  wedges, orange sections, and/or
  apple wedges

2 cups sugar

½ cup honey

½ cup water

1 Cinnamon Stick, 3 inches long

4 Whole Allspice

2 Cardamom Seeds

Cold water

Ice cubes

Crushed ice to serve

1. Prepare fruit and thread each piece on thin 6-inch bamboo skewers. Place skewered fruit on dish, cover lightly, and refrigerate at least 1 hour.

2. Place sugar, honey, ½ cup water, and spices in heavy 2½-quart saucepan and stir to combine. Cook over medium heat, stirring, until sugar has dissolved. Continue heating, without stirring, until mixture reaches 300 to 310°F (hard crack stage) on candy thermometer. To test, drop small amount of syrup into ice water. Syrup will separate into hard brittle threads. Be careful at this point because syrup will burn easily.

3. Turn off heat but leave saucepan on burner.

4. While syrup is cooking, place cold water and lots of ice in bowl large enough to accomodate skewers. Place crushed ice on large serving platter.

5. Place dish of chilled skewered fruit, pan of hot syrup, bowl of ice water, and platter of crushed ice next to each other. Carefully dip skewered fruit, 1 skewer at a time, into hot syrup. Then plunge fruit in and out of ice water, working very quickly. Place glazed skewered fruit on bed of crushed ice and serve immediately.

*Makes 30 bite-size pieces of fruit*

ALLSPICE

# CARIBBEAN

There are times when we all dream of running off to a tropical island — a carefree place where everything is laid-back, casual, and fun.

Invite your guests to escape with you for an evening and share some of these island flavors. (Before you scoff, taste the "Hop, Skip, and Go Naked Punch." It's delightful!)

MENU

## CARIBBEAN

*Reef Soup*

*Drunken Chicken*      *Caribbean Jerk Barbecued Ribs*

*Corn-Shrimp Fritters*

*Island Citrus Dressing*      *Ginger Cream Dressing*
*for Green Salad*      *for Fruit Salad*

*Coconut Muffins*

*Lemon-Ginger Ice*      *Piña Colada Soufflé*

*Hop, Skip, and Go Naked Punch*

ADDITIONAL RECIPES NEEDED
TO PREPARE ABOVE FOOD:
Caribbean Jerk Seasoning *(page 202)*
Caribbean Jerk Paste *(page 202)*

OTHER MENU IDEAS:
Bahamian Jerk Steak *(page 200)*
Caribbean Shipwreck Marinade
   for Pork or Beef *(page 201)*

# Reef Soup

2 tablespoons butter or margarine

2 cups small broccoli florets

1 onion, finely chopped

1 carrot, thinly sliced

1 apple, peeled, cored, and finely
chopped

1 tablespoon Madras Curry Powder

1½ teaspoons Celery Salt

¾ teaspoon Hot Shot! Pepper Blend

½ teaspoon Ground Ginger

2 pounds red snapper or other firm
fish fillets, cut into bite-size pieces

3 bottles (8 ounces each) clam juice

1 can (28 ounces) whole tomatoes,
cut into small pieces

1½ cups water

¼ pound mushrooms, sliced

¼ pound small shrimp, cooked,
peeled, and deveined

1 tablespoon dry vermouth

1 tablespoon Parsley Flakes

1. Melt butter in 4-quart saucepan or Dutch oven over medium-high heat. Add broccoli, onion, carrot, apple, curry powder, celery salt, Hot Shot!, and ginger. Stir-fry until onion is transparent. Add fish, clam juice, tomatoes, water, and mushrooms.

2. Heat to boil, reduce heat, cover, and simmer 10 minutes.

3. Stir in shrimp and vermouth. Keep hot over low heat until shrimp are heated through, but do not allow to boil. Do not overcook shrimp.

4. Sprinkle with parsley and serve.

*Makes 12 servings, 1 cup each*

**CELERY SEED**

# Drunken Chicken

12 boneless, skinless chicken breast halves

¾ cup light rum

3 tablespoons light brown sugar

3 tablespoons lime juice

3 tablespoons soy sauce

1 teaspoon Bon Appétit

½ teaspoon Crushed Red Pepper

¼ teaspoon Ground Nutmeg

¼ teaspoon Ground Ginger

¼ cup butter or margarine

3 cups sliced mushrooms

2 cups dairy sour cream

Long thin strips carrot and celery to garnish

1. Place chicken between 2 pieces of wax paper and pound to ½-inch thickness. Pierce in several places with fork and place in single layer in shallow glass dishes.

2. Place rum, sugar, lime juice, soy sauce, and seasonings in bowl and stir to combine. Pour over chicken. Cover and refrigerate 30 minutes to marinate, turning once.

3. Melt butter in large skillet over medium heat. Remove chicken from marinade and set marinade aside. Sauté chicken in butter. Remove to warm platter.

4. Add mushrooms to skillet and sauté about 3 minutes. Reduce heat, stir in reserved marinade, cover, and cook over low heat 5 minutes.

5. Remove skillet from heat and slowly stir in sour cream. Spoon over chicken. Garnish with strips of carrot and celery.

*Makes 12 servings, ½ chicken breast each, with sauce*

NUTMEG/MACE

# Caribbean Jerk Barbecued Ribs

*4 racks spareribs, 10 pounds*

*2 cups Caribbean Jerk Paste (double recipe page 202)*

*2 cans (8 ounces each) tomato sauce*

*1 cup lime juice*

*½ cup firmly packed dark brown sugar*

1. Preheat oven to 325°F.
2. Half-fill large stockpot with water and heat to boil. Add spareribs and cook 10 minutes. Drain well.
3. Place each rack of ribs on wire rack in shallow roasting pan.
4. Place remaining ingredients in medium-size bowl and mix well. Brush sauce on ribs.
5. Bake in preheated 325°F oven 2 hours, turning ribs and brushing with sauce every 15 to 20 minutes.

*Makes 12 servings, 3 to 4 ribs each*

# Corn-Shrimp Fritters

*4 eggs*

*1 cup milk*

*2 teaspoons olive oil*

*2½ cups all-purpose flour*

*2 tablespoons Caribbean Jerk Seasoning (page 202)*

*4 teaspoons baking powder*

*½ teaspoon salt*

*1 pound shrimp, peeled, deveined, and coarsely chopped*

*½ cup fresh or frozen whole-kernel corn*

*2 tablespoons finely diced red bell pepper*

*2 tablespoons finely diced yellow bell pepper*

*2 tablespoons finely diced green bell pepper*

*2 tablespoons Cilantro Leaves*

*Vegetable oil for frying*

1. Place eggs in 4-quart bowl. Beat eggs, add milk and olive oil, and mix well.
2. Place flour, Jerk Seasoning, baking powder, and salt in bowl and stir until well combined. Add to egg mixture, stirring until smooth. Stir in shrimp, corn, bell peppers, and cilantro.

3. Pour 3 inches oil into 5-inch-deep Dutch oven. Heat oil to 350°F on deep-fry thermometer.

4. Carefully drop batter by tablespoonfuls into hot oil, cooking only 5 or 6 fritters at a time. Fry until browned on 1 side. Turn and brown on second side.

5. Remove with slotted spoon and drain on paper towels. Serve hot.

*Makes 48 to 52 fritters*

# Island Citrus Dressing for Green Salad

*½ cup frozen orange juice concentrate*

*½ medium-size ripe banana*

*½ cup rice wine vinegar*

*¾ teaspoon salt*

*¼ teaspoon Ground Black Pepper*

*⅛ teaspoon Ground Mace*

*¾ cup olive oil*

*12 cups bite-size pieces assorted salad greens*

1. Place orange juice concentrate, banana, vinegar, salt, pepper, and mace in food processor and process until smooth.

2. Add oil in thin stream and continue processing until dressing is smooth and creamy.

3. Place salad greens in large bowl and pour dressing over. Toss gently.

*Makes 12 servings, 1 cup salad each (2 cups dressing)*

**RED PEPPER**

# Ginger Cream Dressing for Fruit Salad

2 cups heavy cream

¼ cup confectioners sugar

1 teaspoon Ground Ginger

½ cup chopped dates

½ cup chopped walnuts

4 teaspoons finely minced Crystallized Ginger

12 cups bite-size pieces assorted fresh fruit

1. Place cream in chilled bowl and beat with electric mixer until cream begins to thicken. Add sugar and ground ginger and whip until stiff.

2. Fold in dates, walnuts, and crystallized ginger. Cover and refrigerate at least 1 hour before serving.

3. Place fruit in large bowl. Pour dressing over fruit and mix gently to coat fruit.

*Makes 12 servings, 1 cup fruit each (4 cups dressing)*

# Coconut Muffins

¾ cup flaked coconut

2½ cups all-purpose flour

⅓ cup sugar

1 tablespoon baking powder

1 teaspoon salt

⅛ teaspoon Ground Mace

1 egg

1¼ cups milk

⅓ cup vegetable oil or vegetable shortening, melted

¼ teaspoon Pure Orange Extract

¼ teaspoon Coconut Extract

1. Preheat oven to 425°F. Lightly grease twelve 2½-inch muffin cups and set aside.

2. Spread coconut in shallow baking pan and toast in preheated 425°F oven 5 minutes or until coconut begins to brown. Remove and set aside. Do not turn oven off.

3. Sift flour, sugar, baking powder, salt, and mace into large bowl. Stir in toasted coconut.

4. Place egg in 1-quart bowl. Beat egg and stir in remaining ingredients. Add to flour mixture and stir just until dry ingredients are moistened. Some small lumps should remain in batter. Do not overmix.

5. Fill prepared muffin cups two-thirds full.

6. Bake in preheated 425°F oven 20 to 25 minutes or until toothpick inserted in center of muffin comes out clean. Remove from pan immediately and serve hot.

*Makes 12 muffins*

# Lemon-Ginger Ice

| | |
|---|---|
| *4 cups water* | *3 tablespoons Crystallized Ginger, ⅛-inch diced* |
| *2 cups sugar* | *2 drops Yellow Food Color* |
| *2 cups lemon juice* | *2 drops Pure Anise Extract* |

1. Place water and sugar in 2-quart saucepan. Heat to boil, stirring until sugar has dissolved. Cook over medium heat 5 minutes without stirring. Remove pan from heat and set aside to cool to room temperature.

2. Stir in remaining ingredients and pour into 13 x 9 x 2-inch metal pan.

3. Cover and freeze at least 4 hours. Remove from freezer every 30 minutes and scrape frozen portion from sides and bottom of pan with metal fork. Break up any large pieces with fork and return to freezer.

4. Keep frozen in covered container until ready to serve.

5. Use fork to scrape frozen chunks into dessert dishes and serve immediately.

*Makes 12 servings, ½ cup each*

# Piña Colada Soufflé

2 envelopes unflavored gelatin

1½ cups canned pineapple juice, chilled, divided

8 eggs

1 cup granulated sugar, divided

½ teaspoon salt

⅛ teaspoon Ground Mace

⅛ teaspoon Ground Cardamom

½ teaspoon Rum Extract

1 cup heavy cream

2 tablespoons confectioners sugar

¼ cup dark rum

1 cup cream of coconut

Sweetened whipped cream or mixture of 3 tablespoons light rum and 6 tablespoons light corn syrup to serve, if desired

1. Soften gelatin in ½ cup cold pineapple juice and set aside.

2. Separate eggs and set egg whites aside. Place egg yolks, ¼ cup granulated sugar, salt, mace, cardamom, and remaining 1 cup pineapple juice in top of double boiler and stir to combine. Cook over (not in) boiling water, stirring constantly, until slightly thickened.

3. Add softened gelatin and rum extract to egg mixture and stir until gelatin has dissolved. Pour into large bowl and set aside to cool to room temperature.

4. Prepare 6-cup soufflé dish by folding 30-inch strip of aluminum foil in half lengthwise. Tie foil around outside of dish with kitchen string to make collar that stands about 5 inches above rim. Tape ends of foil so collar does not spread when dish is filled. Set aside.

5. Place small mixer bowl in freezer to chill.

6. Place egg whites in mixer bowl and beat with electric mixer until foamy. Add remaining ¾ cup granulated sugar and beat just until soft peaks form when beaters are lifted. (Do not overbeat.) Set aside.

7. Place cream in chilled bowl with confectioners sugar. Beat with electric mixer until soft peaks form when beaters are lifted. (Do not overbeat.)

8. Add rum and cream of coconut to gelatin mixture and stir well.

9. Gently fold whipped cream and beaten egg whites into gelatin mixture until mixture is uniform in color and texture. Pour into prepared soufflé dish and refrigerate at least 3 hours or overnight.

*Piña Colada Soufflé (see photo on page 360)*

10. When ready to serve, cut string and carefully remove foil collar.
11. Serve with 1 of following:

Decorate top of soufflé with sweetened whipped cream and spoon onto dessert plates.

**OR**

Combine 3 tablespoons light rum and 6 tablespoons light corn syrup in small bowl and mix well. Spoon soufflé onto dessert plates and pour 1 to 2 teaspoons rum mixture over each serving.

*Makes 16 servings, ½ cup each*

# Hop, Skip, and Go Naked Punch

*4 cans (6 ounces each) frozen limeade concentrate*

*1 liter light rum*

*6 bottles (12 ounces each) light beer*

*2 tablespoons Pure Vanilla Extract*

*2 teaspoons Pure Orange Extract*

*2 Cinnamon Sticks, each 3 inches long, broken in half*

1. Place all ingredients in punch bowl.
2. Stir until limeade concentrate has melted and ingredients are well combined. Remove and discard cinnamon sticks.

*Makes 16 cups, twenty-five 5-ounce servings*

**CARDAMOM**

# *PUGET SOUND*

The Pacific Northwest conjures up images of snowcapped peaks, deep blue water, and cool Canadian sunsets. Food in this "land of blue skies" has a rugged, outdoor aura to it.

    We've tried to capture this atmosphere for you and your guests with these robust recipe suggestions, including our special recipe for Baked Stuffed Salmon. The salmon caught in these waters are world-famous.

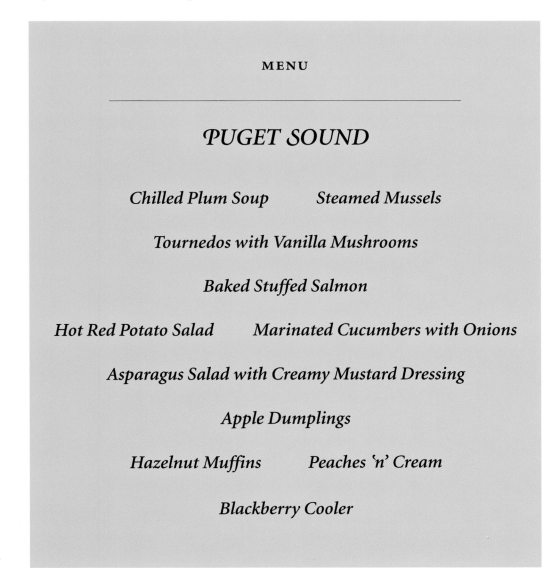

### MENU

## *PUGET SOUND*

*Chilled Plum Soup*      *Steamed Mussels*

*Tournedos with Vanilla Mushrooms*

*Baked Stuffed Salmon*

*Hot Red Potato Salad*      *Marinated Cucumbers with Onions*

*Asparagus Salad with Creamy Mustard Dressing*

*Apple Dumplings*

*Hazelnut Muffins*      *Peaches 'n' Cream*

*Blackberry Cooler*

*Piña Colada Soufflé (see recipe on page 358)*

# Chilled Plum Soup

6 cups apple juice

2 cups sugar

1 cup water

6 Whole Cloves

6 Whole Allspice

1 Cinnamon Stick, 3 inches long

1 Vanilla Bean, 2 inches long

¼ teaspoon salt

16 ripe red plums, halved and pitted

2 to 3 drops Red Food Color

Dairy sour cream to serve, if desired

1. Place apple juice, sugar, water, spices, vanilla bean and salt in large saucepan. Heat to boil, reduce heat immediately, and simmer 10 minutes.

2. Remove and discard whole spices. Add plum halves, return to boil, reduce heat, and simmer 10 minutes or until plums are very soft. Set aside to cool slightly.

3. Drain liquid through strainer into glass or ceramic bowl and set liquid aside.

4. Press plums through food mill or coarse strainer and discard skins. Add plum pulp to reserved liquid. Add red food color and mix well. Refrigerate 2 hours or overnight.

5. Spoon into small soup bowls and top each serving with dollop of sour cream.

*Makes 12 servings, ¾ cup each*

CINNAMON

# Steamed Mussels

6 pounds mussels

1½ cups dry vermouth

1½ cups water

1 tablespoon Instant Minced Garlic

1 tablespoon Instant Chopped Onions

1 tablespoon Coarse Ground
    Black Pepper

1 teaspoon Thyme Leaves

1 teaspoon Basil Leaves

1 Bay Leaf

1. Scrub mussels, remove beards, and discard any mussels not tightly closed.

2. Place remaining ingredients in 6-quart pot and stir to combine. Heat to boil, add mussels, cover, and cook 15 minutes or until shells open.

3. Remove mussels with slotted spoon and reserve broth. Remove and discard bay leaf and discard any mussels that have not opened.

4. Place mussels in serving bowls and pour small amount of reserved broth over each serving.

*Makes 12 servings, 7 to 9 mussels each*

# Tournedos with Vanilla Mushrooms

12 beef tenderloin steaks, cut at least
    1 inch thick

½ cup olive oil

2 tablespoons dry vermouth

2 teaspoons Pure Vanilla Extract

1 teaspoon Bon Appétit

½ teaspoon Ground Black Pepper

1 pound mushrooms

1. Preheat broiler or grill.

2. Broil or grill steaks 4-6 minutes or to desired doneness.

3. While steaks are cooking, heat oil in large skillet over high heat. Stir in vermouth, vanilla, Bon Appétit, and pepper. Add mushrooms and cook, stirring, 3 to 5 minutes.

4. Place steaks on warm serving platter and spoon sauce over. Serve immediately.

*Makes 12 servings, 1 steak each with mushrooms*

# Baked Stuffed Salmon

STUFFING

*4 slices white bread, crusts trimmed*

*½ cup butter or margarine*

*1 pound mushrooms, coarsely chopped*

*1 teaspoon Bon Appétit*

*1 teaspoon lemon juice*

*½ teaspoon Ground Savory*

*½ teaspoon Coarse Ground Black Pepper*

\* \* \*

*8 to 10-pound whole salmon, cleaned and scaled*

BASTING SAUCE

*½ cup butter or margarine*

*¼ cup tomato sauce*

*1 tablespoon soy sauce*

*1 tablespoon Ground Mustard*

*1 tablespoon brown sugar*

*¼ teaspoon Instant Minced Garlic*

1. Preheat oven to 350°F. Grease large piece of aluminum foil and place foil in 14 x 9 x 1-inch baking pan. Set aside.

2. Cut bread into ½-inch cubes.

3. To make stuffing, melt ½ cup butter in large skillet over medium heat. Add bread cubes, mushrooms, Bon Appétit, lemon juice, savory, and pepper. Sauté 10 minutes, stirring occasionally.

4. Spoon stuffing into cavity of salmon, packing tightly. Close opening with small skewers or wooden toothpicks to keep stuffing from falling out. Place fish in prepared pan and set aside.

5. To make sauce, melt ½ cup butter in 1-quart saucepan over low heat. Stir in remaining ingredients and mix well. Simmer 3 to 4 minutes.

6. Use very sharp knife to score skin on top of salmon in diagonal lines to make diamond pattern. Brush with basting sauce.

7. Bake in preheated 350°F oven 1½ hours, brushing frequently with sauce.

*Makes 12 servings, 6 to 8 ounces each*

# Hot Red Potato Salad

3 pounds small red potatoes,
    unpeeled, quartered

2 cans (11 ounces each) whole-kernel
    corn, drained

6 scallions, trimmed and chopped

4 slices bacon, cut into 1-inch pieces

1½ cups dairy sour cream

1 tablespoon Salad Supreme
    Seasoning

¾ teaspoon Onion Powder

½ teaspoon Hot Shot! Pepper
    Blend

1. Place potatoes in large saucepan, cover with water, and boil gently just until tender. Drain and return to pan. Add corn and scallions to pan and keep warm over very low heat.

2. In another pan or microwave-safe utensil, cook bacon until crisp. Drain on paper towels and set aside.

3. Place sour cream, seasoning, onion powder, and Hot Shot! in small bowl and stir to combine. Pour over potato mixture and mix well.

4. Spoon into serving bowl, sprinkle with reserved bacon, and serve hot.

*Makes 12 servings, ¾ cup each*

# Marinated Cucumbers with Onions

4 cups peeled, thinly sliced cucumbers
    (4 small or 2 large cucumbers)

1 teaspoon salt

2 cups thinly sliced fresh onions

½ cup vinegar

½ cup water

2 tablespoons sugar

1 teaspoon Dill Weed

½ teaspoon Cracked Black Pepper

Dash Ground Red Pepper

1. Place cucumber slices in medium-size glass bowl and sprinkle with salt. Cover with cold water and refrigerate 30 minutes. Drain well and return to bowl. Stir in onions.

2. Place remaining ingredients in 2-cup glass measure and beat with fork to combine.

3. Pour over cucumbers and onions and toss lightly. Refrigerate at least 3 hours. Stir before serving.

*Makes 12 servings, ½ cup each*

# Asparagus Salad with Creamy Mustard Dressing

*4 pounds asparagus, about 72 spears*

*1½ cups mayonnaise*

*½ cup Dijon-style mustard*

*1 teaspoon lemon juice*

*¼ teaspoon Dill Weed*

*¼ teaspoon Basil Leaves*

*¼ teaspoon Ground Black Pepper*

1. Wash asparagus and break off stalks as far down as they snap easily. Place in steamer, and cook just until crisp-tender, about 10 minutes. Plunge into cold water immediately to stop cooking. Drain, place on flat dish, cover, and refrigerate to chill.

2. Place remaining ingredients in small bowl and stir to mix well. Cover and refrigerate to chill.

3. When ready to serve, arrange asparagus spears on individual salad plates and place dollop of dressing on side of each plate.

*Makes 12 servings, 6 asparagus spears and 2 tablespoons sauce each*

**DILL WEED**

# Apple Dumplings

12 medium-size baking apples,
    peeled and cored

2 tablespoons lemon juice

SYRUP

2 cups granulated sugar

2 cups water

1 teaspoon Ground Cinnamon

½ teaspoon Ground Nutmeg

¼ teaspoon Ground Cloves

⅛ teaspoon Ground Mace

DOUGH

6 cups all-purpose flour

2 cups whole-wheat flour

8 teaspoons baking powder

2 teaspoons salt

1 teaspoon Ground Cinnamon

1 cup butter or margarine, softened

About 2½ cups milk

\* \* \*

FILLING

½ cup firmly packed brown sugar

2 tablespoons butter or margarine

1 teaspoon Ground Cinnamon

1 teaspoon Ground Nutmeg

1. Place apples in large, deep container. Add enough water to cover. Add lemon juice and set aside.

2. To make syrup, place granulated sugar, water, 1 teaspoon cinnamon, ½ teaspoon nutmeg, cloves, and mace in 2-quart saucepan. Stir to combine and heat to boil. Remove from heat and set aside.

3. To make dough, place all-purpose flour, whole-wheat flour, baking powder, salt, and 1 teaspoon cinnamon in large bowl. Mix well.

4. Add 1 cup butter and cut into flour mixture with pastry blender or 2 knives until mixture resembles coarse meal. Add 1½ cups milk and mix well. Add additional milk as needed to make soft but not sticky dough.

5. Turn out onto lightly floured surface and knead lightly about 15 seconds. Divide dough into 4 equal-size pieces. Roll each piece of dough to 21 x 7-inch rectangle. Cut each rectangle into three 7-inch squares to make 12 squares.

6. Preheat oven to 350°F. Lightly grease shallow baking pan or pans large enough to hold 12 apples. Set aside.

7. Remove 1 apple from water and drain. Place on square of pastry and fill cavity with 2 teaspoons brown sugar, ½ teaspoon butter, and dash each cinnamon and nutmeg. Repeat with remaining apples.

8. Lift edges of dough to meet over top of each apple. Moisten seams and press together. Trim off excess dough. If desired, cut small leaf shapes out of scraps of excess dough. Moisten 1 end of each leaf with water and press gently to attach at top of each dumpling.

9. Place dumplings in prepared baking pan(s). Reheat syrup briefly, if necessary, and pour over dumplings.

10. Bake in preheated 350°F oven 50 to 55 minutes, basting with syrup every 15 minutes. Place in serving bowls and spoon syrup over. Serve warm.

*Makes 12 apple dumplings*

# Hazelnut Muffins

*2 tablespoons Sesame Seed*

*1 cup apple juice*

*½ cup molasses*

*¼ cup butter or margarine, melted*

*¼ cup milk*

*2 eggs, beaten*

*2 cups whole-wheat flour*

*1 cup all-purpose flour*

*¾ cup sugar*

*4 teaspoons baking powder*

*1 teaspoon baking soda*

*1 teaspoon salt*

*¼ teaspoon Ground Ginger*

*⅛ teaspoon Ground Allspice*

*⅛ teaspoon Ground Cardamom*

*½ cup chopped hazelnuts (filberts)*

1. Preheat oven to 400°F. Lightly grease twenty-four 2½-inch muffin cups and set aside.

2. Spread sesame seed on cookie sheet and toast in preheated 400°F oven 10 minutes or until lightly browned. Remove from cookie sheet and set aside. Do not turn off oven.

3. Place apple juice, molasses, melted butter, milk, and eggs in bowl and mix well.

4. Place whole-wheat flour, all-purpose flour, sugar, baking powder, baking soda, salt, and spices in large bowl and stir until well combined.

5. Add liquid ingredients and hazelnuts to dry ingredients and stir just until dry ingredients are moistened. Do not overmix.

6. Spoon into prepared muffin pans, filling cups no more than two-thirds full. Sprinkle ¼ teaspoon reserved, toasted sesame seed over each muffin.

7. Bake in preheated 400°F oven 15 minutes or until toothpick inserted in center of muffin comes out clean. Remove from pan immediately and serve hot.

*Makes 24 muffins*

# Peaches 'n' Cream

4½ teaspoons unflavored gelatin
   (1½ envelopes)

¾ cup cold water

3 cups heavy cream

1½ cups sugar

3 cups dairy sour cream

3 tablespoons peach brandy

¾ teaspoon Pure Vanilla Extract

6 large ripe peaches, peeled, sliced,
   and sugared

1. Lightly oil 2-quart shallow mold and set aside.
2. Sprinkle gelatin over cold water to soften and set aside.
3. Place heavy cream and sugar in 2-quart saucepan and stir to combine. Heat over medium heat, stirring constantly, just until sugar has dissolved and mixture begins to bubble around edges.
4. Add gelatin to saucepan and stir until gelatin has dissolved. Remove from heat and beat in sour cream, peach brandy, and vanilla.
5. Pour into prepared mold and refrigerate overnight.
6. When ready to serve, unmold onto center of serving plate and surround with sliced sugared peaches.

*Makes 12 servings, ½ cup each*

# Blackberry Cooler

1 cup blackberry or raspberry syrup

¼ teaspoon Pure Anise Extract

4 bottles (750ml each) pink
champagne, chilled

1. Place blackberry syrup in 2-cup glass measure and stir in anise extract. Refrigerate to chill.
2. When ready to serve, spoon 2 teaspoons chilled syrup into each goblet or champagne flute. Pour in enough chilled pink champagne to fill glasses about two-thirds full. Stir with swizzle stick and serve immediately.

*Makes 24 servings, 2 teaspoons syrup and 4 ounces champagne each*

TIP:

Unused syrup may be refrigerated in covered container.

# *PACIFIC RIM*

Columbus discovered fiery red pepper plants in the New World. In due course, Portuguese sailors brought them to the Orient where the plants thrived and the red hot pepper pods they produced changed cuisines throughout Asia.

Because so many nations traded with the Orient, the area became a crossroads of diverse tastes. The development of new and exciting flavors spread throughout the world.

This Pacific Rim menu provides an unusual opportunity to delight guests with a mixture of unique flavor combinations. But, in order to keep the menu authentic, at least one dish should have enough red pepper in it to "tease the tongue." Since it was the Chinese who were the first to create sauces for various foods and to invent the noodles we call spaghetti, an appropriate Pacific Rim menu can include a remarkably wide range of different kinds of food.

**RED PEPPER**

MENU

# *PACIFIC RIM*

*Lemony Chicken Soup*

*Green Thai Curry*          *Saté with Peanut-Cashew Sauce*

*Sizzling Five-Spice Beef*

*Indonesian Vegetable Curry*

*Thai Rice*          *Thai Bean Salad*

*Fresh Fruit with Poppy Seed-Yogurt Dressing*

*Oriental Melon Dessert*

*Spiced Tea*

OTHER MENU IDEAS:

Thai Lemon Chicken *(page 219)*

Singapore Curry *(page 220)*

Island Pork *(page 206)*

Tofu with Bell Peppers and
    Peanuts *(page 252)*

Chicken Tikka *(page 220)*

Thai Roasted Vegetables *(page 257)*

Polynesian Pork with Almonds
    *(page 206)*

# Lemony Chicken Soup

3 quarts chicken broth

1½ cups cooked chicken, cut into
  ¼-inch dice

4 ounces (half of 8-ounce package)
  wide egg noodles, broken into
  1-inch pieces

¾ cup lemon juice

2 tablespoons thinly sliced scallion

¾ teaspoon Thai Seasoning

½ teaspoon Mint Flakes

1. Place chicken broth in 4-quart saucepan and heat to boil.

2. Stir in remaining ingredients, reduce heat to low, and simmer 10 minutes.

*Makes 12 servings, 1 cup each*

# Green Thai Curry

2 cans (4 ounces each) chopped
  green chilies

1 small onion, quartered

3 tablespoons lime juice

2 tablespoons olive oil

1 tablespoon Instant Minced Garlic

1 teaspoon Thai Seasoning

1 teaspoon Basil Leaves

1 teaspoon salt

½ teaspoon Ground Black Pepper

½ teaspoon Ground Red Pepper

¼ teaspoon Mint Flakes

¼ teaspoon Caraway Seed

1 cup water

1 cup cream of coconut

3 pounds shrimp, cooked, peeled,
  and deveined

Hot cooked rice to serve, if desired

1. Combine all ingredients except water, cream of coconut, shrimp, and rice in food processor and process to smooth paste.

2. Spoon into 4-quart saucepan. Stir in water and cream of coconut and heat over low heat just until mixture begins to bubble.

3. Stir in shrimp and cook until shrimp are heated through, about 10 minutes. Serve over hot cooked rice.

*Makes 12 servings, 6 ounces each*

# Saté with Peanut-Cashew Sauce

### SATÉ

3-pound top or bottom round
    beef roast

¾ cup soy sauce

1 teaspoon Ground Ginger

1 teaspoon Onion Salt

½ teaspoon Garlic Powder

½ teaspoon Ground Black Pepper

¼ teaspoon Ground Red Pepper

### PEANUT-CASHEW SAUCE

1 cup unsalted dry-roasted peanuts

1 cup unsalted dry-roasted cashews

2 tablespoons peanut oil

¼ teaspoon Ground Red Pepper

4 teaspoons Chicken Flavor Base

1 cup hot water

1. Cut meat into thin strips, 5 x 1 x ¹⁄₁₆-inch, with very sharp knife or on slicing machine. Place meat strips in 13 x 9 x 2-inch glass dish.

2. Mix remaining Saté ingredients in small bowl or cup measure and pour over meat.

3. Cover and refrigerate at least 4 hours or overnight.

4. To make sauce, place peanuts and cashews in food processor. Process until very fine and smooth and transfer to medium-size bowl, scraping into bowl with rubber spatula.

5. Add oil and red pepper. Mix well. Stir flavor base into hot water and add to nut mixture gradually, stirring to mix well after each addition. (If thinner sauce is desired, add additional hot water, 1 tablespoon at a time, mixing well after each addition.)

6. Preheat broiler or grill.

7. Remove meat from marinade and discard marinade. Thread meat strips on thin bamboo skewers and place skewers on broiler pan or grill rack. Broil or grill 5 minutes, turning 2 or 3 times during cooking.

8. Serve meat hot with sauce for dipping.

*Makes 12 servings, 4 ounces meat each (2 cups sauce)*

TIP:

Beef is easier to slice if partially frozen. Cut across grain into bite-size strips.

*Saté with Peanut-Cashew Sauce*

# Sizzling Five-Spice Beef

⅓ cup vegetable oil

3-pound round steak, cut into
2 x ½ x ⅛-inch-thin strips

2 cans (4 ounces each) sliced
mushrooms, drained

2 red bell peppers, cut into 2 x ½-inch
strips

1 tablespoon Chinese Five Spice

3 tablespoons soy sauce

2 tablespoons cornstarch

⅓ cup cold water

Hot cooked rice to serve, if desired

1. Heat oil in large skillet or wok over high heat. Add meat and stir-fry 3 to 4 minutes.

2. Add mushrooms, bell pepper strips, and Chinese Five Spice. Cook, stirring, 1 minute.

3. Place soy sauce, cornstarch, and water in small bowl or cup measure and mix well. Pour over meat and cook, stirring, until sauce is clear and thickened. Serve, sizzling hot, over hot cooked rice.

*Makes 12 servings, 4 ounces each*

# Indonesian Vegetable Curry

½ cup butter or margarine

3 tablespoons all-purpose flour

1 tablespoon Madras Curry Powder

¼ teaspoon Thyme Leaves

¼ cup tomato paste

1 tablespoon Chicken Flavor Base

2 cups water

6 cups steamed mixed vegetables
such as broccoli florets,
cauliflowerets, sliced carrots,
and/or sliced zucchini

1. Melt butter in 1-quart saucepan over low heat . Stir in flour, curry powder, and thyme. Cook, stirring, 2 minutes. Do not brown.

2. Stir in tomato paste and flavor base. Add water gradually and cook, stirring, just until sauce thickens.

3. Pour sauce over hot steamed vegetables and keep warm until ready to serve.

*Makes 12 servings, ½ cup each*

# Thai Rice

1 tablespoon vegetable oil

1 tablespoon Thai Seasoning

¼ cup chopped green bell pepper

¼ cup chopped red bell pepper

¼ cup chopped fresh onion

1 tablespoon chopped scallion,
    white part only

2 cups long grain rice

4 cups water

1 tablespoon Chicken Flavor Base

1 tablespoon chopped scallion,
    green part only

1 tablespoon chopped unsalted
    dry-roasted peanuts

1. Heat oil and Thai seasoning in 4-quart saucepan over medium heat. Add green and red bell peppers, onion, and white portion of scallion. Sauté, stirring occasionally, until onion is transparent.

2. Stir in rice and cook, stirring occasionally, 5 minutes. Add water and flavor base.

3. Heat to boil, reduce heat, cover, and simmer 25 to 30 minutes or until all water has been absorbed.

4. Fluff with fork and spoon into serving dish. Sprinkle with green portion of scallion and peanuts.

*Makes 12 servings, ½ cup each*

# Thai Bean Salad

3 cans (15 ounces each) red kidney
    beans, drained

2 cans (16 ounces each) cut yellow
    wax beans, drained

¾ cup chopped scallions

¾ cup olive oil

3 tablespoons malt vinegar

2 teaspoons Thai Seasoning

2 teaspoons Instant Chopped
    Onions

1½ teaspoons water

1. Place kidney beans, wax beans, and scallions in large bowl and stir to combine.

2. Place remaining ingredients in 2-cup glass measure or small bowl and beat until well combined.

3. Pour over bean mixture and toss to mix well. Cover and refrigerate to chill.

*Makes 12 servings, ½ cup each*

# Fresh Fruit With Poppy Seed-Yogurt Dressing

*1 cup plain yogurt*

*2 tablespoons honey*

*4 teaspoons lime juice*

*1 teaspoon Pure Vanilla Extract*

*1 teaspoon Poppy Seed*

*12 cups cut-up fresh fruit*

1. Place all ingredients except fruit in small bowl and stir until well combined.
2. Spoon fruit into 12 serving dishes and top each with 1 tablespoon yogurt mixture.

*Makes 12 servings, 1 cup fruit each (1¼ cups dressing)*

# Spiced Tea

*8 cups water*

*8 tea bags*

*1 cup sugar*

*1 cup orange juice*

*½ cup lemon juice*

*16 Whole Cloves*

*6 Cinnamon Sticks, each 3 inches long*

*⅛ teaspoon Ground Nutmeg*

*14 very thin lemon slices*

1. Heat water to boil in medium-size glass or stainless steel saucepan, add tea bags, remove from heat, and steep 5 minutes.
2. Remove and discard tea bags. Stir in sugar, orange juice, lemon juice, cloves, cinnamon sticks, and nutmeg.
3. Let stand over low heat 30 minutes. Before serving, remove whole spices.
4. Serve hot with paper-thin lemon slice floating in each cup.

*Makes 12 servings, 5 ounces each*

# Oriental Melon Dessert

*1 round dark green watermelon*

*1 cantaloupe*

*1 honeydew melon*

*1 can (15 ounces) lychee nuts, drained*

*1 jar (10 ounces) kumquats, drained*

*1 cup orange juice*

*½ cup honey*

*¼ teaspoon Pure Anise Extract*

*¼ teaspoon Pure Almond Extract*

1. Cut thin slice from blossom end of watermelon to make stable base. Stand watermelon on cut end.

2. Cut 2-inch slice off top of watermelon. Scoop out fruit and remove and discard seeds. Cut fruit into bite-size pieces, place in large bowl, and set aside.

3. Carve top edge of watermelon all the way around in notched or scalloped pattern.

4. Use point of bamboo skewer or sharp pencil to draw flower and leaf designs on side of watermelon. Carefully remove rind along drawn outlines of designs with small, sharp knife. Cover carved watermelon with plastic wrap.

5. Peel cantaloupe and honeydew, remove seeds, and cut into bite-size pieces. Place in large bowl with reserved watermelon pieces. Add lychees and kumquats.

6. Place remaining ingredients in 2-cup glass measure or small bowl and stir to combine. Pour over fruit and stir gently to coat fruit. Cover and refrigerate with watermelon overnight.

7. When ready to serve, remove fruit from refrigerator and stir gently. Fill carved watermelon with fruit and refrigerate remaining fruit until ready to refill watermelon as needed.

*Makes 12 servings, 1 cup each*

TIP:

Quantity of fruit will vary slightly, depending on size of melons used. If desired, use melon scoop to make melon balls instead of cutting fruit into bite-size pieces.

*Oriental Melon Dessert (see photo on page 380)*

# CASABLANCA

*Casablanca* and other classic movies can provide creative themes for unusual parties. Many of the old movies are filled with fantasy and take place in exotic locales that can be used as wonderful excuses for unusual menus. Add to the fun by persuading your guests to dress up like their favorite film characters. Who wouldn't enjoy pretending to be Humphrey Bogart, Ingrid Bergman, or some other great romantic Hollywood star?

For a "Casablanca" party, rent a video of the movie or get a CD or tape of the musical score. Make a low table by using a 4 x 8-foot piece of ⅝-inch-thick plywood. Use concrete blocks for support at each corner and under the center of the table. Select a brightly colored tablecloth or scarves to cover the table and place pillows on the floor around the table for guests to sit on. Use fruit in colorful bowls or baskets and candles in brass containers to create a centerpiece.

Serve Couscous with Lamb, Coriander Potatoes, Spiced Oranges, and other suggested recipes for a menu, choosing those dishes you think your guests will enjoy most. You can be certain everyone will remember the party "as time goes by."

**CORIANDER**

*Oriental Melon Dessert (see recipe on page 379)*

MENU

## *CASABLANCA*

*Sautéed Sesame Grapes*

*Couscous with Lamb*

*Coriander Potatoes        Garden Vegetable Salad*

*Carrot-Orange Salad*

*Whole-Wheat Pita Bread*

*Spiced Oranges        Date-Filled Squares*

*Mint Tea        Cardamom Coffee*

OTHER MENU IDEAS:

Dilly Bread *(page 276)* — (Make 2 loaves to serve 12)

Game Hens Cardamom *(page 217)*

Seafood Stew *(page 234)*

Couscous with Variations *(page 261)* — (Double recipe to serve 12)

# Sautéed Sesame Grapes

1 pound seedless grapes
    (Thompson preferred)

1 egg

1 tablespoon water

1½ teaspoons Ground Ginger

1½ teaspoons Garlic Powder

½ teaspoon salt

½ cup all-purpose flour

⅓ cup Sesame Seed

⅓ cup dry bread crumbs

2 tablespoons vegetable or canola oil

1. Rinse grapes and set aside in bowl of cold water.

2. Place egg in medium-size bowl and beat with fork. Add water, ginger, garlic powder, and salt and mix well.

3. Place flour in plastic bag.

4. Combine sesame seed and bread crumbs in separate bag.

5. Prepare a few grapes at a time: remove from water but don't dry; shake in flour; dip in egg mixture; and shake in sesame-bread crumb mixture. Place coated grapes on plate and repeat until all grapes have been coated. (Grapes may be prepared up to four hours ahead of time and refrigerated until ready to cook.)

6. When ready to cook, heat oil in large skillet over medium heat. Add grapes and sauté, turning until golden on all sides. Serve hot as appetizer or side dish with ham, poultry, or seafood.

*Makes 40 to 50 sautéed grapes*

SESAME

# Couscous with Lamb

### COUSCOUS

9¼ cups water, divided

1 tablespoon butter or margarine

1 teaspoon Season-All Seasoned Salt

1 pound (3 cups) quick-cooking couscous

⅛ teaspoon Ground Cinnamon

2 tablespoons butter or margarine, melted

### LAMB STEW

¼ cup vegetable oil

2 pounds boneless lamb for stew, cut into 1-inch cubes

4 ripe tomatoes, peeled and quartered

⅓ cup Instant Chopped Onions

1 tablespoon Ground Black Pepper

1 tablespoon Parsley Flakes

1 teaspoon Coriander Seed

1 Cinnamon Stick, 3 inches long

2 cans (16 ounces each) chickpeas, drained

4 carrots, quartered lengthwise and cut into 2-inch pieces

2 turnips, peeled and cut into 1-inch cubes

1 large sweet potato, peeled and cut into 1-inch cubes

½ cup raisins

2 zucchini, each 6 inches long, cut in half lengthwise and then into 1-inch slices

1. Place 3¾ cups water, 1 tablespoon butter, and seasoned salt in 4-quart saucepan and heat to boil. Stir in couscous, remove from heat, cover, and let stand 5 minutes.

2. Stir cinnamon into 2 tablespoons melted butter and drizzle over couscous. Fluff with fork and set aside.

3. Heat oil in 6-quart pot over high heat. Add lamb, tomatoes, chopped onions, pepper, parsley, coriander seed, and cinnamon stick. Cook stirring, 5 minutes.

4. Add 4 cups water, chickpeas, and carrots. Heat to boil, reduce heat to low, cover, and boil gently 35 to 40 minutes. Stir in turnips, sweet potato, remaining 1½ cups water, raisins, and zucchini.

5. Spoon reserved couscous into large colander and place colander over pot containing lamb mixture. Cover colander and, if colander does not fit inside pot, wrap foil around sides of colander. Boil gently over low heat 25 to 30 minutes.

6. Spoon couscous in ring around edge of large platter. Spoon lamb mixture onto center of platter and remove and discard cinnamon stick.

*Makes 12 servings, ⅔ cup couscous and 1 cup stew each*

# Coriander Potatoes

24 small red potatoes, unpeeled,
  cut into ¾-inch slices

2 tablespoons Instant Chopped
  Onions

1 tablespoon Bon Appétit

¼ cup butter or margarine

¼ cup olive oil

2 tablespoons lemon juice

1 tablespoon Parsley Flakes

1 tablespoon Coriander Seed, crushed

2 teaspoons Season-All Seasoned Salt

½ teaspoon Ground Black Pepper

½ teaspoon Mediterranean Oregano
  Leaves

1. Place sliced potatoes, chopped onions, and Bon Appétit in 6-quart pot. Cover with water, heat to boil, and boil 10 minutes or until potatoes are fork tender. Do not overcook. Drain immediately and set aside.

2. Melt butter in 4-quart Dutch oven over low heat.

3. Stir in remaining ingredients. Add reserved potatoes and turn gently in mixture to coat potatoes on all sides.

4. Cover and keep over low heat 5 minutes.

*Makes 12 servings, ¾ cup each*

TIP:

Crush Coriander Seed in mortar and pestle or small electric spice grinder.

# Garden Vegetable Salad

4 cups peeled, cubed, cooked
  potatoes

3 cups cooked lima beans

3 cups cooked peas

2 cups sliced, cooked carrots

1½ cups diced, cooked beets

1½ cups chopped celery

¾ cup vegetable oil

1⅓ cup white vinegar

1 tablespoon Bon Appétit

2 teaspoons Instant Minced Onion

¾ teaspoon Ground Mustard

¼ teaspoon Ground White Pepper

Dash Garlic Powder

1 cup mayonnaise

Lettuce cups to serve

1. Place potatoes, beans, peas, carrots, beets, and celery in large bowl and toss gently to combine.

2. Place oil, vinegar, and seasonings in 2-cup glass measure and beat with fork until well combined. Pour over vegetables, mix gently, cover, and refrigerate 2 hours or overnight.

3. When ready to serve, stir in mayonnaise and spoon into lettuce cups.

*Makes 12 servings, 1 cup each*

# Carrot-Orange Salad

*6 cups shredded carrots
(about 14 carrots)*

*1 can (11 ounces) mandarin oranges*

*1 cup mayonnaise*

*1¼ teaspoons Lemon & Pepper
Seasoning, divided*

*1 teaspoon Bon Appétit*

*½ teaspoon Onion Powder*

*½ teaspoon Ground Mustard*

*¼ teaspoon Ground Cumin*

*Dash Ground Cloves*

*2 teaspoons olive oil*

*½ cup coarsely chopped walnuts*

*¼ teaspoon Madras Curry Powder*

*⅛ teaspoon salt*

1. Place shredded carrots in large bowl.

2. Drain orange sections, reserving ¼ cup liquid. Add oranges to carrots in bowl.

3. Place mayonnaise in small bowl and stir in reserved ¼ cup liquid from oranges. Add 1 teaspoon Lemon & Pepper seasoning, Bon Appétit, onion powder, mustard, cumin, and cloves. Mix well and stir into carrots and oranges.

4. Cover and refrigerate to chill.

5. Spoon carrot salad into shallow serving dish.

6. Heat oil in small skillet over low heat. Stir in remaining ¼ teaspoon Lemon & Pepper seasoning, oil, walnuts, curry powder, and salt. Cook, stirring, 1 minute. Sprinkle over carrot salad just before serving.

*Makes 12 servings, ½ cup each*

# Whole-Wheat Pita Bread

1 package (¼ ounce) active dry yeast

1 teaspoon sugar

2½ cups warm water (105 to 110°F), divided

4 cups all-purpose flour

2 cups whole-wheat flour

1 teaspoon Bon Appétit

Cornmeal for dusting cookie sheets

1. Place yeast, sugar, and ½ cup warm water in small bowl and mix well.

2. Place all-purpose flour, whole-wheat flour, and Bon Appétit in large bowl and stir to combine. Add remaining 2 cups warm water and mix well. Stir in yeast mixture.

3. Cover bowl with damp towel and let rise in warm, draft-free place 1 to 1½ hours or until dough doubles in size.

4. Preheat oven to 450°F. Sprinkle 2 or more cookie sheets with cornmeal and set aside.

5. Divide dough into 12 equal-size pieces. Place dough, 1 piece at a time, on lightly floured surface and roll out each piece of dough to 6 ½-inch round.

6. Place on prepared cookie sheets.

7. Bake in preheated 450°F oven 7 minutes. Bread should be puffy and just beginning to brown.

8. Remove from oven. Let cool. Cut pocket opening along one side and into middle of bread to form pocket for filling.

*Makes 12 pita bread pockets*

# Spiced Oranges

6 large navel oranges

1 cup orange juice

½ cup honey

¼ cup lemon juice

4 Whole Cloves

3 Whole Allspice

1 Cinnamon Stick, 3 inches long

1 Whole Nutmeg

1 Cardamom Seed

1 Bay Leaf

Fresh mint sprigs to garnish

1. Peel oranges with sharp knife, removing all white underskin. Slice each orange crosswise into 4 thick slices and arrange slices in shallow, heatproof glass dish.

2. Place remaining ingredients except mint sprigs in 1-quart saucepan. Mix well. Heat to boil, reduce heat, and simmer 5 minutes. Pour over orange slices.

3. Cover and refrigerate at least 2 hours.

4. When ready to serve, remove whole spices and garnish oranges with mint sprigs.

*Makes 12 servings, 2 orange slices each*

# Date-Filled Squares

*1 cup chopped dates*

*⅓ cup water*

*¼ cup sugar*

*¼ cup chopped walnuts*

*4 teaspoons lemon juice*

*1 teaspoon Pure Vanilla Extract*

*1 cup firmly packed light brown sugar*

*½ cup butter or margarine, softened*

*3 cups rolled oats*

*½ teaspoon Ground Cinnamon*

*¼ teaspoon Ground Allspice*

1. Preheat oven to 350°F.

2. Place dates, water, sugar, walnuts, and lemon juice in saucepan and stir to combine. Cook over low heat, stirring frequently, until thickened, about 5 minutes. Remove from heat, stir in vanilla, and set aside.

3. Cream sugar and butter in large bowl. Stir in rolled oats, cinnamon, and allspice.

4. Press half of oat mixture firmly in bottom of 13 x 9 x 2-inch baking pan. Spread reserved date mixture evenly over and sprinkle with remaining half of oat mixture. Press firmly.

5. Bake in preheated 350°F oven 15 minutes.

6. Cool in pan on wire rack. Cut 4 rows down length of pan and 5 rows across width of pan to make 20 squares, each about 2 x 2 inches.

*Makes 20 squares, approximately 2 x 2 inches each*

# Mint Tea

*¼ cup loose tea or 10 tea bags*
*12 cups boiling water*
*¼ teaspoon Pure Mint Extract*

1. Place tea in 4-quart heatproof glass or stainless steel bowl and pour boiling water over. Let steep 5 minutes.
2. Stir in mint extract.
3. Pour through strainer into serving containers (teapots or thermal carafes).

*Makes 12 cups*

# Cardamom Coffee

Serve strong black coffee in small cups and float 1 Cardamom Seed in each cup. Add sugar, if desired.

Suggest guests stir coffee and remove Cardamom Seed when coffee is flavored to individual taste.

**MINT**

# MAKE-YOUR-OWN-CURRY PARTY

A Bengali feast — an unusual and delightful party your guests can create themselves!

This dinner from India is a great do-it-yourself party. The host is responsible for the preparation of the main ingredients such as seafood, chicken, or meat, as well as providing the spices and condiments. When dinner is served, the guests take over and use their taste buds to create their own curry sauce to accompany the main dish.

Curry, a blend of many spices, is the world's favorite seasoning. The word "curry" actually means sauce, and encouraging your guests to craft their own can be an exciting challenge, and the result, a wonderful taste treat.

Curry is eaten in more cultures than any other sauce. It's different in each setting and is as individualistic as is each Italian family's secret tomato sauce.

We suggest you start the party by serving Sunshine Avocado and Melon Salad. You may want to end the meal in a traditional way by offering Dessert Spices. Wealthy princes used to do this as a sign of their hospitality and vast riches. In order to leave this "good taste in your mouth," a recipe for Dessert Spices has been included.

Our "Make-Your-Own-Curry" Party menu provides suggestions for the things you will need (ingredients, food, and equipment) and the way to present the food. Reading through the following pages will familiarize you with the entire plan for the party and will help you prepare everything ahead of time so you can enjoy the party as much as your guests will.

**CUMIN**

MENU

---

## CURRY PARTY

*Make-Your-Own Curry*

*Sunshine Avocado and Melon Salad*

*Banana and Mango Chutney*

*Spice Ice Cream*

*Dessert Spices*

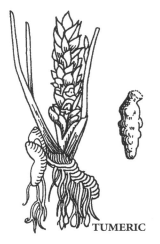

TUMERIC

# Make-Your-Own Curry

PARTY SUPPLY LIST

To serve 12 people, you will need:

1. 3 cups Chicken Broth *(page 396)*
2. 9 cups White Sauce *(page 397)*
3. Spices — 1 bottle each of:

| | |
|---|---|
| *Onion Powder* | *Ground Cinnamon* |
| *Ground Coriander* | *Ground Allspice* |
| *Ground Cumin* | *Ground Ginger* |
| *Ground Turmeric* | *Ground Mustard* |
| *Ground Cloves* | *Ground White Pepper* |
| *Ground Cardamom* | *Ground Red Pepper* |

4. 12 teaspoons for measuring spices
5. 10 to 12 cups cooked white rice
6. 3 to 4 pounds cooked seafood, beef, or chicken, cut into bite-size pieces
7. Condiments:

| | |
|---|---|
| *1 cup flaked coconut* | *½ cup minced Crystallized Ginger* |
| *1 cup chopped hard-cooked egg\** | *4 cups Banana and Mango Chutney* |
| *1 cup chopped peanuts* | *(page 398)* |
| *1 cup diced green bell pepper* | |

8. 12 bouillon or custard cups
9. 12 soup bowls or mugs that will hold 12 ounces each
10. 12 teaspoons for mixing
11. 12 dinner plates
12. Your choice of other food from menu
13. Light cream to tone down flavor in case guest makes a curry too hot and spicy

*\*(To hard-cook eggs, see page 48)*

Here's how we suggest you direct the proceedings:

1. Arrange spices into 3 groups of 4 spices as indicated below.

   BACKGROUND FLAVORS:

   Mark the background flavors by tying a green ribbon around the neck of each bottle. These flavors form the background flavor of the curry.

   Onion Powder - pungent

   Ground Coriander - sweet, slightly lemony

   Ground Cumin - strong, earthy

   Ground Turmeric - golden color, slightly bitter, earthy

   BLENDING FLAVORS:

   Mark the blending spices by tying a yellow ribbon around the neck of each bottle. These spices blend to balance the flavor of the curry.

   Ground Cloves - sweet, pungent

   Ground Cardamom - warm, sweet, mellow, citrus-like

   Ground Cinnamon - spicy, sweet, woody

   Ground Allspice - rich, warm, flavor resembles a mixture of spices

   ROBUST FLAVORS:

   Mark the hot, robust spices by tying a red ribbon around the neck of each bottle. These spices are used to accent the flavor of the curry. They should be added in tiny amounts. BE CAREFUL!

   Ground Ginger - warm, citrus-like, sweet, pungent, hot

   Ground Mustard - pungent, tangy, hot

   Ground White Pepper - earthy, hot

   Ground Red Pepper - very hot

2. Prepare Chicken Broth and White Sauce *(pages 396 and 397)*. Pour each into separate bowl and keep warm.

3. Cook rice, spoon into serving bowls, and keep warm.

4. Cut cooked seafood, beef, or chicken into bite-size pieces, arrange on serving dish, and keep warm.

5. Place 6 condiments in separate small bowls.

6. Arrange curry-making table and seating for your guests.

7. Serve each guest 2 to 3 tablespoons Chicken Broth in bouillon or custard cup.

8. Serve each guest ½ to ¾ cup White Sauce in soup bowl or 12-ounce mug.

*(continued)*

*Make-Your-Own Curry*

9. Demonstrate for your guests how each group of spices should be used in order to blend the rich, warm, earthy, and pungent flavors typical of curry. Explain that the colored ribbons on the spice bottles represent green for mild, yellow for medium, and red for hot. *(For more information on spices, see pages 11 to 44)*

10. Suggest your guests start by adding ¼ teaspoon or less of each green-ribboned spice to the Chicken Broth; ⅛ teaspoon or less of each yellow-ribboned spice; and just a tiny bit of each red-ribboned spice. Remind your guests they can always add more of any spice they like, but it's hard to subtract a flavor if too much has been used — especially red pepper!

11. Advise everyone to smell each spice as it is used — aroma is related to flavor. Once all the spices have been added to the Chicken Broth and mixed well, tell your guests to stir the spiced Chicken Broth into the White Sauce, taste, and correct the seasoning to suit their individual taste. Keep a small pitcher of light cream handy in case one of your guests has used too much red pepper. The sauce can be diluted with the cream and it will help soften the heat of the pepper.

12. Invite your guests to help themselves to rice and meat, chicken, or seafood. Then tell them to pour their curry sauce over the food and garnish it with a selection of condiments.

13. And finally, as host, enjoy your creation and sit back to listen as your guests argue about who has made the best curry. Everyone will enjoy the competition.

# Chicken Broth

*1 tablespoon Chicken Flavor Base*
*3 cups boiling water*

1. Dissolve flavor base in boiling water.
2. Keep over low heat until ready to serve.

*Makes 12 servings, 2 to 3 tablespoons each (3 cups broth)*

# White Sauce

¾ cup butter or margarine

1 tablespoon Onion Powder

2 teaspoons Bon Appétit

2 teaspoons Ground White Pepper

1 cup all-purpose flour

5 cups hot milk

2 cups hot light cream

1½ cups Chablis (dry white wine)

1. Melt butter in 3-quart saucepan over low heat. Stir in onion powder, Bon Appétit, and white pepper and mix well. Stir in flour and cook, stirring 2 minutes. Do not brown.

2. Remove from heat and gradually stir in hot milk, cream, and Chablis.

3. Return to heat and heat to low boil, stirring constantly.

*Makes 12 servings, ¾ cup each (9 cups sauce)*

# Sunshine Avocado and Melon Salad

½ cup orange juice

½ cup olive oil

¼ cup white wine vinegar

2 teaspoons Lemon & Pepper Seasoning

1 teaspoon Ground Coriander

1 teaspoon Orange Peel

4 large ripe avocados

1 honeydew melon

1 cantaloupe

Lettuce cups to serve

1. Combine orange juice, oil, vinegar and seasonings in screw-top jar. Shake to mix well and refrigerate to chill.

2. Cut avocados in half. Remove pits, peel, and slice fruit and place in glass bowl. Shake dressing and pour over avocados.

3. Cut melons in half and remove seeds. Scoop out as many melon balls as possible with melon ball cutter and add to avocados. Toss to mix well.

4. Cover and refrigerate at least 1 hour.

5. When ready to serve, spoon into lettuce cups.

*Makes 12 servings, ½ cup each*

# Banana and Mango Chutney

¾ cup white wine vinegar

¾ cup firmly packed light brown sugar

2 teaspoons Madras Curry Powder

1 teaspoon Ground Black Pepper

½ teaspoon salt

½ teaspoon Ground Cinnamon

¼ teaspoon Ground White Pepper

¼ teaspoon Instant Minced Garlic

⅛ teaspoon Ground Red Pepper

6 medium-size ripe bananas, divided

1 jar (26 ounces) mango slices in
    light syrup, drained and cut
    into ½-inch dice (2 cups), divided

¼ cup raisins

1. Combine vinegar, sugar, curry powder, black pepper, salt, cinnamon, white pepper, minced garlic, and red pepper in 4-quart saucepan or Dutch oven. Heat to simmer, stirring, and cook 1 minute.

2. Peel 4 bananas, slice, and add to saucepan. Add 1 cup diced mangos. Heat fruit mixture, and simmer, uncovered, 10 minutes, stirring occasionally, until mixture thickens.

3. Peel remaining 2 bananas, slice, and stir into chutney. Add remaining 1 cup diced mangos and raisins. Stir to mix well, remove from heat, cover, and let stand 30 minutes.

4. Serve hot or cold with curries or as condiment with meat, fish, or poultry dishes.

*Makes 4 cups*

# Spice Ice Cream

Soften 1 quart vanilla ice cream just enough to stir. Do not allow ice cream to melt. Spoon into large bowl and add 1 of following seasoning options. Mix well, cover, and refreeze immediately.

¼ teaspoon Ground Cloves and
    ⅛ teaspoon Pure Anise Extract

OR

¼ teaspoon Ground Nutmeg

OR

¾ teaspoon Ground Cinnamon

OR

1 tablespoon crushed Green
    Peppercorns, 1 teaspoon
    Coarse Ground Black Pepper,
    and ¼ teaspoon Coconut
    Extract

TIP:

These spices also can be used to flavor chocolate ice cream.

# Dessert Spices

1 cup white raisins

1 tablespoon Pure Vanilla Extract

1 egg white

½ cup confectioners sugar

1 cup whole almonds

1 cup walnut pieces

½ cup crystallized violets or rose petals

½ cup candied orange peel

⅓ cup Crystallized Ginger

⅓ cup Sesame Seed

2 teaspoons Fennel Seed, crushed

2 teaspoons Coriander Seed, crushed

2 teaspoons Ground Cinnamon

1 teaspoon Ground Nutmeg

1. Place raisins in small bowl, sprinkle with vanilla, and set aside.

2. Preheat oven to 250°F. Lightly coat cookie sheet with nonstick vegetable spray and set aside.

3. Place egg white in mixer bowl and beat with electric mixer until soft peaks form when beaters are lifted. Add sugar and beat just until mixed.

4. Add reserved raisins and remaining ingredients. Mix well and spread on prepared cookie sheet.

5. Bake in preheated 250°F oven 5 minutes. Turn off oven but DO NOT open door. Leave spice mixture in oven overnight.

6. Break into small pieces and place in bowl to serve.

*Makes 3 cups*

TIP:

Crush Fennel and Coriander Seed in mortar and pestle or small electric spice grinder.

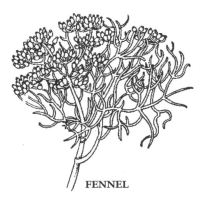

FENNEL

# CHILDREN'S PARTIES

All it takes is imagination, "glue" and baked goods from the supermarket to turn a children's party into an instant success. Birthday parties and parties for other occasions can be easy to prepare and fun for the guests when you use Cake Mate Decorating products and transform baked goods (creme-filled or jelly-filled snack cakes, cookies, cupcakes) into edible "toys" as party favors. For example, ready-made snack cakes can be transformed into race cars, planes, or trains. Cookies or cupcakes can be made into faces, flowers, or even the sun with the addition of Cake Mate Decors, Decorating Icing, Glossy Decorating Gel, Candles, Candy Decorations, and Party Favors.

Children will enjoy using the Cake Mate Decorating products and other food, such as candies, nuts, raisins, marshmallows, maraschino cherries, pretzels, licorice ropes, etc., to design their own creations.

POPPY

# *Before You Start*

Some form of "glue" is needed to attach decorations to snack cakes, cookies, cupcakes, etc. The white Cake Mate Decorating Icing and the interchangeable decorating tips can be used, or you can make your own "glue" and use a pastry bag with the Cake Mate Decorating Tips.

---

# *Icing "Glue"*

*2 egg whites*
*1 tablespoon lemon juice*
*3½ cups confectioners sugar*

1. Place egg whites in mixer bowl and beat with electric mixer until foamy. Add lemon juice. Beat in sugar gradually at high speed until very thick. Spoon into bowl and keep bowl covered with damp towel when not in use.

2. Icing can be spread on parts of cakes or cookies to "glue" parts together; it can be piped onto cakes or cookies where "glue" is needed to attach candy or other decorations; and it can be used to pipe decorations on cakes or cookies.

3. To pipe, use pastry bag or make your own by cutting a resealable plastic bag ⅛ inch in from bottom corner of bag. Put Cake Mate Decorating Tip in open tip of bag.

4. Fill bag with "glue," squeeze out air, and seal bag. Squeeze "glue" through tip onto item to be decorated where needed.

5. Keep leftover "glue" refrigerated in covered jar or plastic container up to 1 week.

*Makes 2 cups*

# To Make Race Cars

SUPPLIES:

*Creme-filled, jelly-filled, or plain yellow snack cake (approximately 4-inches long) for body of each car*

*Assorted Cake Mate Decorating Products: Decorating Icing, Glossy Decorating Gel, Party Favors, Décors, and Candy Decorations*

*"Glue"*

*Thin cookie wafer, broken in half*

*Assorted round candies*

DIRECTIONS:

Place cake on work surface and attach candies or draw wheels with Cake Mate Decorating Icing using 1 of decorating tips. Cut slit in top of cake near front of car, add thin line of "glue" or Decorating Icing and insert half of cookie wafer for windshield. "Glue" round candy or use Icing to draw steering wheel behind windshield. Use Candy Decorations, Décors, Icing, or Gel to add racing numbers, stripes, and other designs. Cake Mate Decorating Icing can also be spread over snack cake to make different color cars.

# *To Make Trains*

SUPPLIES:

*Long piece of cardboard about 4 inches wide and 12 or more inches long*

*Aluminum foil*

*Assorted Cake Mate Decorating Products: Decorating Icing, Glossy Decorating Gel, Party Favors, Décors, Candy Decorations, Candle Holders*

*Creme-filled or plain chocolate or yellow snack cakes*

*"Glue"*

*Assorted candies for decorations*

DIRECTIONS:

Cover cardboard with aluminum foil and draw railroad tracks on foil with Cake Mate Chocolate Decorating Icing. Use whole snack cake for bottom of engine. Cut second snack cake in half crosswise and set 1 piece on back half of whole cake to make housing/cab for engineer. Use whole or parts of cakes for other cars. Use "glue" to attach pieces of cake to each other or to attach candies for decoration. Use round candies for wheels or draw them with Cake Mate Decorating Icing or Glossy Decorating Gels. Cut licorice ropes to desired length and push 1 end into center of back end of front car and other end of licorice into center of front end of next car. Continue with other cars and decorate as desired. Cake Mate Candy Decorations can be used to add animals or scenery around train. Snack cakes can also be covered with Cake Mate Decorating Icing to make different colored cars - red for caboose, blue or yellow for engine.

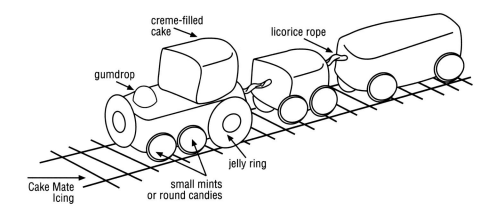

# *To Make Boats*

SUPPLIES:

*Piece of cardboard about 4 inches wide and 6 inches long*

*Aluminum foil*

*Assorted Cake Mate Decorating Products: Decorating Icing,
    Glossy Decorating Gel, Party Favors, Décors, and Candy Decorations*

*Creme-filled, jelly-filled, or plain chocolate or yellow snack cakes*

*"Glue"*

*Assorted candies for decorations*

*Pretzel sticks or Cake Mate Candles for sail posts*

*White or colored paper for sails*

DIRECTIONS:

Cover cardboard with aluminum foil and draw waves on foil with Cake Mate
Decorating Icing. Use l snack cake for each boat, or use l snack cake for base
of boat and "glue" pieces of other snack cakes on base to make wheelhouse or
upperdeck for boat. Set cake on top of waves on aluminum foil. Cake Mate
Décors can be used to add figures, animals, or scenery (make an island with
Cake Mate Decorating Icing
and add Cake Mate Palm Tree Candy
Decoration) around boat. Insert
thin pretzel stick or Cake Mate Candle
into cake for sail post. Punch 2 holes
in paper sail and slide onto sail post.
Decorate as desired.

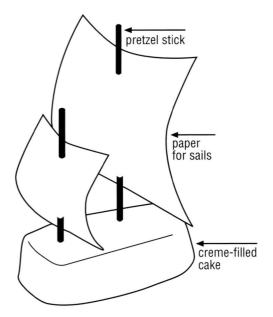

pretzel stick

paper
for sails

creme-filled
cake

# To Make Airplanes

SUPPLIES:

*Assorted Cake Mate Decorating Products: Decorating Icing,
   Glossy Decorating Gel, Party Favors, Décors, and Candy Decorations*

*Creme-filled, jelly-filled, or plain chocolate or yellow snack cakes*

*"Glue"*

*Assorted candies for decorations, gum drops*

*Graham cracker*

*Pretzel sticks*

DIRECTIONS:

Place whole cake on work surface and inset 2 thin pretzels sticks crosswise through center of cake. Cut second cake into 3 equal-size pieces. (When no one is looking — eat center piece!) Spread "glue" on flat, cut ends of both remaining pieces of cut cake. Attach l piece on each side of airplane by pushing flat, cut side of cake onto protruding pretzel sticks to make wings. Cut small triangular piece of graham cracker and spread "glue" on cut edge. Attach to back of airplane for tail. Decorate airplane as desired using Candy Decorations, Décors, Gels, and other candies. Spread "glue" on flat side of gumdrop and attach to front of airplane for nose. Glue 1½-inch piece of pretzel stick on each side of gumdrop for propeller.

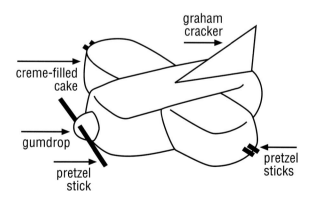

graham cracker

creme-filled cake

gumdrop

pretzel stick

pretzel sticks

# To Make Graham Cracker "Gingerbread" Cookie Houses

Every child who has read the story of "Hansel and Gretel" knows all about the gingerbread house where the wicked witch lived. It's easy to make a "gingerbread house" if you make it with graham crackers and Cake Mate Decorating Icing "glue."

Although Christmas is the traditional time to make a gingerbread house, it can be fun for children to create and decorate a house at any season.  A "Gingerbread" Cookie House always makes a wonderful centerpiece for a party table.

SUPPLIES:

*8 x 10-inch piece of stiff cardboard*

*Aluminum foil*

*Whole graham crackers*

*"Glue"*

*Assorted Cake Mate Decorating Products: Decorating Icing, Glossy Decorating Gel, Party Favors, Décors, and Candy Decorations*
*Other decorations: candies, nuts, etc., as desired*

DIRECTIONS:

Cover cardboard with aluminum foil for base of house. Score and break 2 graham crackers with knife as shown in Diagram 1 below. "Glue" 4 whole graham crackers to base as shown in Diagram 2. Continue to build and "glue" house as shown in Diagram 3. After you get a sense of how to handle graham crackers and "glue," you can design your own house. Decorate house as desired. Use wide Decorating Tip to add shingles to roof; use flaked coconut and white Decorating Icing for snow or use green Decorating Icing for grass; add trees or shrubs around house with items from Candy Decorations; draw sidewalk on aluminum foil with Cake Mate Decorating Icing; add flowers, doorway, and windows to house with Decorating Icing or Gels. Have fun and put your creativity on display!

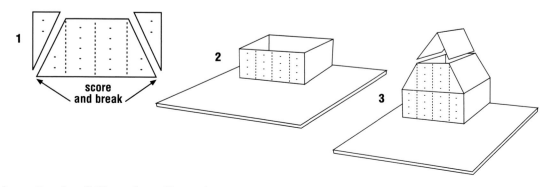

*Graham Cracker "Gingerbread" Cookie House*

# *To Make Decorated Cookies, Graham Crackers, or Cupcakes*

SUPPLIES:

*Assorted cookies in various shapes*

*Graham crackers*

*Cupcakes*

*Snack cakes*

*Cardboard*

*Aluminum foil*

*Assorted Cake Mate Decorating Products: Decorating Icing, Glossy Decorating Gel, Party Favors, Décors, Candles, and Candy Decorations*

*Assorted candies for decorations*

DIRECTIONS:

Tops of cookies or cupcakes can be decorated to look like faces, clowns, or dolls with Cake Mate Candy Decorations, Icing, and Gels. Different shapes of cookies can also be decorated to look like the sun, balloons, flag, footballs, baseballs, and flowers.

Decorate graham crackers with children's names using Decorating Icing and Gels and use decorated crackers for place cards.

Add "strings" and drum sticks to a cupcake with Cake Mate Icing and turn a cupcake into drum.

One whole snack cake plus half a snack cake can be turned into a doll carriage or a baby bootie with addition of Icing, Candies, and Décors.

# INDEX

～

Page numbers in **boldface** indicate photographs or illustrations.